Third Edition

Techniques & Principles in Language Teaching

Diane Larsen-Freeman
and Marti Anderson

OXFORD

UNIVERSITY PRESS

OXFORD
UNIVERSITY PRESS

Great Clarendon Street, Oxford OX2 6DP

Oxford University Press is a department of the University of Oxford.
It furthers the University's objective of excellence in research,
scholarship, and education by publishing worldwide in

Oxford New York

Auckland Cape Town Dar es Salaam Hong Kong Karachi
Kuala Lumpur Madrid Melbourne Mexico City Nairobi
New Delhi Shanghai Taipei Toronto

With offices in

Argentina Austria Brazil Chile Czech Republic France Greece
Guatemala Hungary Italy Japan Poland Portugal Singapore
South Korea Switzerland Thailand Turkey Ukraine Vietnam

OXFORD and OXFORD ENGLISH are registered trade marks of
Oxford University Press in the UK and in certain other countries

ISBN: 978 0 19 442360 1

Printed in China

This book is printed on paper from certified and well-managed sources.

ACKNOWLEDGEMENTS

*The authors and publisher are grateful to those who have given permission to
reproduce the following extract of copyright material*: p.214 Screenshot from
Facebook (http://www.facebook.com). Reproduced by kind permission
of Facebook.

Sources: p.215 www.wikipedia.com; p.205 The British National Corpus

Illustrations by: Chris Pavely pp.26, 38, 53, 56, 72, 87, 89, 106, 118, 135,
153, 172, 183, 188, 193.

This title originally appeared in the series *Teaching Techniques in English
as a Second Language*, edited by Russell N Campbell and William E
Rutherford (First Edition 1986; Second Edition 2000).

Contents

Acknowledgments

We thank the readers of the first and second editions of this book. Your invaluable feedback and input have helped to shape this third edition.

The approach we have used in this book, as in the previous two editions, is based on our experience in teaching the methods/approaches course at the Master of Arts in Teaching Program at the School for International Training. This book would not have been written in the first place if it had not been for the influence of colleagues and students there. We are indeed grateful for the time we spent in this wonderful community.

Marti would like to thank Diane for being an inspiring teacher and mentor as well as beloved colleague and friend. Working with her on this project has been a great privilege.

Diane would like to thank Marti for her willingness to join her in this project and her 'can-do' attitude throughout. Diane is counting on Marti to make this project her own and carry it into the future.

We wish to thank our life partners for their encouragement and support.

For the initial faith they showed and for their continued encouragement and helpful suggestions, Diane acknowledges with gratitude the editors of this series, Russell Campbell and William Rutherford.

It has also been a pleasure working with the professionals at Oxford University Press. For this edition, we want to acknowledge Julia Bell's helpfulness especially, and Ann Hunter's and Keith Layfield's skillful copy-editing.

In addition, this book has benefited from the fact that leading methodologists and colleagues have generously responded to requests for feedback on portions of this manuscript, either the previous edition or the current one. We are indebted to Earl Stevick (To the Teacher Educator), Shakti Gattegno (Silent Way), Georgi Lozanov, Allison Miller, and Tetsuo Nishizawa (Desuggestopedia), Jennybelle Rardin and Pat Tirone (Community Language Learning), James Asher (Total Physical Response), Marjorie Wesche and Ann Snow (Content-based Instruction), Elsa Auerbach (Participatory Approach), and Leo van Lier and Mat Schulze (Technology). Their comments have made us feel more confident of our interpretation and representation. Any errors of interpretation are entirely our responsibility, of course.

List of Acronyms

ALM	Audio-Lingual Method
BNC	British National Corpus
CBI	Content-based Instruction
CLL	Community Language Learning
CLT	Communicative Language Teaching
CALL	Computer-assisted Language Learning
CLIL	Content and Language Integrated Learning
ELF	English as a Lingua Franca
LCD	Liquid Crystal Display
SLA	Second Language Acquisition
SAARRD	Security, Aggression, Attention, Reflection, Retention, and Discrimination
SIOP	Sheltered Instruction Observation Protocol
TL	Target Language
TBLT	Task-based Language Teaching
WL	Whole Language
ZPD	Zone of Proximal Development

To the Teacher Educator

The Work of Language Teaching

The work of teaching is simultaneously mental and social. It is also physical, emotional, practical, behavioral, political, experiential, historical, cultural, spiritual, and personal. In short, teaching is very complex, influenced not only by these 12 dimensions and perhaps others, but also requiring their contingent orchestration in support of students' learning. When *language* teaching in particular is in focus, the complexity is even greater, shaped by teachers' views of the nature of language, of language teaching and learning in general, and by their knowledge of the particular sociocultural setting in which the teaching and learning take place (Adamson 2004). Indeed, research has shown that there is a degree of shared pedagogical knowledge among language teachers that is different from that of teachers of other subjects (Gatbonton 2000; Mullock 2006). Nonetheless, each teacher's own language learning history is also unique. The way that teachers have been taught during their own 'apprenticeship of observation' (Lortie 1975) is bound to be formative. There is also the level of complexity at the immediate local level, due to the specific and unique needs of the students themselves in a particular class at a particular time, and the fact that these needs change from moment to moment. Finally, the reality of educational contexts being what they are, teachers must not only attempt to meet their students' learning needs, but they must also juggle other competing demands on their time and attention.

Because of this complexity, although this is a book about the methods and methodological innovations of recent years, we do not seek to convince readers that one method is superior to another, or that there is or ever will be a perfect method (Prabhu 1990). The work of teaching suggests otherwise. As Brumfit observes:

> A claim that we can predict closely what will happen in a situation as complex as [the classroom] can only be based on either the view that human beings are more mechanical in their learning responses than any recent discussion would allow, or the notion that we can measure and predict the quantities and qualities of all ... factors. Neither of these seems to be a sensible point of view to take.
> (Brumfit 1984: 18–19)

After all, 'If it could be assumed that learners were 'simply' learners, that teachers were 'simply' teachers, and that one classroom was essentially the same as another, there would probably be little need for other than a technological approach to language teaching' (Tudor 2003: 3), with adjustments being made for the age of the learners, specific goals, or class numbers, etc. However, the truth is that

> Learners are not 'simply' learners any more than teachers are 'simply' teachers; teaching contexts, too, differ from one another in a significant number of ways. In other words, language teaching is far more complex than producing cars: we cannot therefore assume that the technology of language teaching will lead in a neat, deterministic manner to a predictable set of learning outcomes.
> (Tudor 2003: 3).

Tudor goes on to observe that this is true even within a given culture. It cannot be assumed that all teachers will share the same conceptions of language, of learning, and of teaching.

> Rather than the elegant realisation of one rationality, then, language teaching is likely to involve the meeting and interaction of different rationalities. Murray (1996) is therefore right in drawing attention to the 'tapestry of diversity' which makes our classrooms what they are.
> (ibid. 2003: 7)

Language Teacher Learning

Recognizing the complex and diverse nature of the work of teaching has stimulated much discussion during the last 15 years around the question of how it is that language teachers learn to teach (Bailey and Nunan 1996; Bartels 2005; Burns and Richards 2009; Freeman and Richards 1996; Hawkins 2004; Johnson 2009; Tedick 2005). In addition, during this same time period, the journal *Language Teaching Research* began publication with Rod Ellis as its editor. Much of the research reported on in these sources can be summed up in what Johnson describes as her current understanding of language teacher learning:

> L2 teacher learning [is] ... socially negotiated and contingent on knowledge of self, subject matter, curricula, and setting ... L2 teachers [are] ... users and creators of legitimate forms of knowledge who make decisions about how best to teach their L2 students within complex socially, culturally, and historically situated contexts.
> (Johnson 2006: 239)

Such a view has radically transformed notions of teacher learning. As Richards (2008: 164) notes: 'While traditional views of teacher-learning often viewed the teachers' task as the application of theory to practice, more recent

views see teacher-learning as the theorization of practice.' Rather than con-
sumers of theory, then, teachers are seen to be both practitioners and theory
builders (Prabhu 1992; Savignon 2007). Given this view of teachers as theory
builders, teacher education must serve two functions: 'It must teach the skills
of reflectivity and it must provide the discourse and vocabulary that can serve
participants in renaming their experience' (Freeman 2002: 11).

   It is these two functions that we believe our study of methods is well-posi-
tioned to address. First of all, by observing classes in action and then analyzing the observations, we intend to help readers cultivate skills in reflectivity,
important for their sense of self-efficacy (Akbari 2007). The point is to illustrate the thinking that goes on beneath the surface behavior enacted in the
classroom in order to understand the rationale for some of the decisions that
teachers make (Woods 1996; Borg 2006). A study of methods is also a means
of socialization into professional thinking and discourse that language teachers require in order to 'rename their experience', to participate in their profession, and to learn throughout their professional lives.

A Study of Methods

Thus, a study of methods is invaluable in teacher education in at least five ways:

1 Methods serve as a foil for reflection that can aid teachers in bringing to
   conscious awareness the thinking that underlies their actions. We know
   that teachers come to teacher training with ideas about the teaching/
   learning process formed from the years they themselves spent as students
   (Lortie 1975). A major purpose of teacher education is to help teachers
   make the tacit explicit (Shulman 1987). By exposing teachers to methods
   and asking them to reflect on the principles of those methods and actively
   engage with the techniques, teacher educators can help teachers become
   clearer about why they do what they do. They become aware of their own
   fundamental assumptions, values, and beliefs. In turn, reflective teachers
   can take positions on issues that result in the improvement of the society
   in which they live (Clarke 2007; Akbari 2007).

2 By becoming clear on where they stand (Clarke 2003), teachers can
   choose to teach differently from the way they were taught. They are able
   to see why they are attracted to certain methods and repelled by others.
   They are able to make choices that are informed, not conditioned.
   They may be able to resist, or at least argue against, the imposition of a
   particular method by authorities. In situations where a method is not
   being imposed, different methods offer teachers alternatives to what
   they currently think and do. It does not necessarily follow that they will
   choose to modify their current practice. The point is that they will have
   the understanding and the tools to do so, if they are able to and want to.

3   A knowledge of methods is part of the knowledge base of teaching. With it, teachers join a community of practice (Lave and Wenger 1991). Being a community member involves learning the professional discourse that community members use so that professional dialogue can take place. Being part of a discourse community confers a professional identity and connects teachers with each other so they are less isolated in their practice.

4   Conversely, by being members of a professional discourse community, teachers may find their own conceptions of how teaching leads to learning challenged. Interacting with others' conceptions of practice helps to keep teachers' teaching alive and to prevent it from becoming stale and overly routinized (Prabhu 1990).

5   A knowledge of methods helps to expand a teacher's repertoire of techniques. This in itself provides a further avenue for professional growth, since some teachers find their way to new pedagogical positions by first trying out new techniques rather than by entertaining new principles. Moreover, effective teachers who are more experienced and expert have a large, diverse repertoire of best practices (Arends 2004), which presumably helps them deal more effectively with the unique qualities and idiosyncrasies of their students.

Criticisms of Methods

Despite these potential gains from a study of methods, it is important to acknowledge that a number of writers in our field have criticized the concept of language teaching methods. Some say that methods are prescriptions for classroom behavior, and that teachers are encouraged by textbook publishers and academics to implement them whether or not the methods are appropriate for a particular context (Pennycook 1989). Others have noted that the search for the best method is ill-advised (Prabhu 1990; Bartolome 1994); that teachers do not think about methods when planning their lessons (Long 1991); that methodological labels tell us little about what really goes on in classrooms (Katz 1996); and that teachers experience a certain fatigue concerning the constant coming and going of fashions in methods (Rajagopalan 2007). Hinkel (2006) also notes that the need for situationally relevant language pedagogy has brought about the decline of methods.

These criticisms deserve consideration. It is possible that a particular method may be imposed on teachers by others. However, these others are likely to be disappointed if they hope that mandating a particular method will lead to standardization. For we know that teaching is more than following a recipe. Any method is going to be shaped by a teacher's own understanding, beliefs, style, and level of experience. Teachers are not mere conveyor belts delivering language through inflexible prescribed and proscribed behaviors

(Larsen-Freeman 1991); they are professionals who can, in the best of all worlds, make their own decisions—informed by their own experience, the findings from research, and the wisdom of practice accumulated by the profession (see, for example, Kumaravadivelu 1994).

Furthermore, a method is decontextualized. How a method is implemented in the classroom is not only going to be affected by who the teacher is, but also by who the students are, what they and the teacher expect as appropriate social roles, the institutional constraints and demands, and factors connected to the wider sociocultural context in which the instruction takes place. Even the 'right' method will not compensate for inadequate conditions of learning, or overcome sociopolitical inequities. Further, decisions that teachers make are often affected by exigencies in the classroom rather than by methodological considerations. Thus, saying that a particular method is practiced certainly does not give us the whole picture of what is happening in the classroom. Since a method is more abstract than a teaching activity, it is not surprising that teachers think in terms of activities rather than methodological choices when they plan their lessons.

What critics of language teaching methods have to offer us is important. Admittedly, at this point in the evolution of our field, there is little empirical support for a particular method, although there may be some empirical support in second language acquisition research for methodological principles (Long 2009). Further, what some of the methods critics have done is to raise our awareness about the importance of critical pedagogy. As Akbari puts it:

> By viewing education as an intrinsically political, power-related activity, supporters of critical pedagogy seek to expose its discriminatory foundations and take steps toward reforming it so that groups who are left out because of their gender, race, or social class are included and represented ... Critical pedagogy puts the classroom context into the wider social context with the belief that 'what happens in the classroom should end up making a difference outside of the classroom' (Baynham 2006).
> (Akbari 2008: 644)

Larsen-Freeman and Freeman concur:

> It is clear that universal solutions that are transposed acritically, and often accompanied by calls for increased standardization, and which ignore indigenous conditions, the diversity of learners, and the agency of teachers are immanent in a modernism that no longer applies, if it ever did.
> (Larsen-Freeman and Freeman 2008: 168)

Widdowson (2004) recognizes the inconclusive cycle of pedagogical fashion in teaching methods, and observes that what is needed is not a universal solution, but rather a 'shift to localization,' in which pedagogic practices are designed in relation to local contexts, needs, and objectives (Larsen-Freeman 2000; Bax 2003; Canagarajah 2005). Such a shift responds to the objections of some critical theorists (such as Pennycook 2001) to attempts to 'export' language teaching methods from developed to developing countries with the assumption that one size fits all. Treating localization of practices as a fundamental 'change in attitude,' Widdowson adds that 'local contexts of actual practice are to be seen not as constraints to be overcome but conditions to be satisfied' (2004: 369). Indeed, Larsen-Freeman and Cameron (2008) suggest that one measure of a method should be its adaptability—the degree to which it can be adapted to satisfy different conditions.

In the end, then, which method is practiced is, or at least should be, a local decision. In this regard, teachers' voices must be heeded. And what teachers have to say about the value of methods is unequivocal:

> Few teachers define methods in the narrow pejorative sense used by post-methodologists. Most teachers think of methods in terms of techniques which realize a set of principles or goals and they are open to any method that offers practical solutions to problems in their particular teaching context.
> (Bell 2007: 141)

Continuing, Bell writes:

> A knowledge of methods is equated with a set of options, which empowers teachers to respond meaningfully to particular classroom contexts. In this way, knowledge of methods is seen as crucial to teacher growth.
> (ibid. 2007: 141–2)

As one teacher in a study conducted by Bell remarked:

> 'I think that teachers should be exposed to all methods and they themselves would 'build' their own methods or decide what principles they would use in their teaching. We cannot ignore methods and all the facts that were considered by those who 'created' or use them in their teaching. We need a basis for building our own teaching.'
> (ibid. 2007: 143)

Thus, while the criticism of methods is helpful in some regards, we do not believe that a study of language teaching methods should be excluded from language teacher education. It is not methods, but how they are used that is at issue. A study of methods need not lead to the de-skilling of teachers but rather can serve a variety of useful functions when used appropriately in teacher education. Studying methods can help teachers articulate, and perhaps transform, their understanding of the teaching–learning process. It can strengthen their confidence in challenging authorities who mandate unacceptable educational policies. Methods can serve as models of the integration of theory and practice (see Introduction Chapter 1, page 1). They can contribute to a discourse that becomes the lingua franca of a professional community, from which teachers can receive both support and challenge, and in which continuing education in the lifelong process of learning to teach can be encouraged (Larsen-Freeman 1998). Teachers and teacher educators should not be blinded by the criticisms of methods and thus fail to see their invaluable contribution to teacher education and continuing development. Key to doing so, though, is moving beyond ideology to inquiry, a movement to which we hope this book will contribute.

New to this Third Edition

Some modest revision has been made throughout the book, including a new discussion in Chapter 13 of Howard Gardner's habits of mind, which he claims students need to develop in order to participate effectively in current and emerging cultural and work environments. Other chapters have remained relatively untouched. This is because these chapters describe methods that are more historical than contemporary, although they are all still being practiced somewhere in the world today. In any case, we believe that educators should have a sense of the history of the field, not only of contemporary practices. As we have already indicated, our goal in this book is to expose readers to the 'tapestry of diversity' that exists in human teaching and learning, not to convince readers of the value of any one method over the others.

There are also several major changes that have been made for this edition. First, three methodological innovations—Content-based, Task-based, and Participatory Approaches—which were dealt with in a single chapter in the previous edition, are each addressed in separate chapters in this edition. These three chapters allow for the more in-depth treatment that these enduring practices warrant. Content-based Instruction, or Content and Language Integrated Learning (CLIL), has seen widespread adoption, both in the education of English language learners in the USA and in language education in other countries, particularly in Europe, where it is increasingly common for governments to encourage the teaching of language and other subjects in tandem in state schools. It was also important to expand the discussion of Task-based Language Teaching, which a new chapter has allowed us to do, as it is the method that has received the most support from second language acquisition research. The third new chapter, the Participatory Approach, has enabled us to elaborate on the political dimensions of language teaching, including how language study can influence a language learner's sociopolitical identity.

In addition, we have added a new chapter on technology. Technological aids to language teaching have been around for some time, of course, but in our opinion, technology has reached a point where it should be considered not only as a supplement to teaching or a resource for teachers, but also as an opportunity for autonomous learning. A technological approach to language teaching rests on its own unique set of principles, including a new understanding of the nature of language.

Terminology

Two notes about terminology are also in order:

1   First, we are using the term 'method' here not to mean a formulaic prescription, but rather a coherent set of principles linked to certain techniques and procedures. Anthony (1963: 64) has made the case for a tripartite hierarchy. As he put it: '… techniques carry out a method which is consistent with an approach'. Following Anthony, in certain of the chapters we will introduce a particular method by showing how it is an example of a more general approach to language teaching. However, not all methods discussed in this book conveniently follow from a general approach. They all do, though, have both a conceptual and an operational component, fitting the definition in the *Dictionary of Language Teaching and Applied Linguistics* (a method is 'a way of teaching a language which is based on systematic principles and procedures'), and thus justifying our use of the term. Admittedly, we have sometimes found it difficult to use the term 'method' with more recent innovations, such as learning strategies, cooperative learning, and technology. At such times, we have resorted to the term 'methodological innovations.'

2   We have used the term 'target language' to mean 'the language being taught' for three reasons. First, we intend for this book to be useful to teachers of all languages, not only English teachers. Second, we acknowledge that many teachers and students are multilingual or plurilingual (to use the Council of Europe's term) and so the use of the term 'second' language does not really apply. Third, we have avoided using the term 'foreign' language because this designation is relative to the speaker and mutable in the context. For instance, in the USA, Spanish has a heterogeneous identity: it could be considered as a 'foreign' language to those with little or no knowledge of it; as a 'second' language to those who use it in addition to their first language; or as a 'native' language to those for whom it is a home or heritage language (Larsen-Freeman and Freeman 2008). Although the term

'target language' is not without its problems, using this term seemed a reasonable compromise.

Finally, although we have made every effort toward a faithful rendering of each method and methodological innovation, there will undoubtedly be those who would not totally accept our rendition. This is understandable and probably inevitable. Our description is, as it must be, a product of our own experience.

It is our sincere hope that this book will both inform and stimulate its readers and that it will encourage them to reflect, inquire, and experiment. If it meets these goals, then it may help to restore faith in the appropriate use of teaching methods in language teacher education.

Brattleboro, Vermont and Ann Arbor, Michigan   Diane Larsen-Freeman

Bangkok, Thailand   Marti Anderson

References/Additional Resources

Akbari, R. 2007. 'Reflections on reflection: A critical appraisal of reflective practices in L2 teacher education.' *System* 35: 192–207.

———. 2008. 'Postmethod discourse and practice.' *TESOL Quarterly* 42/4: 641–52.

Adamson, B. 2004. 'Fashions in language teaching methodology' in A. Davies and C. Elder (eds.). *The Handbook of Applied Linguistics*: 604–22. Malden, MA: Blackwell.

Anthony, E. 1963. 'Approach, method, and technique.' *English Language Teaching* 17: 63–7. Reprinted in H. Allen and R. Campbell (eds.). *Teaching English as a Second Language* (2nd. edn.). 1972. New York: McGraw-Hill.

Arends, R. 2004. *Learning to Teach*. (6th edn.) New York: McGraw-Hill.

Bailey, K. and **D. Nunan** (eds.). 1996. *Voices from the Language Classroom*. Cambridge: Cambridge University Press.

Bartels, N. (ed.). 2005. *Applied Linguistics and Language Teacher Education*. New York: Springer.

Bartolome, L. 1994. 'Beyond the methods fetish: Toward a humanizing pedagogy.' *Harvard Educational Review* 64/2: 173–94.

Bax, S. 2003. 'The end of CLT: A context approach to language teaching.' *ELT Journal* 57/3: 278–87.

Baynham, M. 2006. 'Agency and contingency in the language learning of refugees and asylum seekers.' *Linguistics and Education* 17: 24–39.

Bell, D. 2007. 'Do teachers think that methods are dead?' *ELT Journal* 61/2: 135–43.

Borg, S. 2006. *Teacher Cognition and Language Education.* London: Continuum.

Brumfit, C. 1984. *Communicative Methodology in Language Teaching.* Cambridge: Cambridge University Press.

Burns, A. and J. Richards (eds.). 2009. *The Cambridge Guide to Second Language Teacher Education.* New York: Cambridge University Press.

Canagarajah, A. (ed.). 2005. *Reclaiming the Local in Language Policy and Practice.* Mahwah, NJ: Lawrence Erlbaum.

Clarke, M. 2003. *A Place to Stand: Essays for Educators in Troubled Times.* Ann Arbor, MI: University of Michigan Press.

——. 2007. *Common Ground, Contested Territory. Examining the Roles of English Language Teachers in Troubled Times.* Ann Arbor, MI: University of Michigan Press.

Freeman, D. 2002. 'The hidden side of the work: Teacher knowledge and learning to teach.' *Language Teaching* 35/1: 1–14.

—— and J. Richards (eds.). 1996. *Teacher Learning in Language Teaching.* New York: Cambridge University Press.

Gatbonton, E. 2000. 'Investigating experienced ESL teachers' pedagogical knowledge.' *Canadian Modern Language Review* 56: 585–616.

Hawkins, M. (ed.). 2004. *Language Learning and Teacher Education: A Sociocultural Approach.* Clevedon: Multilingual Matters.

Hinkel, E. 2006. 'Current perspectives on teaching the four skills.' *TESOL Quarterly* 40/1: 109–31.

Johnson, K. 2006. 'The sociocultural turn and its challenges for second language teacher education.' *TESOL Quarterly* 40/1: 235–57.

——. 2009. *Second Language Teacher Education: A Sociocultural Perspective.* New York: Routledge.

Katz, A. 1996. 'Teaching style: A way to understand instruction in language classrooms' in K. Bailey and D. Nunan (eds.). *Voices from the Language Classroom,* 57–87. Cambridge: Cambridge University Press.

Kumaravadivelu, B. 1994. 'The postmethod condition: (E)merging strategies for second/foreign language teaching.' *TESOL Quarterly* 28/1: 27–48.

——. 2006. 'TESOL methods: Changing tracks, challenging trends.' *TESOL Quarterly* 40/1: 59–81.

Larsen-Freeman, D. 1991. 'Research on language teaching methodologies: A review of the past and an agenda for the future' in K. de Bot, R. Ginsberg, and C. Kramsch (eds.). *Foreign Language Research in Cross-Cultural Perspective,* 119–32. Amsterdam/Philadelphia: John Benjamins Publishing Co.

——. 1998. 'Learning teaching is a lifelong process.' *Perspectives* XXIV/2: 5–11.

——. 2000. 'On the appropriateness of language teaching methods in language and development' in J. Shaw, D. Lubelske, and M. Noullet (eds.). *Partnership and Interaction: Proceedings of the Fourth International*

Conference on Language and Development. Hanoi, Vietnam, 65–71. Bangkok: Asian Institute of Technology.

—— and **L. Cameron.** 2008. *Complex Systems and Applied Linguistics.* Oxford: Oxford University Press.

—— and **D. Freeman.** 2008. 'Language moves: The place of "foreign" languages in classroom teaching and learning.' *Review of Research in Education* 32: 147– 86.

Lave, J. and **E. Wenger.** 1991. *Situated Learning: Legitimate Peripheral Participation.* New York: Cambridge University Press.

Long, M. 1991. 'Focus on form: A design feature in language teaching methodology' in K. de Bot, R. Ginsberg, and C. Kramsch (eds.). *Foreign Language Research in Cross-Cultural Perspective,* 39–52. Amsterdam/ Philadelphia: John Benjamins Publishing Co.

——. 2009. 'Methodological principles for language teaching' in M. Long and C. Doughty (eds.). *The Handbook of Language Teaching,* 373–94. Malden, MA: Wiley-Blackwell.

Lortie, D. 1975. *Schoolteacher: A Sociological Study.* Chicago: University of Chicago Press.

Mullock, B. 2006. 'The pedagogical knowledge base of four TESOL teachers.' *Modern Language Journal* 90/1: 48–66.

Murray, D. 1996. 'The tapestry of diversity in our classrooms' in K. Bailey and D. Nunan (eds.). *Voices from the Language Classroom,* 434–48. Cambridge: Cambridge University Press.

Pennycook, A. 1989. 'The concept of method, interested knowledge, and the politics of language teaching.' *TESOL Quarterly* 23/4: 591–615.

——. 2001. *Critical Applied Linguistics: A Critical Introduction.* Mahwah, NJ: Erlbaum.

Prabhu, N. S. 1990. 'There is no best method—Why?' *TESOL Quarterly* 24/2: 161–76.

——. 1992. 'The dynamics of the language lesson.' *TESOL Quarterly* 26/2: 225–41.

Rajagopalan. K. 2007. 'From madness in method to method in madness.' *ELT Journal* 62/1: 84–5.

Richards, J. 2008. 'Second language teacher education today.' *RELC Journal* 39/2: 158–77.

Savignon, S. 2007. 'Beyond communicative language teaching: What's ahead?' *Journal of Pragmatics* 39: 207–20.

Shulman, L. 1987. 'Knowledge-base and teaching: Foundations of the new reform.' *Harvard Educational Review* 57/1: 1–22.

Tedick, D. (ed.). 2005. *Language Teacher Education: International Perspectives on Research and Practice.* Mahwah, NJ: Lawrence Erlbaum Associates.

Tudor, I. 2003. 'Learning to live with complexity: Towards an ecological perspective on language teaching.' *System* 31: 1–12.

Widdowson, H. G. 2004. 'A perspective on recent trends' in A. P. R. Howatt with H. G. Widdowson. *A History of English Language Teaching* (2nd edn.), 353–72. Oxford: Oxford University Press.

Woods, D. 1996. *Teacher Cognition in Language Teaching: Beliefs, Decision-Making and Classroom Practice.* Cambridge: Cambridge University Press.

Introduction

Goals of this Book

One of the goals of this book is for you to learn about many different language teaching methods. We will use the term 'method' to mean a coherent set of links between the actions of a teacher in a classroom and the thoughts that underlie the actions. The actions are the techniques, and the thoughts are the principles in the title of this book: *Techniques and Principles in Language Teaching*.

A second goal is to help you uncover the thoughts that guide your own actions as a teacher. They may not be ones of which you are aware. Seeking to determine which principles of the methods you read about here are most [dis]harmonious with your own thinking will help you to uncover some of your implicit thoughts and beliefs about teaching.

A third goal is to introduce you to a variety of techniques, some of which will be new. Although certain techniques may require further training, others can be immediately implemented. Feel free to experiment and adapt those techniques to your teaching context.

Thought-in-Action Links

It is important to recognize that methods link thoughts and actions, because teaching is not entirely about one or the other. Of course this is as true about your own teaching as it is about any method you will read about in this book. As a teacher of language, you have thoughts[1] about your subject matter—what language is, what culture is—and about your students—who they are as learners and how it is they learn. You also have thoughts about yourself as a teacher and what you can do to help your students to learn. Many of your thoughts

[1] We will use the term 'thoughts' for the sake of simplicity; however, we mean for thoughts to include beliefs, attitudes, values, and awarenesses as well.

have been formed by your own experience as a language learner. It is very important for you to become aware of the thoughts that guide your actions in the classroom. With this awareness, you are able to examine why you do what you do and perhaps choose to think about or do things differently.

As an example, let us relate an anecdote about a teacher with whom Diane Larsen-Freeman was working some time ago. We will call her Heather, although that is not her real name. From her study of methods in Stevick (1980), Heather became interested in how to work with teacher control and student initiative in her teaching. Heather determined that during her student teaching internship, she would exercise less control of the lesson in order to encourage her students to take more initiative. She decided to narrow the goal down to having the students take the initiative in posing the questions in the classroom, recognizing that so often it is the teacher who asks all the questions, not the students.

Diane was Heather's teaching supervisor. When Diane came to observe her, Heather was very discouraged. She felt that the students were not taking the initiative that she was trying to get them to take, but she could not see what was wrong.

When Diane visited her class, she observed the following:

HEATHER: Juan, ask Anna what she is wearing.
JUAN: What are you wearing?
ANNA: I am wearing a dress.
HEATHER: Anna, ask Muriel what she is writing.
ANNA: What are you writing?
MURIEL: I am writing a letter.

This pattern continued for some time. It was clear to see that Heather had successfully avoided the common problem of the teacher asking all the questions in the class. The teacher was not asking the questions—the students were. However, Heather had not achieved her goal of encouraging student initiative, since it was she who took the initiative by prompting the students to ask the questions. Heather and Diane discussed the matter in the post-observation conference.

Heather came to see that if she truly wanted students to take more initiative, then she would have to set up the situation in such a way that her participation in an activity was not essential. Diane talked about several ways Heather might do this. During this discussion, Heather came to another important awareness. She realized that since she was a fairly inexperienced teacher, she felt insecure about having the students make the decisions about who says what to whom, and when. What if the students were to ask her questions that she was unable to answer? Having students take the initiative in the classroom was consonant with her values; however, Heather realized that she needed to think further about what level of student initiative would be comfortable for her at this stage in her career as a teacher. The point was that it was not necessarily simply a matter of Heather improving her technique; she could see that that was one possibility. Another was to rethink the way in which she thought about her teaching (Larsen-Freeman 1993).

The links between thought and action were very important in Heather's teaching. She came to realize that when something was not going as she had intended, she could change her thought or she could change her action. Heather had an idea of what she wanted to accomplish—but the action she chose to carry it out did not achieve her purpose. When she examined her intentions more clearly, she saw that she was not yet ready to have her students take complete initiative in the lesson. So for now, the thinking underlying her approach had to change.

A Coherent Set

Returning to the methods in this book, we will see that it is the link between thoughts and actions that is common to them all. But there is another way in which links are made in methods, and that is the connection between one thought-in-action link and another. A method is a coherent set of such links. Methods are coherent in the sense that there should be some theoretical or philosophical compatibility among the links. It would make little sense, for example, for a methodologist who believes that language is made up of a set of fixed patterns to characterize language acquisition as a creative process, and to employ discovery learning techniques to help learners discover the abstract rules underlying a language in order to enable them to create novel sentences.

To say there is coherence among the links does not mean, however, that the techniques of one method can not be used with another. The techniques may look very different in practice, though, if the thoughts behind them differ. For example, Stevick (1993) has shown that the simple technique of using a picture to provide a context for a dialogue that the students are supposed to learn can lead to very different conclusions about teaching and learning depending on how the technique is managed. If the students first look at the picture, close their eyes while the teacher reads the dialogue, and then repeat the dialogue bit by bit after the teacher, repeating until they have learned it fluently and flawlessly, the students could infer that it is the teacher who is the provider of all language and its meaning in the classroom. They could further infer that they should use that 'part of their brains that copies but not the part that creates' (1993: 432).

If, on the other hand, before they listen to or read the dialogue, the students look at the picture and describe it using words and phrases they can supply, and then guess what the people in the picture might be saying to each other before they hear the dialogue, they might infer that their initiative is welcomed, and that it is all right to be wrong. Further, if they then practice the dialogue in pairs without striving for perfect recall, they might also infer that they should 'use the part of their brains that creates' and that guessing and approximation are acceptable (1993: 432). We can see from this example how a technique might look very different and might lead students to very different inferences about their learning, depending on the thoughts and beliefs of the teacher.

Which Method is Best?

It is not our purpose in this book to promote one method over another. Thus, from our perspective, it is not a question of choosing between intact methods; nor should the presence of any method in this book be construed as an endorsement by us. Our agnostic stance will no doubt irritate some of our readers. However, like Prahbu (1990), we do not believe that there is a single best method. Further, it is not our purpose to have you sift through the methods presented here in order to choose the one with which you feel the most philosophically in tune. Instead, it is intended that you will use what is here as a way to make explicit your own beliefs about the teaching–learning process, beliefs based upon your experience and your professional training, including the research you know about. Unless you become clear about your beliefs, you will continue to make decisions that are conditioned rather than conscious. Engaging with the professional beliefs of others in an ongoing manner is also important for keeping your teaching practice alive. Furthermore, 'if the teacher engages in classroom activity with a sense of intellectual excitement, there is at least a fair probability that learners will begin to participate in the excitement and to perceive classroom lessons mainly as learning events—as experiences of growth for themselves' (Prabhu 1992: 239).

As time passes, new methods are created and others fall into disfavor. Rajagopalan (2007) has observed that teachers experience 'methods fatigue' with the continual coming and going of methodological fashions. This has not been our experience, however. Our experience is that teachers always want to know what is new. They know that teaching is difficult work, and they are always searching for ways to make it more successful. It is also sometimes the case that methods or practices that fall into disfavor in one era are resurrected in another. For instance, for many years, teachers were told that they should never use the students' native language in the classroom—that they should never translate—even when all the students shared a language in common. The motivation for this advice was to maximize students' opportunities to use the language they were studying. Associated with the Direct Method (see Chapter 3), this admonition arose because its immediate predecessor, the Grammar-Translation Method (Chapter 2), made abundant use of translation (as the name suggests), but it did not prepare students to communicate in the language of instruction. However, these days such absolute proscriptions to avoid use of the students' common language have come under attack. For instance, Cook (2010) suggests that such a proscription is isolationist and undermines the possibility for teachers and students to establish a relationship between languages. Further, he notes, it also violates the pedagogical principle of moving from the known (here the common language of the students) to the unknown (the language the students are learning). This principle is firmly embedded in Community Language Learning (Chapter 7), which makes use of translation to establish meaning and correspondence between the languages. It should be clear, then, that some of the methods featured in this book are incompatible with others.

Of course, it is not only the dynamics internal to the field that contribute to changing practices. There are factors external to the field that affect language teaching as well. For instance, population flows among countries of the world have increased multilingualism (Todeva and Cenoz 2009). Then, too, the development and promotion of the Common European Framework (CEFR: Council of Europe 2001) has influenced thinking about language education. Among other things, the Council of Europe has encouraged plurilingualism (an individual's language proficiency in several languages). Use of the CEFR promotes the view that most learners are not complete *tabulae rasae*. They already have some degree of competence in another language or languages, and teachers should take advantage of this (Paradowski 2007). The ongoing development of technology is another of those external influences that has had a major impact in the field, and this is likely to increase in the future. Speaking of external influences, we should also acknowledge that standardized examinations and textbooks, which require adherence to even the smallest details through their teacher guides, mean that, in reality, teachers are not always able to exercise the methodological choices they would wish (Akbari 2007).

Finally, it was not our intent to be comprehensive and to deal with all language teaching methods that have ever been practiced. While we consider the various methods in a rough chronological order, it is also the case that there were methods practiced before the first one discussed in this book, and that many of them are practiced concurrently. To be clear, we are not claiming that newer methods are better in all respects than older methods. What we did choose to do was to include methods[2] that are practiced today, and that reflect a diversity of views on the teaching and learning processes. By confronting such diversity, and by viewing the thought-in-action links that others have made, we hope that you will arrive at your own personal conceptualizations of how thoughts lead to actions in your teaching and how, in turn, your teaching leads to the desired learning outcomes in your students. Thus, ultimately, the choice among techniques and principles depends on learning outcomes, a theme to which we will return in the final chapter of this book.

Doubting Game and Believing Game

Some of what you encounter here will no doubt affirm what you do or believe already; other things you read about may challenge your notions. When our fundamental beliefs are challenged, we are often quick to dismiss the idea. It is too threatening to our well-established beliefs. Diane Larsen-Freeman will never forget one of the first times she heard Caleb Gattegno discuss the Silent Way, a method presented in this book (see Chapter 5). Diane reports that it was at a language teaching convention in New York City in 1976:

> Several things Gattegno talked about that day were contrary to my own beliefs at the time. I found myself listening to him and at the same time hearing this doubtful voice in my head saying 'Wait a minute ...'.
>
> Gattegno said that day that a teacher should never praise a student, not even say 'Good,' or smile. 'Wait a minute,' I heard the voice in my head echoing, 'Everyone knows that being a good teacher means giving positive feedback to students and being concerned about their affective side or their feelings. Besides, how will the students know when they are right if the teacher doesn't tell them so?'
>
> Later, though, I found myself thinking, 'On the other hand, I can see why you are reluctant to give feedback. You have made me think about the power of silence. Without having the teacher to rely on, students have to assume responsibility for the work—just as you so often say, 'only the learner can do the learning.' I can see how this silence (behavior) is in keeping with your belief that the students must do without the overt

---

[2] It should be acknowledged that not all of the originators of the methods presented in this book would call their contribution a 'method' because they note that the term is sometimes associated with formulaic practice. We hope that we have made it clear that for us a method is a way of connecting particular principles with particular techniques into a coherent package, not a 'recipe' to be prescribed to teachers.

approval of the teacher. They must concentrate on developing and then satisfying their own ~~inner criteria~~. ~~Learning to listen to themselves is part of lessening their reliance on the teache~~r. The teacher will not always be there. Also, they will be encouraged to form criteria for correcting their own mistakes—for monitoring their own progress. I also see how you think that if the teacher makes a big deal out of students' success, this implies that what the student is doing is out of the ordinary—and that the job of learning a language must be difficult. Also, I see that in your view, students' security is provided for by their just being accepted without regard for any linguistic successes or difficulties they might be having.

What are the differences between the two voices Diane heard in her head—between the 'Wait a Minute' and the 'On the Other Hand' responses? Well, perhaps it would be clearer if we reflected for a moment on what it requires to uphold each position. What Diane has attempted to illustrate is two games (Larsen-Freeman 1983b). They are described in the article, 'The Doubting Game and the Believing Game,' which appears in an appendix to a book authored by Peter Elbow (1973). Elbow believes that **doubting and believing games** are games because they are rule-governed, ritualized processes, which are not real life. The doubting game, Elbow says, requires logic and evidence. 'It emphasizes a model of knowing as an act of discrimination: putting something on trial to see whether it is wanting or not' (Larsen-Freeman 1983a: 15). We think its practice is something far more common to the academic world than its counterpart—the believing game. As the famous Tibetan Buddhist master, Sogyal Rinpoche, puts it:

> Our contemporary education, then, that indoctrinates us in the glorification of doubt, has created in fact what could almost be called a religion or theology of doubt, in which to be seen to be intelligent we have to be seen to doubt everything, to always point to what's wrong and rarely to ask what is right or good …
> (Sogyal Rinpoche 1993: 123–4).

Many of us are very good at playing the ~~doubting game, but we do so at a cost. We may find fault with a new idea before giving it a proper chanc~~e.

What does playing the believing game require, then? The believing game 'emphasizes a model of knowing as an act of constructing, an act of investment, an act of involvement' (Elbow 1973: 163). It is not just the withholding of doubt. Rather, it asks us to put on the eyeglasses of another person—to adopt his or her perspective—to see the method as the originator sees it. Further, it requires a willingness to explore what is new.

see through another's lens

While it may appear that the believing game is the more desirable of the two games, ~~Elbow is not arguing, nor are we, that we should abandon the doubt~~-

ing game, but rather that you attempt to understand first before you judge. Therefore, do not be quick to dismiss a principle or technique because, at first glance, it appears to be at odds with your own beliefs or to be impossible to apply in your own situation. For instance, in one of the methods we will consider, teachers translate what the students want to know how to say from the students' native language to the language they are studying. If you reject this technique as impractical because you do not know your students' native language or because your students speak a number of different native languages, then you may be missing out on something valuable. You should first ask what the purpose of translating is: Is there a principle behind its use in which you believe? If so, can you apply it another way, say, by inviting a bilingual speaker to come to your class now and again or by having your students act out or paraphrase what they want to be able to say in the language they are studying?

Layout of Chapters

You will learn about the methods by entering a classroom where each method is being practiced. In most chapters in this book, one language teaching method is presented. However, in a few chapters, a more general approach to language teaching is presented, and what are described in the chapter are one or more methods that are examples of the approach[3]. We have assumed that observing a class will give you a greater understanding of a particular method and will give you more of an opportunity to reflect on your own practice than if you were simply to read a description of it. It should be acknowledged, however, that these classroom encounters are idealized. Anyone who is or has been a language teacher or student will immediately recognize that lessons seldom go as smoothly as the ones you will see here. In the real world students do not always catch on as quickly, and teachers have to contend with many other social and classroom management matters than those presented here. As we have already acknowledged, a method does not reflect everything that is happening in the classroom.

We will observe the techniques the teacher is using as well as his or her behavior. (In the even-numbered chapters, the teacher is female; in the odd-numbered chapters, the teacher is male.) After observing a lesson, we will try to infer the principles on which the teacher's behavior and techniques are based. Although in most cases, we will observe only the one beginning or intermediate-level class for each method, once the principles are clear, they can be applied to other situations. To illustrate the application of the prin-

[3] Following Anthony's (1963) use of the term 'approach.'

ciples at more than one level of proficiency, in two instances, with the Silent Way and Desuggestopedia, we will first visit a beginning-level class and then later briefly visit a class at a high-intermediate level. It should be noted that when learners are at the advanced level, methods are often less distinct because advanced learners may have special, well-defined needs, such as learning how to read and write academic texts. However, as we have seen from Stevick's example of using a picture to teach a dialogue, the way the teacher thinks about language teaching and learning will still affect how the teacher works at all levels.

After we have identified the principles, we will consider the answers to 10 questions. The questions are:

1 What are the goals of teachers who use this method?
2 What is the role of the teacher? What is the role of the students?
3 What are some characteristics of the teaching/learning process?
4 What is the nature of student–teacher interaction? What is the nature of student–student interaction?
5 How are the feelings of the students dealt with?
6 How is language viewed? How is culture viewed?
7 What areas of language are emphasized? What language skills are emphasized?
8 What is the role of the students' native language?
9 How is evaluation accomplished?
10 How does the teacher respond to student errors?

The answers to these questions will add to our understanding of each method and allow us to see some salient differences among the methods presented here. Before reading the answers to these questions in the book, you might first try to answer them yourself. This might increase your understanding of a method and give you practice with reflecting on an experience.

Following these questions, the techniques we observed in the lesson will be reviewed and in some cases expanded, so that you can try to put them into practice if you wish. Indeed, as we mentioned earlier, another purpose of this book is to present a variety of techniques, some of which may be new to you, and to encourage you to experiment with them. We know that the more experienced a teacher is, the broader is his or her repertoire of techniques (Arends 2004). Presumably, such versatility allows a teacher to deal more effectively with the unique constellation of students with whom she or he is working at any one time.

In the conclusion to each chapter, you will be asked to think about how all of this information can be of use to you in your teaching. It is you who have to view these methods through the filter of your own beliefs, needs, knowledge, and experience. By playing the believing game, it is our hope that no matter what your assessment of a particular method, you will not have reached it without first 'getting inside the method and looking out'. We should note, though, that this book is not a substitute for actual training in a particular method, and specific training is advised for some of them.

At the end of each chapter are two types of exercise. The first type allows you to check your understanding of what you have read. The second type of exercise asks you to make the connection between what you understand about a method and your own teaching situation. Wherever possible, we encourage you to work with someone else as you consider these. Teaching can be a solitary activity, but collaborating with other teachers can help enrich our experience and nurture our growth.

References/Additional Resources

Akbari, R. 2007. 'Reflections on reflection: A critical appraisal of reflective practices in L2 teacher education.' *System* 35: 192–207.

Anthony, E. 1963. 'Approach, method and technique.' *English Language Teaching* 17: 63–7. Reprinted in H. Allen and R. Campbell (eds.). *Teaching English as a Second Language* (2nd edn.). 1972. New York: McGraw-Hill.

Arends, R. 2004. *Learning to Teach* (6th edn.). New York: McGraw-Hill.

Bailey, K., M. Long, and **S. Peck** (eds.). 1983. *Second Language Acquisition Studies*. Rowley, MA: Newbury House.

Cook, G. 2010. *Translation in Language Teaching–An Argument for Reassessment*. Oxford: Oxford University Press.

Council of Europe. 2001. *Common European Framework of Reference for Languages: Learning, Teaching, Assessment*. Cambridge: Cambridge University Press.

Elbow, P. 1973. *Writing without Teachers*. New York: Oxford University Press.

Larsen-Freeman, D. 1983a. 'Second language acquisition: Getting the whole picture' in K. Bailey, M. Long and S. Peck (eds.). *Second Language Acquisition Studies*. Rowley, MA: Newbury House Publishers, Inc.

——. 1983b. 'Language teaching methods: Getting the whole picture.' Keynote address delivered at the First Annual Summer Conference for Language Teachers, June 24–5, School for International Training, Brattleboro, Vermont.

——. 1993. Foreign language teaching methodology and language teacher education. Plenary address delivered at AILA 1993, Amsterdam.

Paradowski, M. 2007. 'Comparative linguistics and language pedagogy: concise history' in F. Boers, J. Darquennes, and R. Temmerman (eds.). *Multilingualism and Applied Comparative Linguistics*, 1–20. Newcastle: Cambridge Scholars Publishing.

Prabhu, N. S. 1990. 'There is no best method—Why?' *TESOL Quarterly* 24/2: 161–76.

——. 1992. 'The dynamics of the language lesson.' *TESOL Quarterly* 26/2: 225–41.

Rajagopalan, K. 2007. 'From madness in method to method in madness.' *ELT Journal* 62/1: 84–5.

Rinpoche, S. 1993. *The Tibetan Book of Living and Dying.* New York: Harper Collins.

Stevick, E. 1980. *Teaching Languages: A Way and Ways.* Rowley, MA: Newbury House.

——. 1993. 'Social meanings for how we teach' in J. Alatis (ed.). Georgetown University Round Table on Languages and Linguistics. Washington, DC: Georgetown University Press.

Todeva, E. and J. Cenoz (eds.). 2009. *The Multiple Realities of Multilingualism.* Berlin: Mouton de Gruyter.

The Grammar-Translation Method

Introduction

The Grammar-Translation Method is not new. It has had different names, but it has been used by language teachers for many years. At one time it was called the Classical Method since it was first used in the teaching of the classical languages, Latin and Greek. Earlier in the 20ᵗʰ century, this method was used for the purpose of helping students to read and appreciate foreign language literature. It was also hoped that through the study of the grammar of the target language[1] students would become more familiar with the grammar of their native language and that this familiarity would help them speak and write their native language better. Finally, it was thought that foreign language learning would help students grow intellectually; it was recognized that students would probably never use the target language, but the mental exercise of learning it would be beneficial anyway.

   Let us try to understand the Grammar-Translation Method by observing a class where the teacher is using it. The class is a high-intermediate level English class at a university in Colombia. There are 42 students in the class. Two-hour classes are conducted three times a week.

Experience

As we enter the classroom, the class is in the middle of reading a passage in their textbook. The passage is an excerpt entitled 'The Boys' Ambition' from Mark Twain's *Life on the Mississippi*. Each student is called on to read a few

[1] The term *target language* is used to refer to either a second or a foreign language that is being taught. Since many students are plurilingual or multilingual already, the term 'second language' does not make sense, nor does the term 'foreign language' because often the study of language is taking place within a locale where it is spoken, not in some 'foreign' country. The term 'target language', therefore, though not without problems, seems an acceptable compromise.

lines from the passage. After he has finished reading, he is asked to translate the few lines he has just read into Spanish. The teacher helps him with new vocabulary items. When the students have finished reading and translating the passage, the teacher asks them in Spanish if they have any questions. One girl raises her hand and says, 'What is paddle wheel?' The teacher replies, '*Es una rueda de paletas*.' Then she continues in Spanish to explain how it looked and worked on the steamboats which moved up and down the Mississippi River during Mark Twain's childhood. Another student says, 'No understand "gorgeous".' The teacher translates, '*primoroso*.'

Since the students have no more questions, the teacher asks them to write the answers to the comprehension questions which appear at the end of the excerpt. The questions are in English, and the students are instructed to write the answers to them in English as well. They do the first one together as an example. A student reads out loud, 'When did Mark Twain live?' Another student replies, 'Mark Twain lived from 1835 to 1910.' '*Bueno*,' says the teacher, and the students begin working quietly by themselves.

In addition to questions that ask for information contained within the reading passage, the students answer two other types of questions. For the first type, they have to make inferences based on their understanding of the passage. For example, one question is: 'Do you think the boy was ambitious? Why or why not?' The other type of question requires the students to relate the passage to their own experience. For example, one of the questions based on this excerpt asks them, 'Have you ever thought about running away from home?'

After one-half hour, the teacher, speaking in Spanish, asks the students to stop and check their work. One by one, each student reads a question and then reads his or her response. If the answer is correct, the teacher calls on another student to read the next question. If the student is incorrect, the teacher selects a different student to supply the correct answer, or the teacher herself gives the right answer.

Announcing the next activity, the teacher asks the students to turn over the page in their text. There is a list of words there. The introduction to the exercise tells the students that these are words taken from the passage they have just read. The students see the words 'ambition,' 'career,' 'wharf,' 'tranquil,' 'gorgeous,' 'loathe,' 'envy,' and 'humbly.' They are told that some of these are review words and that others are new to them. The students are instructed to give the Spanish word for each of them. This exercise the class does together. If no one knows the Spanish equivalent, the teacher gives it. In Part 2 of this exercise, the students are given English words like 'love,' 'noisy,' 'ugly,' and 'proudly,' and are directed to find the opposites of these words in the passage.

Exercise 2A

These words are taken from the passage you have just read. Some of them are review words and others are new. Give the Spanish translation for each of them. You may refer back to the reading passage.

ambition	gorgeous
career	loathe
wharf	envy
tranquil	humbly

Exercise 2B

These words all have **antonyms** in the reading passage. Find the antonym for each:

love	ugly
noisy	proudly

Figure 2.1 An example of a Grammar-Translation exercise

When they have finished this exercise, the teacher reminds them that English words that look like Spanish words are called **cognates**. The English '-ty,' she says, for example, often corresponds to the Spanish endings -*dad* and -*tad*. She calls the students' attention to the word 'possibility' in the passage and tells them that this word is the same as the Spanish *posibilidad*. The teacher asks the students to find other examples in the excerpt. Hands go up; a boy answers, 'Obscurity.' '*Bien*,' says the teacher. When all of these cognates from the passage have been identified, the students are told to turn to the next exercise in the chapter and to answer the question, 'What do these cognates mean?' There is a long list of English words ('curiosity,' 'opportunity,' 'liberty,' etc.), which the students translate into Spanish.

The next section of the chapter deals with grammar. The students follow in their books as the teacher reads a description of two-word (phrasal) verbs. This is a review for them as they have encountered phrasal verbs before. Nevertheless, there are some new two-word verbs in the passage the students haven't learned yet. These are listed following the description, and the students are asked to translate them into Spanish. Then they are given the rule for use of a direct object with two-word verbs:

If the two-word verb is separable, the direct object may come between the verb and its particle. However, separation is necessary when the direct object is a pronoun. If the verb is inseparable, then there is no separation of the verb and particle by the object. For example:

John put away his book.

or

John put his book away/John put it away.

but not

*John put away it.
(because 'put away' is a separable two-word verb)

The teacher went over the homework.

but not

*The teacher went the homework over.
(because 'go over' is an inseparable two-word verb).

After reading over the rule and the examples, the students are asked to tell which of the following two-word verbs, taken from the passage, are separable and which inseparable. They refer to the passage for clues. If they cannot tell from the passage, they use their dictionaries or ask their teacher.

turn up	wake up	get on	take in
run away	fade out	lay up	
go away	break down	turn back	

Finally, they are asked to put one of these phrasal verbs in the blank of each of the 10 sentences they are given. They do the first two together.

1   Mark Twain decided to _____ because his parents wouldn't let him get a job on the river.
2   The steamboatmen _____ and discharge freight at each port on the Mississippi River.

When the students are finished with this exercise, they read their answers aloud.

At the end of the chapter there is a list of vocabulary items that appeared in the passage. The list is divided into two parts: the first contains words, and the second, idioms like 'to give someone the cold shoulder.' Next to each is a Spanish word or phrase. For homework, the teacher asks the students to memorize the Spanish translation for the first 20 words and to write a sentence in English using each word.

In the two remaining lessons of the week, the students will be asked to:

1   Write out the translation of the reading passage in Spanish.
2   State the rule for the use of a direct object with two-word verbs, and apply it to other phrasal verbs.
3   Do the remaining exercises in the chapter that include practice with one set of irregular past participle forms. The students will be asked to

memorize the present tense, past tense, and past participle forms of this irregular paradigm:

drink	drank	drunk
sing	sang	sung
swim	swam	swum
ring	rang	rung
begin	began	begun

4   Write a composition in the target language about an ambition they have.
5   Memorize the remaining vocabulary items and write sentences for each.
6   Take a quiz on the grammar and vocabulary of this chapter. They will be asked to translate a Spanish paragraph about steamboats into English.

Thinking about the Experience

This has been just a brief introduction to the Grammar-Translation Method, but it is probably true that this method is not new to many of you. You may have studied a language in this way, or you may be teaching with this method right now. Whether this is true or not, let us see what we have learned about the Grammar-Translation Method. We are able to make a number of observations about the class we attended. Our observations will be listed in the left column; from them we will try to identify the principles of the Grammar-Translation Method. The principles will be listed in the right column. We will make our observations in order, following the lesson plan of the class we observed.

Observations	Principles
1 The class is reading an excerpt from Mark Twain's *Life on the Mississippi*.	A fundamental purpose of learning a language is to be able to read literature written in it. Literary language is superior to spoken language. Students' study of the target culture is limited to its literature and fine arts.
2 Students translate the passage from English into Spanish.	An important goal is for students to be able to translate each language into the other. If students can translate from one language into another, they are considered successful language learners.

3 The teacher asks students in their native language if they have any questions. A student asks one and is answered in her native language.	The ability to communicate in the target language is not a goal of language instruction.
4 Students write out the answers to reading comprehension questions.	The primary skills to be developed are reading and writing. Little attention is given to speaking and listening, and almost none to pronunciation.
5 The teacher decides whether an answer is correct or not. If the answer is incorrect, the teacher selects a different student to supply the correct answer or the teacher herself gives the right answer.	The teacher is the authority in the classroom. It is very important that students get the correct answer.
6 Students translate new words from English into Spanish.	It is possible to find native language equivalents for all target language words.
7 Students learn that English '-ty' corresponds to -dad and -tad in Spanish.	Learning is facilitated through attention to similarities between the target language and the native language.
8 Students are given a grammar rule for the use of a direct object with two-word verbs.	It is important for students to learn about the grammar or form of the target language.
9 Students apply a rule to examples they are given.	**Deductive** application of an explicit grammar rule is a useful pedagogical technique.
10 Students memorize vocabulary.	Language learning provides good mental exercise.
11 The teacher asks students to state the grammar rule.	Students should be conscious of the grammatical rules of the target language.
12 Students memorize present tense, past tense, and past participle forms of one set of irregular verbs.	Wherever possible, verb conjugations and other grammatical paradigms should be committed to memory.

There were other activities planned for the remainder of the week, but in this book we will follow the practice of not listing an observation unless it leads to our discovering a different principle of the method.

Reviewing the Principles

The principles of the Grammar-Translation Method are organized below by answering the 10 questions posed in Chapter 1. Not all the questions are addressed by the Grammar-Translation Method; we will list all the questions, however, so that a comparison among the methods we study will be easier for you to make.

1 **What are the goals of teachers who use the Grammar-Translation Method?**
According to the teachers who use the Grammar-Translation Method, a fundamental purpose of learning a language is to be able to read literature written in the target language. To do this, students need to learn about the grammar rules and vocabulary of the target language. In addition, it is believed that studying another language provides students with good mental exercise, which helps develop their minds.

2 **What is the role of the teacher? What is the role of the students?**
The roles are very traditional. The teacher is the authority in the classroom. The students do as she says so they can learn what she knows.

3 **What are some characteristics of the teaching/learning process?**
Students are taught to translate from one language into another. Often what they translate are readings in the target language about some aspect of the culture of the target language community. Students study grammar deductively; that is, they are given the grammar rules and examples, are told to memorize them, and then are asked to apply the rules to other examples. They also learn grammatical paradigms such as verb conjugations. They memorize native language equivalents for target language vocabulary words.

4 **What is the nature of student–teacher interaction? What is the nature of student–student interaction?**
Most of the interaction in the classroom is from the teacher to the students. There is little student initiation and little student–student interaction.

5 **How are the feelings of the students dealt with?**
There are no principles of the method which relate to this area.

6 How is the language viewed? How is culture viewed?

Literary language is considered superior to spoken language and is therefore the language the students study. Culture is viewed as consisting of literature and the fine arts.

7 What areas of language are emphasized? What language skills are emphasized?

Vocabulary and grammar are emphasized. Reading and writing are the primary skills that the students work on. There is much less attention given to speaking and listening. Pronunciation receives little, if any, attention.

8 What is the role of the students' native language?

The meaning of the target language is made clear by translating it into the students' native language. The language that is used in class is mostly the students' native language.

9 How is evaluation accomplished?

Written tests in which students are asked to translate from their native language into the target language or vice versa are often used. Questions about the target culture or questions that ask students to apply grammar rules are also common.

10 How does the teacher respond to student errors?

Having the students get the correct answer is considered very important. If students make errors or do not know an answer, the teacher supplies them with the correct answer.

Reviewing the Techniques

Ask yourself if any of the answers to the above questions make sense to you. If so, you may choose to try some of the techniques of the Grammar-Translation Method from the review that follows. On the other hand, you may find that you agree very little with the answers to these questions, but that there are still some techniques from the Grammar-Translation Method that you can usefully adapt. Below is an expanded description of some of these techniques.

- **Translation of a Literary Passage**

  Students translate a reading passage from the target language into their native language. The reading passage then provides the focus for several classes: vocabulary and grammatical structures in the passage are studied in subsequent lessons. The passage may be excerpted from some work from the target language literature, or a teacher may write a passage carefully designed to include particular grammar rules and vocabulary. The translation may be written or spoken or both. Students should not translate idioms and the like literally, but rather in a way that shows that they understand their meaning.

Reading Comprehension Questions

Students answer questions in the target language based on their understanding of the reading passage. Often the questions are sequenced so that the first group of questions asks for information contained within the reading passage. In order to answer the second group of questions, students will have to make inferences based on their understanding of the passage. This means they will have to answer questions about the passage even though the answers are not contained in the passage itself. The third group of questions requires students to relate the passage to their own experience.

Antonyms/Synonyms

Students are given one set of words and are asked to find antonyms in the reading passage. A similar exercise could be done by asking students to find **synonyms** for a particular set of words. Or students might be asked to define a set of words based on their understanding of them as they occur in the reading passage. Other exercises that ask students to work with the vocabulary of the passage are also possible.

Cognates

Students are taught to recognize cognates by learning the spelling or sound patterns that correspond between the languages. Students are also asked to memorize words that look like cognates but have meanings in the target language that are different from those in the native language. This technique, of course, would only be useful in languages that share cognates.

Deductive Application of Rules

Grammar rules are presented with examples. Exceptions to each rule are also noted. Once students understand a rule, they are asked to apply it to some different examples.

- **Fill-in-the-blanks Exercise**

  Students are given a series of sentences with words missing. They fill in the blanks with new vocabulary items or with items of a particular grammar type, such as prepositions or verbs with different tenses.

- **Memorization**

  Students are given lists of target language vocabulary words and their native language equivalents and are asked to memorize them. Students are also required to memorize grammatical rules and grammatical paradigms such as verb conjugations.

- **Use Words in Sentences**

  In order to show that students understand the meaning and use of a new vocabulary item, they make up sentences in which they use the new words.

- **Composition**

  The teacher gives the students a topic to write about in the target language. The topic is based upon some aspect of the reading passage of the lesson. Sometimes, instead of creating a composition, students are asked to prepare a précis of the reading passage.

Conclusion

You have now had an opportunity to examine the principles and some of the techniques of the Grammar-Translation Method. Try to make a connection between what you have understood and your own teaching situation and beliefs.

Do you believe that a fundamental reason for learning another language is to be able to read the literature written in the target language? Do you think it is important to learn about the target language? Should culture be viewed as consisting of literature and the fine arts? Do you agree with any of the other principles underlying the Grammar-Translation Method? Which ones?

Is translation a valuable exercise? Is answering reading comprehension questions of the type described here helpful? Should grammar be presented deductively? Are these or any of the other techniques of the Grammar-Translation Method ones which will be useful to you in your own teaching? Which ones?

Activities

> ### (A) Check your understanding of the Grammar-Translation Method.
>
> 1 It has been said that the Grammar-Translation Method teaches students about the target language, but not how to use it. Explain the difference in your own words.
> 2 What are the clues that this method had its origin in the teaching of the classical languages, Latin and Greek?

> ### (B) Apply what you have understood about the Grammar-Translation Method.
>
> 1 Think of a particular group of students you have recently taught or are currently teaching. Choose a reading passage from a literary work or a textbook or write one yourself. Make sure it is at a level your students can understand, yet not at a level that would be too simple for them. Try translating it yourself as a test of its difficulty. Identify the vocabulary you would choose to work on. Plan vocabulary exercises you would use to help your students associate the new words with their native language equivalents.
> 2 Pick a grammatical point or two contained in the same passage. Provide the explicit grammar rule that relates to each one and give some examples. Design exercises that require your students to apply the rule to some different examples.

References/Additional Resources

Chastain, K. 1988. *Developing Second-language Skills* (3rd edn.). Chicago: Rand McNally College Publishing Company.

Coleman, A. 1929. 'The teaching of modern foreign languages in the United States.' Vol. 12. American and Canadian Committees on Modern Languages.

Kelly, L. 1969. *25 Centuries of Language Teaching*. Rowley, MA: Newbury House.

Plotz, K. 1887. *Elementarbuch der Französischen Sprache*. Berlin: F. A. Herbig.

Stern, H. 1983. *Fundamental Concepts of Language Teaching*. Oxford: Oxford University Press.

Thomas, C. (ed.). 1901. Report of the committee of twelve of the Modern Language Association of America. Boston: DC Heath.

The Direct Method

Introduction

As with the Grammar-Translation Method, the Direct Method is not new. Its principles have been applied by language teachers for many years. Most recently, it was revived as a method when the goal of instruction became learning how to use another language to communicate. Since the Grammar-Translation Method was not very effective in preparing students to use the target language communicatively, the Direct Method became popular.

The Direct Method has one very basic rule: No translation is allowed. In fact, the Direct Method receives its name from the fact that meaning is to be conveyed directly in the target language through the use of demonstration and visual aids, with no recourse to the students' native language.

We will now try to come to an understanding of the Direct Method by observing an English teacher using it in a *scuola media* (lower-level secondary school) class in Italy. The class has 30 students who attend English class for one hour, three times a week. The class we observe is at the end of its first year of English language instruction in a *scuola media*.

Experience

The teacher is calling the class to order as we find seats toward the back of the room. He has placed a big map of the USA in the front of the classroom. He asks the students to open their books to a certain page number. The lesson is entitled 'Looking at a Map.' As the students are called on one by one, they read a sentence from the reading passage at the beginning of the lesson. The teacher points to the part of the map the sentence describes after each has read a sentence. The passage begins:

We are looking at a map of the United States of America. Canada is the country to the north of the United States, and Mexico is the country to the south of the United States. Between Canada and the United States are the Great Lakes. Between Mexico and the United States is the Rio Grande River. On the East Coast is the Atlantic Ocean, and on the West Coast is the Pacific Ocean. In the east is a mountain range called the Appalachian Mountains. In the west are the Rocky Mountains.

After the students finish reading the passage, they are asked if they have any questions. A student asks what a mountain range is. The teacher turns to the whiteboard and draws a series of inverted cones to illustrate a mountain range.

Figure 3.1   The teacher drawing on the board to illustrate the meaning of 'mountain range'

The student nods and says, 'I understand.' Another student asks what 'between' means. The teacher replies, 'You are sitting between Maria Pia and Giovanni. Paolo is sitting between Gabriella and Cettina. Now do you understand the meaning of "between"?' The student answers, 'Yes, I understand.'

After all of the questions have been answered, the teacher asks some of his own. 'Class, are we looking at a map of Italy?'

The class replies in chorus, 'No!'

The teacher reminds the class to answer in a full sentence.

'No, we aren't looking at a map of Italy,' they respond.

The teacher asks, 'Are we looking at a map of the United States?'

'Yes. We are looking at a map of the United States.'

'Is Canada the country to the south of the United States?'

'No. Canada isn't the country south of the United States.'
'Are the Great Lakes in the North of the United States?'
'Yes. The Great Lakes are in the North.'
'Is the Rio Grande a river or a lake?'
'The Rio Grande is a river.'
'It's a river. Where is it?'
'It's between Mexico and the United States.'
'What color is the Rio Grande on the map?'
'It's blue.'
'Point to a mountain range in the west. What mountains are they?'
'They are the Rocky Mountains.'

The question and answer session continues for a few more minutes. Finally, the teacher invites the students to ask questions. Hands go up, and the teacher calls on students to pose questions one at a time, to which the class replies. After several questions have been posed, one girl asks, 'Where are the Appalachian Mountains?' Before the class has a chance to respond, the teacher works with the student on the pronunciation of 'Appalachian.' Then he includes the rest of the class in this practice as well, expecting that they will have the same problem with this long word. After insuring that the students' pronunciation is correct, the teacher allows the class to answer the question.

Later another student asks, 'What is the ocean in the West Coast?' The teacher again interrupts before the class has a chance to reply, saying, 'What is the ocean *in* the West Coast? … or *on* the West Coast?' The student hesitates, then says, 'On the West Coast.'

'Correct,' says the teacher. 'Now, repeat your question.'
'What is the ocean on the West Coast?'
The class replies in chorus, 'The ocean on the West Coast is the Pacific.'

After the students have asked about 10 questions, the teacher begins asking questions and making statements again. This time, however, the questions and statements are about the students in the classroom, and contain one of the prepositions 'on,' 'at,' 'to,' 'in,' or 'between,' such as, 'Antonella, is your book on your desk?' 'Antonio, who is sitting between Luisa and Teresa?' 'Emanuela, point to the clock.' The students then make up their own questions and statements and direct them to other students.

The teacher next instructs the students to turn to an exercise in the lesson which asks them to fill in the blanks. They read a sentence out loud and supply the missing word as they are reading, for example:

The Atlantic Ocean is _____ the East Coast.
The Rio Grande is _____ Mexico and the United States.
Edoardo is looking _____ the map.

Finally, the teacher asks the students to take out their notebooks, and he gives them a dictation. The passage he dictates is one paragraph long and is about the geography of the United States.

During the remaining two classes of the week, the class will:

1 Review the features of United States geography.
2 Following the teacher's directions, label blank maps with these geographical features. After this, the students will give directions to the teacher, who will complete a map on the board.
3 Practice the pronunciation of 'river', paying particular attention to the /ɪ/ in the first syllable (and contrasting it with /iː/) and to the pronunciation of /r/.
4 Write a paragraph about the major geographical features of the United States.
5 Discuss the proverb 'Time is money'. Students will talk about this is in order to understand the fact that Americans value punctuality. They will compare this attitude with their own view of time.

Thinking about the Experience

Let us make some observations about our experience. These will be in the column on the left. The principles of the Direct Method that can be inferred from our observations will be listed in the column on the right.

Observations	Principles
1 The students read aloud a passage about the geography of the United States of America.	Reading in the target language should be taught from the beginning of language instruction; however, the reading skill will be developed through practice with speaking. Language is primarily speech. Culture consists of more than the fine arts (e.g. in this lesson we observed the students studying geography and cultural attitudes).
2 The teacher points to a part of the map after each sentence is read.	Objects (e.g. realia or pictures) present in the immediate classroom environment should be used to help students understand the meaning.

3 The teacher uses the target language to ask the students if they have a question. The students use the target language to ask their questions.	The native language should not be used in the classroom.
4 The teacher answers the students' questions by drawing on the whiteboard or giving examples.	The teacher should demonstrate, not explain or translate. It is desirable that students make a direct association between the target language form and meaning.
5 The teacher asks questions about the map in the target language, to which the students reply in a complete sentence in the target language.	Students should learn to think in the target language as soon as possible. Vocabulary is acquired more naturally if students use it in full sentences, rather than memorizing word lists.
6 Students ask questions about the map.	The purpose of language learning is communication (therefore students need to learn how to ask questions as well as answer them).
7 The teacher works with the students on the pronunciation of 'Appalachian.'	Pronunciation should be worked on right from the beginning of language instruction.
8 The teacher corrects a grammar error by asking the students to make a choice.	Self-correction facilitates language learning.
9 The teacher asks questions about the students; students ask each other questions.	Lessons should contain some conversational activity—some opportunity for students to use language in real contexts. Students should be encouraged to speak as much as possible.
10 The students fill in blanks with prepositions practiced in the lesson.	Grammar should be taught **inductively**. There may never be an explicit grammar rule given.
11 The teacher dictates a paragraph about United States geography.	Writing is an important skill, to be developed from the beginning of language instruction.

12 All of the lessons of the week involve United States geography.	The syllabus is based on situations or topics, not usually on linguistic structures.
13 A proverb is used to discuss how Americans view punctuality.	Learning another language also involves learning how speakers of that language live.

Reviewing the Principles

Now let us consider the principles of the Direct Method as they are arranged in answer to the 10 questions posed earlier:

1 What are the goals of teachers who use the Direct Method?

Teachers who use the Direct Method intend that students learn how to communicate in the target language. In order to do this successfully, students should learn to think in the target language.

2 What is the role of the teacher? What is the role of the students?

Although the teacher directs the class activities, the student role is less passive than in the Grammar-Translation Method. The teacher and the students are more like partners in the teaching–learning process.

3 What are some characteristics of the teaching/learning process?

Teachers who use the Direct Method believe students need to associate meaning with the target language directly. In order to do this, when the teacher introduces a new target language word or phrase, he demonstrates its meaning through the use of realia, pictures, or pantomime; he never translates it into the students' native language. Students speak in the target language a great deal and communicate as if they were in real situations. In fact, the syllabus used in the Direct Method is based upon situations (for example, one unit would consist of language that people would use at a bank, another of the language that they use when going shopping) or topics (such as geography, money, or the weather). Grammar is taught inductively; that is, the students are presented with examples and they figure out the rule or generalization from the examples. An explicit grammar rule may never be given. Students practice vocabulary by using new words in complete sentences.

4 What is the nature of student–teacher interaction? What is the nature of student–student interaction?

The initiation of the interaction goes both ways, from teacher to students and from students to teacher, although the latter is often teacher-directed. Students converse with one another as well.

5 How are the feelings of the students dealt with?

There are no principles of the method which relate to this area.

6 How is language viewed? How is culture viewed?

Language is primarily spoken, not written. Therefore, students study common, everyday speech in the target language. They also study culture consisting of the history of the people who speak the target language, the geography of the country or countries where the language is spoken, and information about the daily lives of the speakers of the language.

7 What areas of language are emphasized? What language skills are emphasized?

Vocabulary is emphasized over grammar. Although work on all four skills (reading, writing, speaking, and listening) occurs from the start, oral communication is seen as basic. Thus the reading and writing exercises are based upon what the students practice orally first. Pronunciation also receives attention right from the beginning of a course.

8 What is the role of the students' native language?

The students' native language should not be used in the classroom.

9 How is evaluation accomplished?

We did not actually see any formal evaluation in the class we observed; however, in the Direct Method, students are asked to use the language, not to demonstrate their knowledge about the language. They are asked to do so, using both oral and written skills. For example, the students might be interviewed orally by the teacher or might be asked to write a paragraph about something they have studied.

10 How does the teacher respond to student errors?

The teacher, employing various techniques, tries to get students to self-correct whenever possible.

Reviewing the Techniques

Are there answers to the 10 questions with which you agreed? Then the following techniques may also be useful. Of course, even if you did not agree with all the answers, there may be some techniques of the Direct Method you can adapt to your own approach to teaching. The following expanded review of techniques provides you with some details, which will help you do this.

- **Reading Aloud**
  Students take turns reading sections of a passage, play, or dialogue out loud. At the end of each student's turn, the teacher uses gestures, pictures, realia, examples, or other means to make the meaning of the section clear.

- **Question and Answer Exercise**
  This exercise is conducted only in the target language. Students are asked questions and answer in full sentences so that they practice new words and grammatical structures. They have the opportunity to ask questions as well as answer them.

- **Getting Students to Self-correct**
  The teacher of this class has the students self-correct by asking them to make a choice between what they said and an alternative answer he supplied. There are, however, other ways of getting students to self-correct. For example, a teacher might simply repeat what a student has just said, using a questioning voice to signal to the student that something was wrong with it. Another possibility is for the teacher to repeat what the student said, stopping just before the error. The student then knows that the next word was wrong.

- **Conversation Practice**
  The teacher asks students a number of questions in the target language, which they have to understand to be able to answer correctly. In the class we observed, the teacher asked individual students questions about themselves. The questions contained a particular grammar structure. Later, the students were able to ask each other their own questions using the same grammatical structure.

- **Fill-in-the-blanks Exercise**
  This technique has already been discussed in the Grammar-Translation Method, but differs in its application in the Direct Method. All the items are in the target language; furthermore, no explicit grammar rule would be applied. The students would have induced the grammar rule they need to fill in the blanks from examples and practice with earlier parts of the lesson.

- **Dictation**

  The teacher reads the passage three times. The first time the teacher reads it at a normal speed, while the students just listen. The second time he reads the passage phrase by phrase, pausing long enough to allow students to write down what they have heard. The last time the teacher again reads at a normal speed, and students check their work.

- **Map Drawing**

  The class included one example of a technique used to give students listening comprehension practice. The students were given a map with the geographical features unnamed. Then the teacher gave the students directions such as the following, 'Find the mountain range in the West. Write the words "Rocky Mountains" across the mountain range.' He gave instructions for all the geographical features of the United States so that students would have a completely labeled map if they followed his instructions correctly. The students then instructed the teacher to do the same thing with a map he had drawn on the board. Each student could have a turn giving the teacher instructions for finding and labeling one geographical feature.

- **Paragraph Writing**

  The teacher in this class asked the students to write a paragraph in their own words on the major geographical features of the United States. They could have done this from memory, or they could have used the reading passage in the lesson as a model.

Conclusion

Now that you have considered the principles and the techniques of the Direct Method, see what you can find of use for your own teaching situation.

Do you agree that the goal of target language instruction should be to teach students how to communicate in the target language? Does it make sense to you that the students' native language should not be used to give meaning to the target language? Do you agree that the culture that is taught should be about people's daily lives in addition to the fine arts? Should students be encouraged to self-correct? Are there any other principles of the Direct Method which you believe in? Which ones?

Is dictation a worthwhile activity? Have you used question-and-answer exercises and conversation practice as described here before? If not, should you? Is paragraph writing a useful thing to ask students to do? Should grammar be presented inductively? Are there any other techniques of the Direct Method which you would consider adopting? Which ones?

Activities

Ⓐ Check your understanding of the Direct Method.

1   In the previous chapter on the Grammar-Translation Method, we learned that grammar was treated deductively. In the Direct Method, grammar is treated inductively. Can you explain the difference between deductive and inductive treatments of grammar?

2   What are some of the characteristics of the Direct Method that make it so distinct from the Grammar-Translation Method?

3   It has been said that it may be advantageous to a teacher using the Direct Method not to know his students' native language. Do you agree? Why?

Ⓑ Apply what you have understood about the Direct Method.

1   Choose a particular situation (such as at the bank, at the railroad station, or at the doctor's office) or a particular topic (such as articles of clothing, holidays, or the weather) and write a short passage or a dialogue on the theme you have chosen. Now think about how you will convey its meaning to students without using their native language.

2   Select a grammar point from the passage. Plan how you will get students to practice the grammar point. What examples can you provide them with so that they can induce the rule themselves?

3   Practice writing and giving a dictation as it is described in this chapter.

References/Additional Resources

Berlitz, M. 1887. *Méthode Berlitz*. New York: Berlitz and Company.

de Sauzé, E. 1929. *The Cleveland Plan for the Teaching of Modern Languages with Special Reference to French* (Revised edn.). Philadelphia: Winston, 1959.

Diller, K. 1978. *The Language Teaching Controversy*. Rowley, MA: Newbury House.

Gatenby, E. 1958. *A Direct Method English Course* (3rd edn.). London: Longman.

Gouin, F. 1880. *The Art of Teaching and Studying Languages* (H. Swan and V. Betts trs.). London: Philip.

Krause, C. 1916. *The Direct Method in Modern Languages*. New York: Charles Scribner.

SKU	ISBN/UPC	Title & Author/Artist	Shelf ID	Qty	OrderSKU
S339922400	9780194423601	Techniques and Principles in Language Teac... Anderson, Marti,Larsen-Freeman, Diane	11--15--3	1	‖‖‖‖‖

SHIPPED STANDARD TO:
Julian Bocanegra
5350 SE Del Rio CT
Hillsboro Oregon 97123
59m2wh49bd0yl1t@marketplace.amazon.com

ORDER# 111-3143949-0320202
AmazonMarketplaceUS

4

The Audio-Lingual Method

Introduction

The Audio-Lingual Method, like the Direct Method we have just examined, is also an oral-based approach. However, it is very different, in that rather than emphasizing vocabulary acquisition through exposure to its use in situations, the Audio-Lingual Method drills students in the use of grammatical sentence patterns. Also, unlike the Direct Method, it has a strong theoretical base in linguistics and psychology. Charles Fries (1945) of the University of Michigan led the way in applying principles from structural linguistics in developing the method, and for this reason, it has sometimes been referred to as the 'Michigan Method.' Later in its development, principles from behavioral psychology (Skinner 1957) were incorporated. It was thought that the way to acquire the sentence patterns of the target language was through **conditioning**—helping learners to respond correctly to stimuli through shaping and reinforcement, so that the learners could overcome the habits of their native language and form the new habits required to be target language speakers.

In order to come to an understanding of this method, let us now enter a classroom where the Audio-Lingual Method is being used. We will sit in on a beginning-level English class in Mali. There are 34 students, 13–15 years of age. The class meets for one hour a day, five days a week.

Experience

As we enter the classroom, the first thing we notice is that the students are attentively listening as the teacher is presenting a new dialogue, a conversation between two people. The students know they will be expected eventually to memorize the dialogue the teacher is introducing. All of the teacher's instructions are in English. Sometimes she uses actions to convey meaning, but not one word of the students' native language is uttered. After she acts out the dialogue, she says:

'All right, class. I am going to repeat the dialogue now. Listen carefully, but no talking please.

Two people are walking along a sidewalk in town. They know each other, and as they meet, they stop to talk. One of them is named Sally and the other one is named Bill. I will talk for Sally and for Bill. Listen to their conversation:

SALLY: Good morning, Bill.
BILL: Good morning, Sally.
SALLY: How are you?
BILL: Fine, thanks. And you?
SALLY: Fine. Where are you going?
BILL: I'm going to the post office.
SALLY: I am, too. Shall we go together?
BILL: Sure. Let's go.

Listen one more time. This time try to understand all that I am saying.'

Now she has the whole class repeat each of the lines of the dialogue after her model. They repeat each line several times before moving on to the next line. When the class comes to the line, 'I'm going to the post office,' they stumble a bit in their repetition. The teacher, at this point, stops the repetition and uses a backward build-up drill (expansion drill). The purpose of this drill is to break down the troublesome sentence into smaller parts. The teacher starts with the end of the sentence and has the class repeat just the last two words. Since they can do this, the teacher adds a few more words, and the class repeats this expanded phrase. Little by little the teacher builds up the phrases until the entire sentence is being repeated.

TEACHER: Repeat after me: post office.
CLASS: Post office.
TEACHER: To the post office.
CLASS: To the post office.
TEACHER: Going to the post office.
CLASS: Going to the post office.
TEACHER: I'm going to the post office.
CLASS: I'm going to the post office.

Through this step-by-step procedure, the teacher is able to give the students help in producing the troublesome line. Having worked on the line in small pieces, the students are also able to take note of where each word or phrase begins and ends in the sentence.

After the students have repeated the dialogue several times, the teacher gives them a chance to adopt the role of Bill while she says Sally's lines. Before the class actually says each line, the teacher models it. In effect, the class is experiencing a repetition drill where the students have to listen carefully and attempt to mimic the teacher's model as accurately as possible.

Next, the class and the teacher switch roles in order to practice a little more: The teacher says Bill's lines and the class says Sally's. Then the teacher divides the class in half so that each half on their own gets to try to say either Bill's or Sally's lines. The teacher stops the students from time to time when she feels they are straying too far from the model, and once again provides a model, which she has them attempt to copy. To further practice the lines of this dialogue, the teacher has all the boys in the class take Bill's part and all the girls take Sally's.

She then initiates a chain drill with four of the lines from the dialogue. A chain drill gives students an opportunity to say the lines individually. The teacher listens and can tell which students are struggling and will need more practice. A chain drill also lets students use the expressions in communication with someone else, even though the communication is very limited. The teacher addresses the student nearest her with, 'Good morning, Adama.' He, in turn, responds, 'Good morning, teacher.' She says, 'How are you?' Adama answers, 'Fine, thanks. And you?' The teacher replies, 'Fine.' He understands through the teacher's gestures that he is to turn to the student sitting beside him and greet her. That student, in turn, says her lines in reply to him. When she has finished, she greets the student on the other side of her. This chain continues until all of the students have a chance to ask and answer the questions. The last student directs the greeting to the teacher.

Finally, the teacher selects two students to perform the entire dialogue for the rest of the class. When they are finished, two others do the same. Not everyone has a chance to say the dialogue in a pair today, but perhaps they will sometime later in the week.

The teacher moves next to the second major phase of the lesson. She continues to drill the students with language from the dialogue, but these drills require more than simple repetition. The first drill the teacher leads is a single-slot substitution drill in which the students will repeat a sentence from the dialogue and replace a word or phrase in the sentence with the word or phrase the teacher gives them. This word or phrase is called the cue.

The teacher begins by reciting a line from the dialogue, 'I am going to the post office.' Following this she shows the students a picture of a bank and says the phrase, 'the bank.' She pauses, then says, 'I am going to the bank.'

From her example the students realize that they are supposed to take the cue phrase ('the bank'), which the teacher supplies, and put it into its proper place in the sentence.

Now she gives them their first cue phrase, 'the drugstore.' Together the students respond, 'I am going to the drugstore.' The teacher smiles. 'Very good!' she exclaims. The teacher cues, 'the park.' The students chorus, 'I am going to the park.'

Other cues she offers in turn are 'the café,' 'the supermarket,' 'the bus station,' 'the football field,' and 'the library.' Each cue is accompanied by a picture as before. After the students have gone through the drill sequence three times, the teacher no longer provides a spoken cue phrase. Instead, she simply shows the pictures one at a time, and the students repeat the entire sentence, putting the name of the place in the picture in the appropriate slot in the sentence.

Figure 4.1 Using pictures to conduct a sentence drill

A similar procedure is followed for another sentence in the dialogue, 'How are you?' The subject pronouns 'he,' 'she,' 'they,' and 'you' are used as cue words. This substitution drill is slightly more difficult for the students since they have to change the form of the verb 'be' to 'is' or 'are,' depending on which subject pronoun the teacher gives them. The students are apparently familiar with the subject pronouns since the teacher is not using any pictures. Instead, after going through the drill a few times supplying oral cues, the teacher points to a boy in the class and the students understand they are to use the pronoun 'he' in the sentence. They chorus, 'How is he?' 'Good!' says the teacher. She points to a girl and waits for the class's response, then points to other students to elicit the use of 'they.'

Finally, the teacher increases the complexity of the task by leading the students in a multiple-slot substitution drill. This is essentially the same type of drill as the single-slot the teacher has just used. However with this drill, students must recognize what part of speech the cue word is and where it fits into the sentence. The students still listen to only one cue from the teacher. Then they must make a decision concerning where the cue word or phrase belongs in a sentence also supplied by the teacher. The teacher in this class starts off by having the students repeat the original sentence from the dialogue, 'I am going to the post office.' Then she gives them the cue 'she.' The students understand and produce, 'She is going to the post office.' The next cue the teacher offers is 'to the park.' The students hesitate at first; then they respond by correctly producing, 'She is going to the park.' She continues in this manner, sometimes providing a subject pronoun, other times naming a location.

The substitution drills are followed by a transformation drill. This type of drill asks students to change one type of sentence into another—an affirmative sentence into a negative or an active sentence into a passive, for example. In this class, the teacher uses a substitution drill that requires the students to change a statement into a *yes/no* question. The teacher offers an example, 'I say, "She is going to the post office." You make a question by saying, "Is she going to the post office?"'

The teacher models two more examples of this transformation, then asks, 'Does everyone understand? OK, let's begin: "They are going to the bank."' The class replies in turn, 'Are they going to the bank?' They transform approximately fifteen of these patterns, and then the teacher decides they are ready to move on to a question-and-answer drill.

The teacher holds up one of the pictures she used earlier, the picture of a football field, and asks the class, 'Are you going to the football field?' She answers her own question, 'Yes, I'm going to the football field.' She poses the next question while holding up a picture of a park, 'Are you going to the park?' And again answers herself, 'Yes, I'm going to the park.' She holds up a third picture, the one of a library. She poses a question to the class, 'Are you going to the library?' They respond together, 'Yes, I am going to the library.'

'Very good,' the teacher says. Through her actions and examples, the students have learned that they are to answer the questions following the pattern she has modeled. The teacher drills them with this pattern for the next few minutes. Since the students can handle it, she poses the question to selected individuals rapidly, one after another. The students are expected to respond very quickly, without pausing.

The students are able to keep up the pace, so the teacher moves on to the next step. She again shows the class one of the pictures, a supermarket this time. She asks, 'Are you going to the bus station?' She answers her own question, 'No, I am going to the supermarket.'

The students understand that they are required to look at the picture and listen to the question and answer negatively if the place in the question is not the same as what they see in the picture. 'Are you going to the bus station?' The teacher asks while holding up a picture of a café. 'No, I am going to the café,' the class answers.

'Very good!' exclaims the teacher. After posing a few more questions that require negative answers, the teacher produces the pictures of the post office and asks, 'Are you going to the post office?' The students hesitate a moment and then chorus, 'Yes, I am going to the post office.'

'Good,' comments the teacher. She works a little longer on this question-and-answer drill, sometimes providing her students with situations that require a negative answer and sometimes giving encouragement to each student. She holds up pictures and poses questions one right after another, but the students seem to have no trouble keeping up with her. The only time she changes the rhythm is when a student seriously mispronounces a word. When this occurs she restates the word and works briefly with the student until his pronunciation is closer to her own.

For the final few minutes of the class, the teacher returns to the dialogue with which she began the lesson. She repeats it once, then has the half of the class to her left do Bill's lines and the half of the class to her right do Sally's. This time there is no hesitation at all. The students move through the dialogue briskly. They trade roles and do the same. The teacher smiles, 'Very good. Class dismissed.'

The lesson ends for the day. Both the teacher and the students have worked hard. The students have listened to and spoken only English for the period. The teacher is tired from all her action, but she is pleased for she feels the lesson went well. The students have learned the lines of the dialogue and to respond without hesitation to her cues in the drill pattern.

In lessons later in the week, the teacher will do the following:

1　Review the dialogue.
2　Expand upon the dialogue by adding a few more lines, such as 'I am going to the post office. I need a few stamps.'
3　Drill the new lines and introduce some new vocabulary items through the new lines, for example:

> I am going to the supermarket.　　I need a little butter.
> 　　　　　… library.　　　　　　　　… few books.
> 　　　　　… drugstore.　　　　　　　… little medicine.

4　Work on the difference between mass and count nouns, contrasting 'a little/a few' with mass and count nouns respectively. No grammar rule will ever be given to the students. The students will be led to figure out the rules from their work with the examples the teacher provides.

5 A contrastive analysis (the comparison of two languages, in this case, the students' native language and the target language, English) has led the teacher to expect that the students will have special trouble with the pronunciation of words such as 'little,' which contain /ɪ/. The students do indeed say the word as if it contained /iː/. As a result, the teacher works on the contrast between /ɪ/ and /iː/ several times during the week. She uses **minimal pair** words, such as ship/sheep, live/leave, and his/he's to get her students to hear the difference in pronunciation between the words in each pair. Then, when she feels they are ready, she drills them in saying the two sounds—first, the sounds on their own, and later, the sounds in words, phrases, and sentences.

6 Sometime towards the end of the week, the teacher writes the dialogue on the blackboard. She asks the students to give her the lines and she writes them out as the students say them. They copy the dialogue into their notebooks. They also do some limited written work with the dialogue. In one exercise, the teacher has erased 15 selected words from the expanded dialogue. The students have to rewrite the dialogue in their notebooks, supplying the missing words without looking at the complete dialogue they copied earlier. In another exercise, the students are given sequences of words such as 'I,' 'go,' 'supermarket' and 'he,' 'need,' 'butter,' and they are asked to write complete sentences like the ones they have been drilling orally.

7 On Friday the teacher leads the class in the 'supermarket alphabet game.' The game starts with a student who needs a food item beginning with the letter 'A.' The student says, 'I am going to the supermarket. I need a few apples.' The next student says, 'I am going to the supermarket. He needs a few apples. I need a little bread' (or 'a few bananas,' or any other food item you could find in the supermarket beginning with the letter 'B'). The third student continues, 'I am going to the supermarket. He needs a few apples. She needs a little bread. I need a little cheese.' The game continues with each player adding an item that begins with the next letter in the alphabet. Before adding his or her own item, however, each player must mention the items of the previous students. If the student has difficulty thinking of an item, the other students or the teacher helps.

8 A presentation by the teacher on supermarkets in the United States follows the game. The teacher tries very hard to get meaning across in English. The teacher answers the students' questions about the differences between supermarkets in the United States and open-air markets in Mali. They also discuss briefly the differences between American and Mali football. The students seem very interested in the

discussion. The teacher promises to continue the discussion of popular American sports the following week.

Thinking about the Experience

Although it is true that this was a very brief experience with the Audio-Lingual Method (ALM), let us see if we can make some observations about the behavior of the teacher and the techniques she used. From these we should be able to figure out the principles underlying the method. We will make our observations in order, following the lesson plan of the class we observed.

Observations	Principles
1 The teacher introduces a new dialogue.	Language forms do not occur by themselves; they occur most naturally within a context.
2 The language teacher uses only the target language in the classroom. Actions, pictures, or realia are used to give meaning otherwise.	The native language and the target language have separate linguistic systems. They should be kept apart so that the students' native language interferes as little as possible with the students' attempts to acquire the target language.
3 The language teacher introduces the dialogue by modeling it two times; she introduces the drills by modeling the correct answers; at other times, she corrects mispronunciation by modeling the proper sounds in the target language.	One of the language teacher's major roles is that of a model of the target language. Teachers should provide students with an accurate model. By listening to how it is supposed to sound, students should be able to mimic the model.
4 The students repeat each line of the new dialogue several times.	Language learning is a process of habit formation. The more often something is repeated, the stronger the habit and the greater the learning.
5 The students stumble over one of the lines of the dialogue. The teacher uses a backward build-up drill with this line.	It is important to prevent learners from making errors. Errors lead to the formation of bad habits. When errors do occur, they should immediately be corrected by the teacher.

6 The teacher initiates a chain drill in which each student greets another.	The purpose of language learning is to learn how to use the language to communicate.
7 The teacher uses single-slot and multiple-slot substitution drills.	Particular parts of speech occupy particular 'slots' in sentences. In order to create new sentences, students must learn which part of speech occupies which slot.
8 The teacher says, 'Very good,' when the students answer correctly.	Positive reinforcement helps the students to develop correct habits.
9 The teacher uses spoken cues and picture cues.	Students should learn to respond to both verbal and nonverbal stimuli.
10 The teacher conducts transformation and question-and-answer drills.	Each language has a finite number of patterns. Pattern practice helps students to form habits which enable the students to use the patterns.
11 When the students can handle it, the teacher poses the questions to them rapidly.	Students should 'overlearn,' i.e. learn to answer automatically without stopping to think.
12 The teacher provides the students with cues; she calls on individuals; she smiles encouragement; she holds up pictures one after another.	The teacher should be like an orchestra leader—conducting, guiding, and controlling the students' behavior in the target language.
13 New vocabulary is introduced through lines of the dialogue; vocabulary is limited.	The major objective of language teaching should be for students to acquire the structural patterns; students will learn vocabulary afterward.
14 Students are given no grammar rules; grammatical points are taught through examples and drills.	The learning of another language should be the same as the acquisition of the native language. We do not need to memorize rules in order to use our native language. The rules necessary to use the target language will be figured out or induced from examples.

15 The teacher does a contrastive analysis of the target language and the students' native language in order to locate the places where she anticipates her students will have trouble.	The major challenge of language teaching is getting students to overcome the habits of their native language. A comparison between the native and target language will tell the teacher in which areas her students will probably experience difficulty.
16 The teacher writes the dialogue on the blackboard toward the end of the week. The students do some limited written work with the dialogue and the sentence drills.	Speech is more basic to language than the written form. The 'natural order' (the order children follow when learning their native language) of skill acquisition is: listening, speaking, reading, and writing.
17 The supermarket alphabet game and a discussion of American supermarkets and football are included.	Language cannot be separated from culture. Culture is not only literature and the arts, but also the everyday behavior of the people who use the target language. One of the teacher's responsibilities is to present information about that culture.

Reviewing the Principles

At this point we should turn to the 10 questions we have answered for each method we have considered so far.

1 What are the goals of teachers who use the Audio-Lingual Method?

Teachers want their students to be able to use the target language communicatively. In order to do this, they believe students need to overlearn the target language, to learn to use it automatically without stopping to think. Their students achieve this by forming new habits in the target language and overcoming the old habits of their native language.

2 What is the role of the teacher? What is the role of the students?

The teacher is like an orchestra leader, directing and controlling the language behavior of her students. She is also responsible for providing her students with a good model for imitation.

Students are imitators of the teacher's model or the tapes she supplies of model speakers. They follow the teacher's directions and respond as accurately and as rapidly as possible.

3 What are some characteristics of the teaching/learning process?

New vocabulary and structural patterns are presented through dialogues. The dialogues are learned through imitation and repetition. Drills (such as repetition, backward build-up, chain, substitution, transformation, and question-and-answer) are conducted based upon the patterns present in the dialogue. Students' successful responses are positively reinforced. Grammar is induced from the examples given; explicit grammar rules are not provided. Cultural information is contextualized in the dialogues or presented by the teacher. Students' reading and written work is based upon the oral work they did earlier.

4 What is the nature of student–teacher interaction? What is the nature of student–student interaction?

There is student-to-student interaction in chain drills or when students take different roles in dialogues, but this interaction is teacher-directed. Most of the interaction is between teacher and students and is initiated by the teacher.

5 How are the feelings of the students dealt with?

There are no principles of the method that relate to this area.

6 How is the language viewed? How is culture viewed?

The view of language in the Audio-Lingual Method has been influenced by descriptive linguists. Every language is seen as having its own unique system. The system comprises several different levels: phonological, morphological, and syntactic. Each level has its own distinctive patterns.

Everyday speech is emphasized in the Audio-Lingual Method. The level of complexity of the speech is graded, however, so that beginning students are presented with only simple patterns. Culture consists of the everyday behavior and lifestyle of the target language speakers.

7 What areas of language are emphasized? What language skills are emphasized?

Vocabulary is kept to a minimum while the students are mastering the sound system and grammatical patterns. A grammatical pattern is not the same as a sentence. For instance, underlying the following three sentences is the same grammatical pattern: 'Meg called,' 'The Blue Jays won,' 'The team practiced.'

The natural order of skills presentation is adhered to: listening, speaking, reading, and writing. The oral/aural skills receive most of the attention. What students write they have first been introduced to orally. Pronunciation is taught from the beginning, often by students working in language laboratories on discriminating between members of minimal pairs.

8 What is the role of the students' native language?

The habits of the students' native language are thought to interfere with the students' attempts to master the target language. Therefore, the target language is used in the classroom, not the students' native language. A contrastive analysis between the students' native language and the target language will reveal where a teacher should expect the most interference.

9 How is evaluation accomplished?

The answer to this question is not obvious because we didn't actually observe the students in this class taking a formal test. If we had, we would have seen that it was discrete-point in nature, that is, each question on the test would focus on only one point of the language at a time. Students might be asked to distinguish between words in a minimal pair, for example, or to supply an appropriate verb form in a sentence.

10 How does the teacher respond to student errors?

Student errors are to be avoided if at all possible, through the teacher's awareness of where the students will have difficulty, and restriction of what they are taught to say.

Reviewing the Techniques

If you agree with the above answers, you may wish to implement the following techniques. Of course, even if you do not agree, there may be techniques described below that you are already using or can adapt to your approach.

- **Dialogue Memorization**

  Dialogues or short conversations between two people are often used to begin a new lesson. Students memorize the dialogue through mimicry; students usually take the role of one person in the dialogue, and the teacher the other. After the students have learned the first person's lines, they switch roles and memorize the other person's part. Another way of practicing the two roles is for half of the class to take one role and the other half to take the other. After the dialogue has been memorized, pairs of individual students might perform the dialogue for the rest of the class.

  In the Audio-Lingual Method, certain sentence patterns and grammar points are included within the dialogue. These patterns and points are later practiced in drills based on the lines of the dialogue.

- **Backward Build-up (Expansion) Drill**

  This drill is used when a long line of a dialogue is giving students trouble. The teacher breaks down the line into several parts. The students repeat a part of the sentence, usually the last phrase of the line. Then, following the teacher's cue, the students expand what they are repeating part by part until they are able to repeat the entire line. The teacher begins with the part at the end of the sentence (and works backward from there) to keep the intonation of the line as natural as possible. This also directs more student attention to the end of the sentence, where new information typically occurs.

- **Repetition Drill**

  Students are asked to repeat the teacher's model as accurately and as quickly as possible. This drill is often used to teach the lines of the dialogue.

- **Chain Drill**

  A chain drill gets its name from the chain of conversation that forms around the room as students, one by one, ask and answer questions of each other. The teacher begins the chain by greeting a particular student, or asking him a question. That student responds, then turns to the student sitting next to him. The first student greets or asks a question of the second student and the chain continues. A chain drill allows some controlled communication, even though it is limited. A chain drill also gives the teacher an opportunity to check each student's speech.

- **Single-slot Substitution Drill**

  The teacher says a line, usually from the dialogue. Next, the teacher says a word or a phrase (called the cue). The students repeat the line the teacher has given them, substituting the cue into the line in its proper place. The major purpose of this drill is to give the students practice in finding and filling in the slots of a sentence.

- **Multiple-slot Substitution Drill**

  This drill is similar to the single-slot substitution drill. The difference is that the teacher gives cue phrases, one at a time, that fit into different slots in the dialogue line. The students must recognize what part of speech each cue is, or at least, where it fits into the sentence, and make any other changes, such as subject–verb agreement. They then say the line, fitting the cue phrase into the line where it belongs.

- **Transformation Drill**

  The teacher gives students a certain kind of sentence pattern, an affirmative sentence for example. Students are asked to transform this sentence into a negative sentence. Other examples of transformations to ask of students are: changing a statement into a question, an active sentence into a passive one, or direct speech into reported speech.

- **Question-and-answer Drill**
  This drill gives students practice with answering questions. The students should answer the teacher's questions very quickly. Although we did not see it in our lesson here, it is also possible for the teacher to cue the students to ask questions as well. This gives students practice with the question pattern.

- **Use of Minimal Pairs**
  The teacher works with pairs of words which differ in only one sound; for example, 'ship/sheep.' Students are first asked to perceive the difference between the two words and later to be able to say the two words. The teacher selects the sounds to work on after she has done a contrastive analysis, a comparison between the students' native language and the language they are studying.

- **Complete the Dialogue**
  Selected words are erased from a dialogue students have learned. Students complete the dialogue by filling the blanks with the missing words.

- **Grammar Game**
  Games like the Supermarket Alphabet Game described in this chapter are used in the Audio-Lingual Method. The games are designed to get students to practice a grammar point within a context. Students are able to express themselves, although in a limited way. Notice there is also a lot of repetition in this game.

Conclusion

We have looked at both the techniques and the principles of the Audio-Lingual Method. Try now to make the bridge between this method and your teaching situation.

Does it make sense to you that language acquisition results from habit formation? If so, will the habits of the native language interfere with target language learning? Should errors be prevented as much as possible? Should the major focus be on the structural patterns of the target language? Which of these or the other principles of the Audio-Lingual Method are acceptable to you?

Is a dialogue a useful way to introduce new material? Should it be memorized through mimicry of the teacher's model? Are structure drills valuable pedagogical activities? Is working on pronunciation through minimal-pair drills a worthwhile activity? Would you say these techniques (or any others of this method) are ones that you can use as described? Could you adapt any of them to your own teaching approach and situation?

Activities

A **Check your understanding of the Audio-Lingual Method.**

1 Which of the techniques below follows from the principles of the Audio-Lingual Method, and which ones do not? Explain the reasons for your answer.

a The teacher asks beginning-level students to write a composition about the system of transportation in their home countries. If they need a vocabulary word that they do not know, they are told to look in a bilingual dictionary for a translation.

b Toward the end of the third week of the course, the teacher gives students a reading passage. The teacher asks the students to read the passage and to answer certain questions based upon it. The passage contains words and structures introduced during the first three weeks of the course.

c The teacher tells the students that they must add an 's' to third person singular verbs in the present tense in English. She then gives the students a list of verbs and asks them to change the verbs into the third person singular present tense form.

2 Some people believe that knowledge of a first and second language can be helpful to learners who are trying to learn a third language. What would an Audio-Lingual teacher say about this? Why?

B **Apply what you have understood about the Audio-Lingual Method.**

1 Read the following dialogue. What subsentence pattern is it trying to teach?

SAM   Lou's going to go to college next fall.

BETTY   Where is he going to go?

SAM   He's going to go to Stanford.

BETTY   What is he going to study?

SAM   Biology. He's going to be a doctor.

Prepare a series of drills (backward build-up, repetition, chain, single-slot substitution, multiple-slot substitution, transformation, and question-and-answer) designed to give beginning-level English language learners some practice with this structure. If the target language that you teach is not English, you may wish to write your own dialogue first. It is not easy to prepare drills, so you might want to try giving them to some other teachers to check.

2   Prepare your own dialogue to introduce your students to a sentence or subsentence pattern in the target language you teach.

References/Additional Resources

Brooks, N. 1964. *Language and Language Learning: Theory and Practice* (2nd edn.). New York: Harcourt Brace.

Chastain, K. 1988. *Developing Second-language Skills* (3rd edn.). Chicago: Rand McNally College Publishing.

Finocchiaro, M. 1974. *English as a Second Language: From Theory to Practice* (2nd edn.). 62–72, 168–72. New York: Regents Publishing.

Fries, C. 1945. *Teaching and Learning English as a Foreign Language*. Ann Arbor: University of Michigan Press.

Lado, R. 1957. *Linguistics Across Cultures: Applied Linguistics for Language Teachers*. Ann Arbor: University of Michigan Press.

——. 1964. *Language Teaching: A Scientific Approach*. New York: McGraw-Hill.

Paulston, C. 1971. 'The sequencing of structural pattern drills.' *TESOL Quarterly* 5/3, 197–208.

Prator, C. 1965. 'Development of a manipulative-communication scale' in R. Campbell and H. Allen (eds.). *Teaching English as a Second Language*. New York: McGraw-Hill.

Rivers, W. 1968. *Teaching Foreign Language Skills*. Chicago: University of Chicago Press.

Skinner, B. F. 1957. *Verbal Behavior*. New York: Appleton-Century-Crofts.

5

The Silent Way

Introduction

Although people did learn languages through the Audio-Lingual Method, and indeed the method is still practiced today, one problem with it was students' inability to readily transfer the habits they had mastered in the classroom to communicative use outside it. Furthermore, the idea that learning a language meant forming a set of habits was seriously challenged in the early 1960s. Linguist Noam Chomsky argued that language acquisition could not possibly take place through habit formation since people create and understand utterances they have never heard before. Chomsky proposed instead that speakers have a knowledge of underlying abstract rules, which allow them to understand and create novel utterances. Thus, Chomsky reasoned, language must not be considered a product of habit formation, but rather of rule formation. Accordingly, language acquisition must be a procedure whereby people use their own thinking processes, or cognition, to discover the rules of the language they are acquiring.

The emphasis on human cognition led to the establishment of the **Cognitive Code Approach**. Rather than simply being responsive to stimuli in the environment, learners were seen to be much more actively responsible for their own learning, engaged in formulating hypotheses in order to discover the rules of the target language. Errors were inevitable and were signs that learners were actively testing their hypotheses. For a while in the early 1970s, there was great interest in applying this new Cognitive Code Approach to language teaching. Materials were developed with deductive (learners are given the rule and asked to apply it) and inductive (learners discover the rule from the examples and then practice it) grammar exercises. However, no language teaching method ever really developed directly from the approach; instead, a number of 'innovative methods' emerged. In the next few chapters we will take a look at these.

[handwritten margin notes: Behaviorists ↓ 1960's Chomsky]

Although Caleb Gattegno's Silent Way, which we will consider in this chapter, did not stem directly from the Cognitive Code Approach, it shares certain principles with it. For example, one of the basic principles of the Silent Way is that 'Teaching should be subordinated to learning.' In other words, Gattegno believed that to teach means to serve the learning process rather than to dominate it. This principle is in keeping with the active search for rules ascribed to the learner in the Cognitive Code Approach. Gattegno looked at language learning from the perspective of the learner by studying the way babies and young children learn. He concluded that learning is a process which we initiate by ourselves by mobilizing our inner resources (our perception, awareness, cognition, imagination, intuition, creativity, etc.) to meet the challenge at hand. In the course of our learning, we integrate into ourselves whatever 'new' that we create, and use it as a stepping stone for further learning.

In order to explore the Silent Way, we will observe the first day of an English class in Brazil. There are 24 secondary school students in this class. The class meets for two hours a day, three days a week.

Experience

As we take our seats, the teacher has just finished introducing the Silent Way in Portuguese. The teacher walks to the front of the room, takes out a metal pointer and points to a chart taped to the wall. The chart has a black background and is covered with small rectangular blocks arranged in rows. Each block is in a different color. This is a sound–color chart. Each rectangle represents one English sound. There is a white horizontal line approximately halfway down the chart separating the upper rectangles, which represent vowel sounds, from those below the line, which represent consonant sounds.

Figure 5.1   The teacher using a sound–color chart to teach the sounds of English

Without saying anything, the teacher points to five different blocks of color above the line. There is silence. The teacher repeats the pattern, pointing to the same five blocks of color. Again, no one says anything. The third time the teacher does the pointing, he says /ɑ/ as he touches the first block. The teacher continues and taps the four other blocks of color with the pointer. As he does this, several students say /e/, /i/, /ɒ/, /u/. He begins with these vowels since they are the ones students will already know. (These five sounds are the simple vowels of Portuguese and every Brazilian schoolchild learns them in this order.)

The teacher points to the rectangle that represents /e/. He puts his two palms together, then spreads them apart to indicate that he wants the students to lengthen this vowel sound. By moving his pointer, he shows that there is a smooth gliding of the tongue necessary to change this Portuguese /e/ into the English diphthong /eɪ/. He works with the students until he is satisfied that their pronunciation of /eɪ/ closely approximates the English vowel. He works in the same way with /iː/, /əʊ/, and /uː/. Then the teacher hands the pointer to a girl in the front row. She comes to the front of the room and points to the white block in the top row. The class responds with /eɪ/. One by one, as she points to the next three blocks, the class responds correctly with /eɪ/, /iː/, /əʊ/. But she has trouble finding the last block of color and points to a block in the third row. A few students yell, 'NO!' She tries another block in the same row; her classmates yell, 'NO!' again. Finally a boy from the front row says, '*À esquerda*' (Portuguese for 'to the left'). As the girl moves the pointer one block to the left, the class shouts /u:/. The teacher signals for the girl to do the series again. This time she goes a bit more quickly and has no trouble finding the block for /u:/. The teacher signals to another student to replace the girl and point to the five blocks as the class responds. Then the teacher brings individuals to the front of the room, each one tapping out the sequence of the sounds as he says them. The teacher works with the students through gestures, and sometimes through instructions in Portuguese, to get them to produce the English vowel sounds as accurately as possible. He does not say the sounds himself.

Apparently satisfied that the students can produce the five sounds accurately, the teacher next points to the five blocks in a different order. A few students hesitate, but most of the students seem able to connect the colored blocks with the correct sounds. The teacher varies the sequence several times and the students respond appropriately. The teacher then points to a boy sitting in the second row. The teacher moves to the chart and points to five colored blocks. Two of the blocks are above the line and are the /eɪ/ and /u:/ they have already worked on. The three other blocks are below the line and are new to them. Two or three of the students yell, '*Pedro*,' which is the boy's name. The other students help him as he points to the colored blocks that represent the sounds of his name: /p/, /e/, /d/, /r/, /u/. Two or three other students do the same. In this way, the students have learned that English has a /p/, /d/, and /r/ and the location of these sounds on the sound–color chart. The students have a little problem with the pronunciation of the /r/, so the teacher works with them before moving on.

The teacher next points to a girl and taps out eight colored rectangles. In a chorus, the students say her name, '*Carolina*,' and practice the girl's name as they did Pedro's. With this the students have learned the colors that represent three other sounds: /k/, /l/, /n/. The teacher follows a similar procedure with a third student whose name is Gabriela. The students know now the location of /g/ and /b/ as well. The teacher has various students tap out the sounds for the names of their three classmates.

After quite a few students have tapped out the three names, the teacher takes the pointer and introduces a new activity. He asks eight students to sit with him around a big table in the front of the room as the rest of the class gathers behind them. The teacher puts a pile of blue, green, and pink wooden rods of varying lengths in the middle of the table. He points to one of the rods, then points to three rectangles of color on the sound–color chart. Some students attempt to say 'rod.' They are able to do this since they have already been introduced to these sound–color combinations. The teacher points again to the blocks of color, and this time all of the students say, 'rod.' The teacher then points to the block of color representing 'a'. He points to his mouth and shows the students that he is raising his jaw and closing his mouth, thus showing the students how to produce a new English sound by starting with a sound they already know. The students say something approximating /ə/, which is a new sound for them. The teacher follows this by pointing first to a new block of color, then quickly in succession to four blocks of color; the students chorus, 'a rod.' He turns to a different chart on the wall; this one has words on it in different colors. He points to the words 'a' and 'rod,' and the students see that each letter is in the same color as the sound the letter signifies.

After pointing to 'a' and 'rod,' the teacher sits down with the students at the table, saying nothing. Everyone is silent for a minute until one girl points to a rod and says, 'a rod.' The teacher hands her the pointer and she goes first to the sound–color chart to tap out the sounds, and second to the word chart to point to the words 'a' and 'rod.' Several other students follow this pattern.

Next, the teacher points to a particular rod and taps out 'a blue rod.' Then he points to the word 'blue' on the word chart. A boy points to the rod and say, 'A blue rod.' He goes to the word chart and finds the three words of this phrase there. Other students do the same. The teacher introduced the word 'green' similarly, with students tapping out the pattern after he is through.

The teacher then points to a pink rod and taps out /pɪnk/ on the chart. The /ɪ/ vowel is a new one for the students. It does not exist in Portuguese. The teacher points to the block of color which represents /i/ and he indicates through his gesture that the students are to shorten the glide and open their mouths a bit more to say this sound.

The first student who tries to say 'a pink rod' has trouble with the pronunciation of 'pink.' He looks to the teacher and the teacher gestures towards the other students. One of them says 'pink' and the teacher accepts her pronunciation. The first student tries again and this time the teacher accepts what he says. Another student seems to have trouble with the phrase. Using a finger to represent each word of the phrase, the teacher shows her how the phrase is segmented. Then by tapping his second finger, he indicates that her trouble is with the second word:

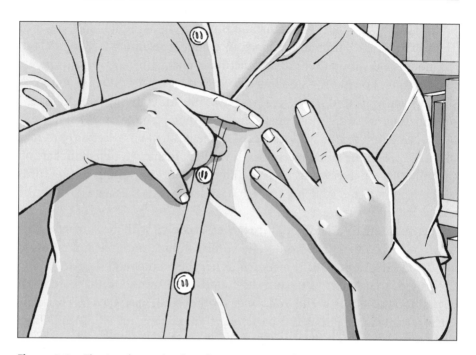

Figure 5.2   The teacher using hand movements to locate a student's error

The teacher then mouths the vowel sound and, with gestures, shows the student that the vowel is shorter than what she is saying. She tries to shape her mouth as he does and her pronunciation does improve a little, although it still does not appear to be as close to the target language sounds as some of the other students'. With the other students watching, he works with her a bit longer. The students practice saying and tapping out the three color words and the phrase, with the teacher listening attentively and occasionally intervening to help them to correct their pronunciation.

The teacher has another group of students take the places of the first eight at the table. The teacher turns to one of the students and says, 'Take a green rod.' The student doesn't respond; the teacher waits. Another student picks up a green rod and says the same sentence. Through gestures from the teacher, he understands that he should direct the command to another student. The second student performs the action and then says, 'Take a blue rod,' to a third student. He takes one. The other students then take turns issuing and complying with commands to take a rod of a certain color.

Next the teacher puts several blue and green rods in the center of the table. He points to the blue rod and to one of the students, who responds, 'Take a blue rod.' The teacher then says 'and' and points to the green rod. The same student says, 'and take a green rod.' The teacher indicates to the student that she should say the whole sentence and she says, 'Take a blue rod and take a green rod.' As the girl says each word, the teacher points to one of his fingers.

When she says the second 'take,' he gestures that she should remove the 'take' from the sentence. She tries again, 'Take a blue rod and a green rod,' which the teacher accepts. The students now practice forming and complying with commands with similar compound objects.

The teacher then points to the word chart and to one of the students, who taps out the sentences on the chart as the other students produce them. Later, students take turns tapping out the sentences of their choice on the word chart. Some students tap out simple commands and some students tap out commands with compound objects.

The students return to their desks. The teacher turns to the class and asks the class in Portuguese for their reactions to the lesson. One student replies that he has learned that language learning is not difficult. Another says that he is finding it difficult; he feels that he needs more practice associating the sounds and colors. A third student adds that she felt as if she were playing a game. A fourth student says he is feeling confused.

At this point the lesson ends. During the next few classes, the students will:

1   Practice with their new sounds and learn to produce accurate intonation and stress patterns with the words and sentences.
2   Learn more English words for colors and where any new sounds are located on the sound–color chart.
3   Learn to use the following items:

   Give it to me/her/him/them
   too
   this/that/these/those
   one/ones
   the/a/an
   put ... here/there
   is/are
   his/her/my/your/their/our

4   Practice making sentences with many different combinations of these items.
5   Practice reading the sentences they have created on the wall charts.
6   Work with **Fidel Charts**, which are charts summarizing the spellings of all the different sounds in English.
7   Practice writing the sentences they have created.

Before we analyze the lesson, let us peek in on another class being taught by the Silent Way.[1] This class is at a high-intermediate level. The students are sitting around a table on which the teacher has used rods to construct

[1] This high-intermediate lesson is based on Donald Freeman's lesson in the Department of State's Language Teaching Methods video.

a floor plan of a 'typical' house. He establishes the 'front' and 'back' of the house by having the students label the 'front' and 'back' doors. He points to each of four rooms and is able to elicit from the students: 'the living room,' 'the dining room,' 'the kitchen,' and 'the bedroom.' Then the teacher points to the walls of each room in turn. This introduces the need for 'inside/outside wall.' By simply pointing to each wall, the teacher gives the students a lot of practice producing phrases like 'the front wall of the living room,' 'the outside wall of the dining room,' etc. Next the teacher picks up a rod and says 'table.' He shrugs his shoulders to indicate to students that they should tell him where to put it. One student says 'the dining room,' but the teacher indicates that he needs more specific directions. The student says 'Put the table in the middle of the dining room.' The teacher does this. He then picks up another, smaller rod. Another student says 'chair.' The teacher indicates that the student should tell him where to put the chair. The teacher works with her, using the charts to introduce new words until she can say, 'Put the chair in the dining room at the head of the table.' The lesson continues in this way, with the teacher saying very little, and the students practicing a great deal with complex sentences such as 'Put the table at one end of the sofa near the outside wall of the living room.'

Thinking about the experience

Since the Silent Way may not be familiar to many of you, let us review in detail our observations and examine its principles.

Observations	Principles
1 The teacher points to five blocks of color without saying anything. The blocks of color represent the sounds of five English vowels close to the five simple vowels of Portuguese.	The teacher should start with something the students already know and build from that to the unknown. Languages share a number of features, sounds being the most basic.
2 The teacher points again to the five blocks of color. When the students say nothing, the teacher points to the first block of color and says /ɑ/. Several students say /e/, /i/, /o/, /u/ as the teacher points to the other four blocks.	Language learners are intelligent and bring with them the experience of already learning a language. The teacher should give only what help is necessary.

3	The teacher does not model the new sounds, but rather uses gestures to show the students how to modify the Portuguese sounds.	Language is not learned by repeating after a model. Students need to develop their own 'inner criteria' for correctness—to trust and to be responsible for their own production in the target language.
4	Students take turns tapping out the sounds.	Students' actions can tell the teacher whether or not they have learned.
5	One student says, 'À esquerda,' to help another.	Students should learn to rely on each other and themselves.
6	The teacher works with gestures, and sometimes instructions in the students' native language, to help the students to produce the target language sounds as accurately as possible.	The teacher works with the students while the students work on the language.
7	The students learn the sounds of new blocks of color by tapping out the names of their classmates.	The teacher makes use of what students already know. The more the teacher does for the students what they can do for themselves, the less they will do for themselves.
8	The teacher points to a rod and then to three blocks of color on the sound–color chart. The students respond, 'rod.'	Learning involves transferring what one knows to new contexts.
9	The teacher points to the words 'a' and 'rod' on the word chart.	Reading is worked on from the beginning but follows from what students have learned to say.
10	The teacher sits down at the table and is silent. After a minute, a girl points to a rod and says, 'a rod.'	Silence is a tool. It helps to foster autonomy, or the exercise of initiative. It also removes the teacher from the center of attention so he can listen to and work with students. The teacher speaks, but only when necessary. Otherwise, the teacher gets out of the way so that it is the students who receive the practice in using the language.

11 The teacher points to a particular rod and taps out 'a blue rod' on the sound–color chart.	Meaning is made clear by focusing students' perceptions, not through translation.
12 One student tries to say 'a pink rod' and has trouble. He looks to the teacher, but the teacher remains silent and looks to the other students.	Students can learn from one another. The teacher's silence encourages group cooperation.
13 The first student tries to say 'a pink rod' again. This time the teacher accepts the student's correct pronunciation.	If the teacher praises (or criticizes) students, they will be less self-reliant. The teacher's actions can interfere with students' developing their own criteria.
14 Another student has trouble pronouncing part of the phrase 'a pink rod.' Using gestures, the teacher isolates the trouble spot for her.	Errors are important and necessary to learning. They show the teacher where things are unclear.
15 After locating the error for the student, the teacher does not supply the correct language until all self-correction options have failed.	If students are simply given answers, rather than being allowed to self-correct, they will not retain them.
16 The teacher mouths the correct sound, but does not vocalize it.	Students need to learn to listen to themselves.
17 The student's pronunciation is improved but is still not as close to the target language sounds as some of the students are able to come. The teacher works with her a bit longer before the lesson proceeds.	At the beginning, the teacher needs to look for progress, not perfection. Learning takes place in time. Students learn at different rates.
18 The teacher listens attentively.	A teacher's silence frees the teacher to closely observe the students' behavior.
19 The teacher says, 'Take the green rod,' only once.	Students learn they must give the teacher their attention in order not to miss what he says. Student attention is a key to learning.

affective filter ?

20 The students take turns issuing and complying with commands to take a rod of a certain color.	Students should engage in a great deal of meaningful practice without repetition.
21 The students practice commands with compound objects.	The elements of the language are introduced logically, expanding upon what students already know.
22 The students take turns tapping out the sentences of their choice on the word charts.	Students gain autonomy in the language by exploring it and by making choices.
23 Some students choose to tap out simple commands; others tap out more complex ones.	Language is for self-expression.
24 The teacher asks the students for their reactions to the lesson.	The teacher can gain valuable information from student feedback; for example, he can learn what to work on next. Students learn how to accept responsibility for their own learning.
25 There is no homework assigned.	Some learning takes place naturally as we sleep. Students will naturally work on the day's lesson then.
26 In subsequent lessons, the students will learn to use a number of different linguistic structures.	The syllabus is composed of linguistic structures.
27 The students will practice making sentences with different combinations of these structures.	The structures of the syllabus are not arranged in a linear fashion, but rather are constantly being recycled.
28 Students will practice writing the sentences they create.	The skills of speaking, reading, and writing reinforce one another.

Reviewing the Principles

As you can see, the Silent Way has a great many principles. Perhaps we can come to a fuller understanding of them if we consider the answers to our 10 questions.

1 What are the goals of teachers who use the Silent Way?
Students should be able to use the language for self-expression—to express their thoughts, perceptions, and feelings. In order to do this, they need

to develop independence from the teacher, to develop their own inner criteria for correctness.

Students become independent by relying on themselves. The teacher, therefore, should give them only what they absolutely need to promote their learning.

2 What is the role of the teacher? What is the role of the students?

The teacher is a technician or engineer. 'Only the learner can do the learning,' but the teacher, relying on what his students already know, can give what help is necessary, 'focus the students' perceptions, 'force their awareness,' and 'provide exercises to insure their facility' with the language. The teacher should respect the autonomy of the learners in their attempts at relating and interacting with the new challenges.

The role of the students is to make use of what they know, to free themselves of any obstacles that would interfere with giving their utmost attention to the learning task, and to actively engage in exploring the language. No one can learn for us, Gattegno would say; to learn is our personal responsibility.

As Gattegno says, 'The teacher works with the student; the student works on the language.'

3 What are some characteristics of the teaching/learning process?

Students begin their study of the language through its basic building blocks, its sounds. These are introduced through a language-specific sound–color chart. Relying on what sounds students already know from their knowledge of their native language, teachers lead their students to associate the sounds of the target language with particular colors. Later, these same colors are used to help students learn the spellings that correspond to the sounds (through the color-coded Fidel Charts) and how to read and pronounce words properly (through the color-coded word charts).

The teacher sets up situations that focus student attention on the structures of the language. The situations provide a vehicle for students to perceive meaning. The situations sometimes call for the use of rods and sometimes do not; they typically involve only one structure at a time. With minimal spoken cues, the students are guided to produce the structure. The teacher works with them, striving for pronunciation that would be intelligible to a native speaker of the target language. The teacher uses the students' errors as evidence of where the language is unclear to students and, hence, where to work.

The students receive a great deal of practice with a given target language structure without repetition for its own sake. They gain autonomy in the language by exploring it and making choices. The teacher asks the students to describe their reactions to the lesson or what they have learned. This provides valuable information for the teacher and encourages students to take responsibility for their own learning. Some further learning takes place while they sleep.

4 What is the nature of student–teacher interaction? What is the nature of student–student interaction?

For much of the student–teacher interaction, the teacher is silent. He is still very active, however—setting up situations to 'force awareness,' listening attentively to students' speech, and silently working with them on their production through the use of nonverbal gestures and the tools he has available. When the teacher does speak, it is to give clues, not to model the language.

Student–student verbal interaction is desirable (students can learn from one another) and is therefore encouraged. The teacher's silence is one way to do this.

5 How are the feelings of the students dealt with?

The teacher constantly observes the students. When their feelings interfere, the teacher tries to find ways for the students to overcome them. Also, through feedback sessions at the end of lessons, students have an opportunity to express how they feel. The teacher takes what they say into consideration and works with the students to help them overcome negative feelings which might otherwise interfere with their learning. Finally, because students are encouraged throughout each lesson to cooperate with one another, it is hoped that a relaxed, enjoyable learning environment will be created.

6 How is the language viewed? How is culture viewed?

Languages of the world share a number of features. However, each language also has its own unique reality, or spirit, since it is the expression of a particular group of people. Their culture, as reflected in their own unique world view, is inseparable from their language.

7 What areas of language are emphasized? What language skills are emphasized?

Since the sounds are basic to any language, pronunciation is worked on from the beginning. It is important that students acquire the melody of the language. There is also a focus on the structures of the language, although explicit grammar rules may never be supplied. Vocabulary is somewhat restricted at first.

There is no fixed, linear, structural syllabus. Instead, the teacher starts with what the students know and builds from one structure to the next. As the learners' repertoire is expanded, previously introduced structures are continually being recycled. The syllabus develops according to learning needs.

All four skills are worked on from the beginning of the course, although there is a sequence in that students learn to read and write what they have already produced orally. The skills reinforce what students are learning.

8 What is the role of the students' native language?

Meaning is made clear by focusing the students' perceptions, not by translation. The students' native language can, however, be used to give instructions when necessary, to help a student improve his or her pronunciation, for instance. The native language is also used (at least at beginning levels of proficiency) during the feedback sessions.

More important, knowledge students already possess of their native language can be exploited by the teacher of the target language. For example, the teacher knows that many of the sounds in the students' native language will be similar, if not identical, to sounds in the target language; he assumes, then, that he can build upon this existing knowledge to introduce the new sounds in the target language.

9 How is evaluation accomplished?

Although the teacher may never give a formal test, he assesses student learning all the time. Since 'teaching is subordinated to learning,' the teacher must be responsive to immediate learning needs. The teacher's silence frees him to attend to his students and to be aware of these needs. The needs will be apparent to a teacher who is observant of his students' behavior. One criterion of whether or not students have learned is their ability to transfer what they have been studying to new contexts.

The teacher does not praise or criticize student behavior since this would interfere with students' developing their own inner criteria. He expects students to learn at different rates. The teacher looks for steady progress, not perfection.

10 How does the teacher respond to student errors?

Student errors are seen as a natural, indispensable part of the learning process. Errors are inevitable since the students are encouraged to explore the language. The teacher uses student errors as a basis for deciding where further work is necessary.

The teacher works with the students in getting them to self-correct. Students are not thought to learn much if the teacher merely supplies the correct language. Students need to learn to listen to themselves and to compare their own production with their developing inner criteria. If the students are unable to self-correct and peers cannot help, then the teacher would supply the correct language, but only as a last resort.

Reviewing the Techniques

Many of the ideas in this chapter may be new to you. Some of these ideas may be immediately attractive to you, whereas others may not. Give yourself time to think about all of them before you decide their value to you.

In the review that follows, the materials surveyed in this chapter (the charts and rods) have been included. While you may not have access to the actual materials discussed here, the materials may give you other ideas of what you can use.

- **Sound–Color Chart**

  The chart contains blocks of color, each one representing a sound in the target language. The teacher, and later the students, points to blocks of color on the chart to form syllables, words, and even sentences. Although we did not see it in this lesson, sometimes the teacher will tap a particular block of color very hard when forming a word. In this way the teacher can introduce the stress pattern for the word. The chart allows students to produce sound combinations in the target language without doing so through repetition. The chart draws the students' attention and allows them to concentrate on the language, not on the teacher. When a particular sound contrast is new for students, and they are unable to perceive which sound of the two they are producing, the sound–color chart can be used to give them feedback on which sound they are making.

  Finally, since the sound–color chart presents all of the sounds of the target language at once, students know what they have learned and what they yet need to learn. This relates to the issue of learner autonomy.

- **Teacher's Silence**

  The teacher gives just as much help as is necessary and then is silent. Or the teacher sets up an unambiguous situation, puts a language structure into circulation (for example, 'Take a _____ rod'), and then is silent. Even in error correction, the teacher will only supply a verbal answer as a last resort.

- **Peer Correction**

  Students are encouraged to help another student when he or she is experiencing difficulty. It is important that any help be offered in a cooperative manner, not a competitive one. The teacher monitors the aid so that it is helpful, not interfering.

- **Rods**

  Rods can be used to provide visible actions or situations for any language structure, to introduce it, or to enable students to practice using it. The rods trigger meaning: Situations with the rods can be created in such a way that the meaning is made clear; then the language is connected to the meaning. At the beginning level, the rods can be used to teach colors and numbers. Later on they can be used for more complicated structures; for example, statements with prepositions ('The blue rod is between the green one and the yellow one') and conditionals ('If you give me a blue rod, then I'll give you two green ones'). They can be used abstractly as well; for instance, for students to make a clock when learning to tell time in the target language, to create a family tree, or to make a floor plan of their house, which they later describe to their classmates. Sometimes, teachers will put the rods down on the desk in a line, using a different rod to represent each word in a sentence. By pointing to each rod in turn, while remaining silent, the teacher can elicit the sentence from the students. He can also make concrete for students aspects of the structure, for example, the need to invert the subject and auxiliary verb in order to form questions.

  The rods are therefore very versatile. They can be used as rods or more abstractly to represent other realities. They allow students to be creative and imaginative, and they allow for action to accompany language.

- **Self-correction Gestures**

  We already examined some self-correction techniques in the chapter on the Direct Method. Some of the particular gestures of the Silent Way could be added to this list. For example, in the class observed, the teacher put his palms together and then moved them outwards to signal to students the need to lengthen the particular vowel they were working on. In another instance, the teacher indicated that each of his fingers represented a word in a sentence and used this to locate the trouble spot for the student.

- **Word Chart**

  The teacher, and later the students, points to words on the wall charts in a sequence so that students can read aloud the sentences they have spoken. The way the letters are colored (the colors from the sound–color chart are used) helps the students with their pronunciation. There are twelve English charts containing about 500 words. The charts contain the functional vocabulary of English. There are others available for other languages. Although we did not see them in this lesson, students also work with Silent Way wall pictures and books to further expand their vocabularies and facility with the language.

- **Fidel Charts**

  The teacher, and later the students, points to the color-coded Fidel Charts in order that students associate the sounds of the language with their spelling. For example, listed together and colored the same as the color block for the sound /eɪ/ are 'ay,' 'ea,' 'ei,' 'eigh,' etc. showing that these are all ways of spelling the /eɪ/ sound in English (as in the words 'say,' 'steak,' 'veil,' 'weigh'). Because of the large number of ways sounds in English can be spelled, there are eight Fidel Charts in all. There are a number of charts available for other languages as well.

- **Structured Feedback**

  Students are invited to make observations about the day's lesson and what they have learned. The teacher accepts the students' comments in a non-defensive manner, hearing things that will help give him direction for where he should work when the class meets again. The students learn to take responsibility for their own learning by becoming aware of and controlling how they use certain **learning strategies** in class. The length and frequency of feedback sessions vary depending on the teacher and the class.

Conclusion

In this chapter we saw a beginning lesson and an intermediate lesson, but the Silent Way is used with advanced students, too. For these students the same principles apply, and the same charts are used. In addition, there are pictures for topical vocabularies, books for American cultural settings, and an introduction to literature.

We have avoided referring to the Silent Way as a method since Caleb Gattegno says it is not one. Proponents of the Silent Way claim its principles are far-reaching, affecting not only education, but the way one perceives the living of life itself. Nevertheless, there clearly are implications for language teaching, and you should ask yourself whether there are implications for you.

Do you believe teaching should be subordinated to learning? Does it make sense to you that learners should be encouraged to be independent of the teacher and autonomous in making their own choices? Do you think students can learn from one another? Should a teacher look for progress, not perfection? Are there any other principles of the Silent Way you believe in? Which ones?

Are there Silent Way materials which would be of use to you? Should a teacher remain silent as much as possible? Is structured feedback a useful thing for teachers to elicit from their students? Which techniques can you adapt to your own approach to language teaching?

Activities

Ⓐ Check your understanding of the Silent Way.

1 There are many reasons for the teacher's silence in the Silent Way. Some of these have been stated explicitly in this chapter; others have been implied. Can you state the reasons?
2 What does the phrase, 'Teaching is subordinated to learning,' mean?
3 One of the mottos of the Silent Way is 'The teacher works with the students; the students work on the language.' What do you think this means?

Ⓑ Apply what you have understood about the Silent Way.

1 Teach some students a short target language verse which contains some unfamiliar sounds. What nonverbal gestures or cues can you develop to guide your students to produce the correct sounds, intonation, and rhythm as they learn the verse?
2 Choose a grammar structure. It is probably better at first to choose something elementary like the demonstrative adjectives ('this,' 'that,' 'these,' 'those' in English) or the possessive adjectives ('my,' 'your,' 'his,' 'her,' 'its,' 'our,' 'their' in English). Plan a lesson to teach the structures where:
    a   You will remain as silent and interfere as little as possible.
    b   The meaning will be clear to the students.
    c   They will receive a good deal of practice without repetition.
3 Think of students with a particular native language background. How will you sequence the sounds of the target language in order to teach them to these students, building on what they already know?

References/Additional Resources

Gattegno, C. 1972. *Teaching Foreign Languages in Schools: The Silent Way* (2nd edn.). New York: Educational Solutions, Inc.

——. 1976. *The Common Sense of Teaching Foreign Languages.* New York: Educational Solutions, Inc.

Richards, J. and **T. Rodgers.** 1986. *Approaches and Methods in Language Teaching.* Cambridge: Cambridge University Press.

Stevick, E. 1990. *Humanism in Language Teaching.* Oxford: Oxford University Press.

——. 1998. *Working with Teaching Methods: What's at Stake?* Boston: Heinle & Heinle.

6

Desuggestopedia

Introduction

The originator of the method we will be exploring in this chapter, Georgi Lozanov, believes, as does Silent Way's Caleb Gattegno, that language learning can occur at a much faster rate than ordinarily transpires. The reason for our inefficiency, Lozanov asserts, is that we set up psychological barriers to learning: We fear that we will be unable to perform, that we will be limited in our ability to learn, that we will fail. One result is that we do not use the full mental powers that we have. According to Lozanov and others, we may be using only five to ten percent of our mental capacity. In order to make better use of our reserve capacity, the limitations we think we have need to be 'desuggested.' Desuggestopedia,[1] the application of the study of suggestion to pedagogy, has been developed to help students eliminate the feeling that they cannot be successful and/or the negative association they may have toward studying and thus to help them overcome the barriers to learning. One of the ways the students' mental reserves are stimulated is through integration of the fine arts, an important contribution to the method made by Lozanov's colleague Evelina Gateva.

desuggest our fears

fine arts

Let us now see for ourselves how the principles of Desuggestopedia are applied to language teaching. We will visit a university class in Egypt being taught English by this method. The students are beginners. The class meets for two hours, three mornings a week.

Experience[2]

The first thing we notice when we enter the classroom is how different this room is compared with all the other classrooms we have been in so far.

---

[1] Suggestopedia is now called Desuggestopedia to reflect the importance placed on desuggesting limitations on learning (Lozanov and Miller, personal communication).
[2] The lesson described here is in part based on ones the authors observed taught by Dan Dugas and Lynn Dhority, respectively. It has been somewhat modified in light of comments by Alison Miller and Georgi Lozanov.

Everything is bright and colorful. There are several posters on the walls. Most of them are travel posters with scenes from the United Kingdom; a few, however, contain grammatical information. One has the conjugation of the verb 'be' and the subject pronouns; another has the object and possessive pronouns. There is also a table with some rhythm instruments on it. Next to them are some hats, masks, and other props.

Figure 6.1   Students looking at posters on the wall

The teacher greets the students in Arabic and explains that they are about to begin a new and exciting experience in language learning. She says confidently, 'You won't need to try to learn. It will just come naturally.'

'First, you will all get to pick new names—English ones. It will be fun,' she says. Besides, she tells them, they will need new identities (ones they can play with) to go along with this new experience. She shows the class a poster with different English names printed in color in the Roman alphabet. The students are familiar with the Roman alphabet from their earlier study of French. There are men's names in one column and women's names in another. She tells them that they are each to choose a name. She pronounces each name and has the students repeat the pronunciation. One by one the students say which name they have chosen.

Next, she tells them that during the course they will create an imaginary biography about the life of their new identity. But for now, she says, they should just choose a profession to go with the new name. Using pantomime to help the students understand, the teacher acts out various occupations, such as pilot, singer, carpenter, and artist. The students choose what they want to be.

The teacher greets the students, using their new names and asks them a few *yes/no* questions in English about their new occupation. Through her actions the students understand the meaning, and they reply 'yes' or 'no.' She then teaches them a short English dialogue in which two people greet each other and inquire what each other does for a living. After practicing the dialogue with the group, they introduce themselves to the teacher. Then they play the rhythm instruments as they sing a name song.

[margin notes: minimal response, -read dialog, -group, -indivi]

Next the teacher announces to the class that they will be beginning a new adventure. She distributes a 20-page handout. The handout contains a lengthy dialogue entitled 'To want to is to be able to,' which the teacher translates into Arabic. She has the students turn the page. On the right page are two columns of print: in the left one is the English dialogue; in the right, the Arabic translation. On the left page are some comments in Arabic about certain of the English vocabulary items and grammatical structures the students will encounter in the dialogue on the facing page. These items have been boldfaced in the dialogue. Throughout the 20 pages are reproductions of classical paintings.

[margin notes: use of L1, explain in L1]

Partly in Arabic, partly in English, and partly through pantomime, the teacher outlines the story in the dialogue. She also calls her students' attention to some of the comments regarding vocabulary and grammar on the left-hand pages. Then she tells them in Arabic that she is going to read the dialogue to them in English and that they should follow along as she reads. She will give them sufficient time to look at both the English and the Arabic. 'Just enjoy,' she concludes.

The teacher puts on some music—Mozart's Violin Concerto in A. After a couple of minutes, in a quiet voice she begins to read the text. Her reading appears to be molded by the music as she varies her intonation and keeps rhythm with the music. The students follow along with the voice of the teacher, who allows them enough time to read the translation of the dialogue in their native language silently. They are encouraged to highlight and take notes during the session. The teacher pauses from time to time to allow the students to listen to the music, and for two or three minutes at a time, the whole group stands and repeats after the teacher, joining their voices to the music.

[margin note: calm music]

Following this musical session, the students take a break. When they return from the break, they see that the teacher has hung a painting of a calming scene in nature at the front of the room. The teacher then explains that she will read the dialogue again. This time she suggests that the students put down their scripts and just listen. The second time she reads the dialogue,

[margin note: calm music and picture]

she appears to be speaking at a normal rate. She has changed the music to Handel's Water Music. She makes no attempt this time to match her voice to the music. With the end of the second reading, the class is over. There is no homework assigned; however, the teacher suggests that if the students want to do something, they could read over the dialogue once before they go to bed and once when they get up in the morning.

We decide to attend the next class to see how the teacher will work with the new material she has presented. After greeting the students and having them introduce themselves in their new identities once again, the teacher asks the students to take out their dialogue scripts.

Next, the teacher pulls out a hat from a bag. She puts it on her head, points to herself, and names a character from the dialogue. She indicates that she wants someone else to wear the hat. A girl volunteers to do so. Three more hats are taken out of the teacher's bag and, with a great deal of playfulness, they are distributed. The teacher turns to the four students wearing the hats and asks them to read a portion of the dialogue, imagining that they are the character whose hat they wear. When they finish their portion of dialogue, four different students get to wear the hats and continue reading the script. This group is asked to read it in a sad way. The next group of four read it in an angry way, and the last group of four in a cheerful way.

The teacher then asks for four new volunteers. She tells them that they are auditioning for a role in a Broadway play. They want very much to win the role. In order to impress the director of the play, they must read their lines very dramatically. The first group reads several pages of the dialogue in this manner, and following groups do this as well.

Next, the teacher asks questions in English about the dialogue. She also asks students to give her the English translation of an Arabic sentence from the dialogue and vice versa. Sometimes she asks the students to repeat an English line after her; still other times, she addresses a question from the dialogue to an individual student.

Then she teaches the students a children's alphabet song containing English names and occupations, 'A, my name is Alice; my husband's name is Alex. We live in Australia, and we sell apples. B, my name is Barbara; my husband's name is Bert. We live in Brazil, and we sell books.' The students are laughing and clapping as they sing along.

After the song, the teacher has the students stand up and get in a circle. She takes out a medium-sized soft ball. She throws the ball to one student and, while she is throwing it, she asks him what his name is in English. He catches the ball as he says, 'My name is Richard.' She indicates that he is to throw the ball to another student while posing a question to him. Richard asks, 'What you do?' The teacher corrects in a very soft voice saying 'What do you do?'

The student replies, 'I am a conductor.' The game continues on in this manner with the students posing questions to one another as they throw the ball. The second class is now over. Again, there is no homework assigned, other than to read over the dialogue if a student so wishes.

During the third class of the week, the students will continue to work with this dialogue. They will move away from reading it, however, and move toward using the new language in a creative way. They will play some competitive games, do role-plays (see description in the techniques review) and skits. The following week, the class will be introduced to a new dialogue, and the basic sequence of lessons we observed here will be repeated.

In the classroom next door, an intermediate class is studying. The students are seated around a rectangular table. On the table there are a few toys and instruments. Again there are posters around the room, this time of more complicated grammar. As we listen in, the teacher is introducing a story from a reader. She gives synonyms or descriptions for the new words. She reads parts of the story and the students do choral and individual reading of other sections. New words, families of words, and expressions are listed at the end of the story for reference. The intermediate students are encouraged to add their own new words and phrases to the lesson with their translations. The students use more complex tenses and language structures.

The teacher presents the first story and lists of related words and structures to the accompaniment of a Beethoven piano concerto in much the same way as the beginners' dialogue is read, followed by a shorter second reading to Bach. The following days include reading, singing, discussions, story-telling, grammar and pronunciation games, and writing, all orchestrated in a creative and playful fashion.

Thinking about the Experience

Let us now investigate Desuggestopedia in our usual fashion. First, we will list our observations. From these, we will attempt to uncover the principles of Desuggestopedia.

Observations	Principles
1 The classroom is bright and colorful.	Learning is facilitated in a cheerful environment.
2 Among the posters hanging around the room are several containing grammatical information.	A student can learn from what is present in the environment, even if his attention is not directed to it (peripheral learning).

3 The teacher speaks confidently.	If the students trust and respect the teacher's authority, they will accept and retain information better.
4 The teacher gives the students the impression that learning the target language will be easy and enjoyable.	The teacher should recognize that learners bring certain psychological barriers with them to the learning situation. She should attempt to 'desuggest' these.
5 The students choose new names and identities.	Assuming a new identity enhances students' feeling of security and allows them to be more open. They feel less inhibited since their performance is really that of a different person.
6 The students introduce themselves to the teacher.	The dialogue that the students learn contains language they can use immediately.
7 They play rhythmic instruments as they sing a song.	Songs are useful for 'freeing the speech muscles' and evoking positive emotions.
8 The teacher distributes a lengthy handout to the class. The title of the dialogue is 'To want to is to be able to.'	The teacher should integrate indirect positive suggestions ('there is no limit to what you can do') into the learning situation.
9 The teacher briefly mentions a few points about English grammar and vocabulary. These are in bold print in the dialogue.	The teacher should present and explain the grammar and vocabulary, but not dwell on them. The bold print allows the students' focus to shift from the whole text to the details before they return to the whole text again. The dynamic interplay between the whole and the parts is important.
10 There are reproductions of classical paintings throughout the text.	Fine art provides positive suggestions for students.
11 In the left column is the dialogue in the target language. In the right column is the native language translation.	One way that meaning is made clear is through native language translation.

Sasha Fierce (handwritten note)

12 The teacher reads the dialogue with a musical accompaniment. She matches her voice to the rhythm and intonation of the music.	Communication takes place on 'two planes': on one the linguistic message is encoded; and on the other are factors which influence the linguistic message. On the **conscious plane**, the learner attends to the language; on the **subconscious plane**, the music suggests that learning is easy and pleasant. When there is a unity between conscious and subconscious, learning is enhanced.
13 The teacher reads the script a second time as the students listen. This is done to different music.	A calm state, such as the state one experiences when listening to a concert, is ideal for overcoming psychological barriers and for taking advantage of learning potential.
14 For homework, the students are to read the dialogue at night and in the morning.	At these times, the distinction between the conscious and the subconscious is most blurred and, therefore, learning can occur.
15 The teacher gives the students hats to wear for the different characters in the dialogue. The students take turns reading portions of the dialogue.	Dramatization is a particularly valuable way of playfully activating the material. Fantasy reduces barriers to learning.
16 The teacher tells the students that they are auditioning for a play.	The fine arts (music, art, and drama) enable suggestions to reach the subconscious. The arts should, therefore, be integrated as much as possible into the teaching process.
17 The teacher leads the class in various activities involving the dialogue, for example, question-and-answer, repetition, and translation.	The teacher should help the students 'activate' the material to which they have been exposed. The means of doing this should be varied so as to avoid repetition as much as possible. Novelty aids acquisition.

18 She teaches the students a children's song.	Music and movement reinforce the linguistic material. It is desirable that students achieve a state of **infantilization** so that they will be more open to learning. If they trust the teacher, they will reach this state more easily.
19 The teacher and students play a question-and-answer game.	In an atmosphere of play, the conscious attention of the learner does not focus on linguistic forms, but rather on using the language. Learning can be fun.
20 The student makes an error by saying, 'How you do?' The teacher corrects the error in a soft voice.	Errors are corrected gently, not in a direct, confrontational manner.

Reviewing the Principles

Let us now follow our usual procedure of reviewing the principles of a method by answering our 10 questions.

1 What are the goals of teachers who use Desuggestopedia?

Teachers hope to accelerate the process by which students learn to use another language for everyday communication. In order to do this, more of the students' mental powers must be tapped. This is accomplished by desuggesting the psychological barriers learners bring with them to the learning situation.

2 What is the role of the teacher? What is the role of the students?

The teacher is the authority in the classroom. In order for the method to be successful, the students must trust and respect her. The students will retain information better from someone in whom they have confidence since they will be more responsive to her 'desuggesting' their limitations and suggesting how easy it will be for them to succeed. Once the students trust the teacher, they can feel more secure. If they feel secure, they can be more spontaneous and less inhibited.

3 What are some characteristics of the teaching/learning process?

The course is conducted in a classroom that is bright and cheerful. Posters displaying grammatical information about the target language are hung around the room in order to take advantage of students' peripheral learning. The posters are changed every few weeks.

Students select target language names and choose new occupations. During the course, they create whole biographies to go along with their new identities.

The texts students work from are handouts containing lengthy dialogues (as many as 800 words) in the target language. Next to the dialogue is a translation in the students' native language. There are also some notes on vocabulary and grammar which correspond to boldfaced items in the dialogue.

The teacher presents the dialogue during two 'concerts.' These represent the first major phase (the receptive phase). In the first concert the teacher reads the dialogue, matching her voice to the rhythm and pitch of the music. In this way, the whole brain (both the left and the right hemispheres) of the students become activated. The students follow the target language dialogue as the teacher reads it out loud. They also check the translation. During the second concert, the students listen calmly while the teacher reads the dialogue at normal speed. For homework, the students read over the dialogue just before they go to sleep, and again when they get up the next morning.

What follows is the second major phase (the active phase), in which students engage in various activities designed to help them gain facility with the new material. The activities include dramatizations, games, songs, and question-and-answer exercises.

4 What is the nature of student–teacher interaction? What is the nature of student–student interaction?

The teacher initiates interactions with the whole group of students and with individuals right from the beginning of a language course. Initially, the students can only respond nonverbally or with a few target language words they have practiced. Later, the students have more control of the target language and can respond more appropriately and even initiate interaction themselves.

5 How are the feelings of the students dealt with?

A great deal of attention is given to students' feelings in this method. One of the fundamental principles of the method is that if students are relaxed and confident, they will not need to try hard to learn the language. It will just come naturally and easily.

It is considered important in this method that the psychological barriers that students bring with them be desuggested. Indirect positive suggestions are made to enhance students' self-confidence and to convince them that success is obtainable.

Students also choose target language names on the assumption that a new identity makes students feel more secure and thus more open to learning.

6 How is language viewed? How is culture viewed?

Language is the first of two planes in the two-plane process of communication. In the second plane are the factors which influence the linguistic message. For example, the way one dresses or the nonverbal behavior one uses affects how one's linguistic message is interpreted.

The culture which students learn concerns the everyday life of people who speak the language. The use of the fine arts is also important in Desuggestopedia classes.

7 What areas of language are emphasized? What language skills are emphasized?

Vocabulary is emphasized. Claims about the success of the method often focus on the large number of words that can be acquired. Grammar is dealt with explicitly but minimally. In fact, it is believed that students will learn best if their conscious attention is focused, not on the language forms, but on using the language.

Speaking communicatively is emphasized. Students also read in the target language (for example, dialogues) and write in it (for example, imaginative compositions).

8 What is the role of the students' native language?

Native language translation is used to make the meaning of the dialogue clear. The teacher also uses the native language in class when necessary. As the course proceeds, the teacher uses the native language less and less.

9 How is evaluation accomplished?

Evaluation usually is conducted on students' normal in-class performance and not through formal tests, which would threaten the relaxed atmosphere considered essential for accelerated learning.

10 How does the teacher respond to student errors?

Errors are corrected gently, with the teacher using a soft voice.

Reviewing the Techniques

If you find Desuggestopedia's principles meaningful, you may want to try some of the following techniques, or to alter your classroom environment. Even if not all of them appeal to you, there may be some elements you could usefully adapt to your own teaching style.

- **Classroom Set-up**
  The challenge for the teacher is to create a classroom environment that is bright and cheerful. This was accomplished in the classroom we visited where the walls were decorated with scenes from a country where the target language is spoken. These conditions are not always possible. However, the teacher should try to provide as positive an environment as possible.

- **Peripheral Learning**
  This technique is based upon the idea that we perceive much more in our environment than we consciously notice. It is claimed that, by putting posters containing grammatical information about the target language on the classroom walls, students will absorb the necessary facts effortlessly. The teacher may or may not call attention to the posters. They are changed from time to time to provide grammatical information that is appropriate to what the students are studying.

- **Positive Suggestion**
  It is the teacher's responsibility to orchestrate the suggestive factors in a learning situation, thereby helping students break down the barriers to learning that they bring with them. Teachers can do this through direct and indirect means. Direct suggestion appeals to the students' consciousness: A teacher tells students they are going to be successful. But indirect suggestion, which appeals to the students' subconscious, is actually the more powerful of the two. For example, indirect suggestion was accomplished in the class we visited through the choice of a dialogue entitled, 'To want to is to be able to.'

- **Choose a New Identity**
  The students choose a target language name and a new occupation. As the course continues, the students have an opportunity to develop a whole biography about their fictional selves. For instance, later on they may be asked to talk or write about their fictional hometown, childhood, and family.

- **Role-play**
  Students are asked to pretend temporarily that they are someone else and to perform in the target language as if they were that person. They are often asked to create their own lines relevant to the situation. In the lesson we observed, the students were asked to pretend that they were someone else and to introduce themselves as that person.

- **First Concert**
  The two concerts are components of the receptive phase of the lesson. After the teacher has introduced the story as related in the dialogue and has called her students' attention to some particular grammatical points that arise in it, she reads the dialogue in the target language. The students have copies of the dialogue in the target language and their native language and refer to it as the teacher is reading.

  Music is played. After a few minutes, the teacher begins a slow, dramatic reading, synchronized in intonation with the music. The music is classical; the early Romantic period is suggested. The teacher's voice rises and falls with the music.

- **Second Concert**
  In the second phase, the students are asked to put their scripts aside. They simply listen as the teacher reads the dialogue at normal speed. The teacher is seated and reads with the musical accompaniment. Thus, the content governs the way the teacher reads the script, not the music, which is pre-Classical or Baroque. At the conclusion of this concert, the class ends for the day.

- **Primary Activation**
  This technique and the one that follows are components of the active phase of the lesson. The students playfully reread the target language dialogue out loud, individually or in groups. In the lesson we observed, three groups of students read parts of the dialogue in a particular manner: the first group, sadly; the next, angrily; the last, cheerfully.

- **Creative Adaptation**
  The students engage in various activities designed to help them learn the new material and use it spontaneously. Activities particularly recommended for this phase include singing, dancing, dramatizations, and games. The important thing is that the activities are varied and do not allow the students to focus on the form of the linguistic message, just the communicative intent.

Conclusion

What connection, if any, can you make between Desuggestopedia and your approach to teaching? Does it make sense to you that when your students are relaxed and comfortable, their learning will be facilitated? Should the teacher's role be one of being a respected and trusted authority? Should direct and indirect suggestions be used? Should learning be made as enjoyable as possible? Which, if any, of the other principles of Desuggestopedia do you accept?

Do you think students can learn peripherally? Would it be useful for your students to develop a new target language identity? Would you consider presenting new material with a musical accompaniment? Are any of the activities of the activation phase of use to you?

Activities

Ⓐ Check your understanding of Desuggestopedia.

1 What are some of the ways that direct positive suggestions were present in the lesson? Indirect positive suggestions?
2 How are the arts integrated into the lesson we observed?

Ⓑ Apply what you have understood about Desuggestopedia.

1 Most teachers do not have control of the classrooms in which they teach. This does not mean that they cannot provide an environment designed to reduce the barriers their students bring with them, however. Can you think of ways that you might do this?
2 Make a list of 10 grammatical points about the target language that you would want to display on posters to encourage beginning students' peripheral learning.

References/Additional Resources

Dhority, L. 1991. *The ACT Approach: The Use of Suggestion for Integrative Learning.* Amsterdam: Gordon and Breach Science Publishers.

Gateva, E. 1991. *Creating Wholeness through Art. Global Artistic Creation of the Educational Training Process.* Aylesbury, UK: Accelerated Learning Systems.

Iki, S. 1993. Interview: 'Georgi Lozanov and Evelyna Gateva.' *The Language Teacher,* 17/7: 3–17.

Lozanov, G. 1978. *Outlines of Suggestology and Suggestopedy*. London: Gordon and Breach.

—— and E. Gateva. 1988. *The Foreign Language Teacher's Suggestopedic Manual*. New York: Gordon and Breach Science Publishers.

Schiffler, L. 1992. *Suggestopedic Methods and Applications* (English edn.). Amsterdam: Gordon and Breach Science Publishers.

Stevick, E. 1998. *Working with Teaching Methods: What's at Stake?* Boston, MA: Heinle & Heinle.

7

Community Language Learning

Introduction[1]

The method we will examine in this chapter advises teachers to consider their students as 'whole persons.' **Whole-person learning** means that teachers consider not only their students' intellect, but they also have some understanding of the relationship among students' feelings, physical reactions, instinctive protective reactions, and desire to learn. The Community Language Learning Method takes its principles from the more general Counseling-Learning approach developed by Charles A. Curran.

Curran studied adult learning for many years. He found that adults often feel threatened by a new learning situation. They are threatened by the change inherent in learning and by the fear that they will appear foolish. Curran believed that a way to deal with the fears of students is for teachers to become language **counselors**. A language counselor does not mean someone trained in psychology; it means someone who is a skillful 'understander' of the struggle students face as they attempt to internalize another language. The teacher who can understand can indicate his acceptance of the student. By understanding students' fears and being sensitive to them, he can help students overcome their negative feelings and turn them into positive energy to further their learning.

Let us see how Curran's ideas are put into practice in the Community Language Learning Method. We will observe a class in a private language institute in Indonesia. Most of the students work during the day and come for language instruction in the evening. The class meets two evenings a week for two hours a session. This is the first class.

[1] In this chapter, the authors have benefited enormously from the careful reading and helpful comments of Jennybelle Rardin and Pat Tirone of the Counseling-Learning Institutes.

Experience

The students arrive and take their seats. The chairs are in a circle around a table that has a tape recorder on it. After greeting the students, the teacher introduces himself and has the students introduce themselves. In Indonesian, he tells the students what they will be doing that evening: They are going to have a conversation in English with his help. The conversation will be tape-recorded, and afterward, they will create a written form of the conversation—a transcript. He tells the class that the rest of the evening will be spent doing various activities with the language on the transcript. He then explains how the students are to have the conversation.

'Whenever one of you would like to say something, raise your hand and I will come behind you. I will not be a participant in the conversation except to help you say in English what you want to say. Say what you want to say in Indonesian; I will give you the English translation. I will give you the translation in phrases, or "chunks". Record only the chunks, one at a time. After the conversation, when we listen to the recording, your sentence will sound whole. Only your voices in English will be on the tape. Since this is your first English conversation, you may want to keep it simple. We have ten minutes for this activity.'

No one speaks at first. Then a young woman raises her hand. The teacher walks to her chair. He stands behind her. 'Selamat sore,' she says. The teacher translates, 'Good ….' After a little confusion with the switch on the microphone, she puts 'Good' on the tape and turns the switch off. The teacher then gives 'evening,' and she tries to say 'evening' into the microphone but only gets out 'eve ….' The teacher says again in a clear and warm voice, somewhat exaggerating the word, 'Eve … ning.' The woman tries again. She shows some signs of her discomfort with the experience, but she succeeds in putting the whole word 'evening' onto the recording.

Another student raises his hand. The teacher walks to him and stands behind his chair. 'Selamat sore,' the second student says to the first student. 'Apa kabar?' he asks of a third. The teacher, already sensing that this student is a bit more secure, gives the entire translation, 'Good evening.' 'Good evening,' the student says, putting the phrase on the tape. 'How are you?' the teacher continues. 'How …,' the student says into the microphone, then turns, obviously seeking help for the rest of the phrase. The teacher, realizing he needed to give smaller chunks, repeats each word separately. 'How,' repeats the teacher. 'How,' says the student into the microphone. 'Are,' repeats the teacher. 'Are,' the student says. 'You,' completes the teacher. 'You,' the student records.

Figure 7.1   A student recording her contribution to the conversation

The student to whom the question was directed raises his hand and the teacher stands behind him. '*Kabar baik. Terima kasih*,' he responds. 'Fine,' the teacher says. 'Fine,' the student records. 'Thank you,' the teacher completes. 'Thank you,' the student confidently puts on the tape.

A fourth student asks of another, '*Nama saudara siapa?*' The teacher steps behind her and says, 'What's … your … name?' pausing after each word to give the student time to put her question successfully on the tape.

The other student replies, '*Nama saya Saleh.*' 'My name is Saleh,' the teacher says in English. '*Apa kabar?*' another student asks Saleh. 'How are you?' the teacher translates. '*Saya tidak sehat*,' Saleh answers. 'I am not well,' the teacher translates. '*Mengapa?*' asks another student 'Why?' says the teacher. '*Sebab kepala saya pusing*,' Saleh replies. 'Because I have a headache,' translates the teacher. Each of these English utterances is recorded in the manner of the earlier ones, the teacher trying to be sensitive to what size chunk each student can handle with confidence. The teacher then announces that they have five minutes left. During this time the students ask questions like why someone is studying English, what someone does for a living, and what someone's hobbies are. In this conversation, each student around the table records some English utterance on the tape.

After the conversation has ended, the teacher sits in the circle and asks the students to say in Indonesian how they feel about the experience. One student says that he does not remember any of the English he has just heard. The teacher accepts what he says and responds, 'You have a concern that you haven't learned any English.' The student says, 'Yes.' Another student says he, too, has not learned any English; he was just involved in the conversation. The teacher accepts this comment and replies, 'Your attention was on the conversation, not on the English.' Another student says that she does not mind the fact that she cannot remember any English; she has enjoyed the conversation. The teacher accepts her comment and reassures her and all the students that they will yet have an opportunity to learn the English words—that he does not expect them to remember the English phrases at this time. 'Would anyone else like to say anything?' the teacher asks. Since there is silence, the teacher continues, 'OK, then. Let's listen to your conversation. I will play the tape. Just listen to your voices in English.' The students listen. 'OK,' the teacher says. 'I am going to play the tape again and stop it at the end of each sentence. See if you can recall what you said, and say it again in Indonesian to be sure that everyone understands what was said. If you can't recall your own sentence, we can all help out.' They have no trouble recalling what was said.

Next the teacher asks them to move their chairs into a semicircle and to watch as he writes the conversation on the board. The teacher asks if anyone would like to operate the tape recorder and stop it at the end of each sentence. No one volunteers, so the teacher operates it himself. The teacher then writes line by line, numbering each English sentence. One student asks if he can copy the sentences. The teacher asks him to stay focused on the words being written up at this point and reassures him that there will be time for copying later, if not in this class session, then in the next.

The teacher writes all the English sentences. Before going back to put in the Indonesian equivalents, he quietly underlines the first English word and then pauses. He asks the students to give the Indonesian equivalents. Since no one volunteers the meaning, after a few seconds he writes the literal Indonesian translation. He continues this way until all the sentences are translated, leaving out any unnecessary repetition.

Next, the teacher tells the students to sit back and relax as he reads the transcript of the English conversation. He reads it three times, varying the instructions each time. The first time, students just listen. The next time they close their eyes and listen. The last time they silently mouth the words as the teacher reads the conversation.

Figure 7.2 The teacher writing up the student conversation

For the next activity, the **Human Computer**™, the students are told in a warm manner, 'For the next five to ten minutes I am going to turn into a 'human computer' for you. You may use me to practice the pronunciation of any English word or phrase or entire sentence on the transcript. Raise your hand, and I'll come behind you. Then you say either the sentence number or the word you want to practice in English or Indonesian. As the computer, I am programmed to give back only correct English, so you will have to listen carefully to see if what you say matches what I am saying. You may repeat the word, phrase, or sentence as many times as you want. I will stop only when you stop. You control me; you turn the computer on and off.'

A student raises his hand and says, 'Thank you.' He has trouble with the sound at the beginning of 'thank.' The teacher repeats the phrase after him and the student says it again. The teacher repeats it. Three more times the student starts the computer by saying, 'Thank you.' After the teacher has said it for the third time, the student stops, which in turn stops the computer.

Another student raises his hand and says, 'What do you do?' a question from the transcript. Again the teacher moves behind the student and repeats the question the student has chosen to practice. The student works on this question several times just as the first student did. Several others practice saying some part of the transcript in a similar manner.

The teacher then asks the students to work in groups of three to create new sentences based upon the words and phrases of the transcript. Each group writes its sentences down. The teacher walks from group to group to help. The first group writes the sentence 'Adik not work in a bank.' The teacher gives the correct sentence to the group: 'Adik does not work in a bank.' The second group writes 'What is my name?' 'OK,' says the teacher. After the teacher finishes helping the group, each group reads its sentences to the class. The teacher replays the tape two more times while the students listen.

Finally, the teacher tells the class they have 10 minutes left in the session. He asks them to talk in Indonesian about the experience they have had that evening, their English, and/or their learning process. As students respond, the teacher listens carefully and reflects back to the students in such a way that each feels he or she has been understood. Most of the students are positive about the experience, one student saying that it is the first time she has felt so comfortable in a beginning language class. 'I now think I can learn English,' she says.

For the next two classes the teacher decides to have the students continue to work with the conversation they created. Some of the activities are as follows:

1 The teacher selects the verb 'be' from the transcript, and together he and the students conjugate it for person and number in the present tense. They do the same for the verb 'do' and for the regular verb 'work.'
2 The students work in small groups to make sentences with the new forms. They share the sentences they have created with the rest of the class.
3 Students take turns reading the transcript, one student reading the English and another reading the Indonesian. They have an opportunity to work on their English pronunciation again as well.
4 The teacher puts a picture of a person on the whiteboard, and the students ask questions of that person as if they have just met him.
5 The students reconstruct the conversation they have created.
6 They create a new dialogue using words they have learned to say during their conversation.

When they finish these activities, the class has another conversation, records it, and uses the new transcript as the basis for subsequent activities.

Thinking about the Experience

Let us now turn our attention to analyzing what we saw. On the left, we can list our observations, and on the right, we can list the principles we derive from our observations.

Observations	Principles
1 The teacher greets the students, introduces himself, and has the students introduce themselves.	Building a relationship with and among students is very important.
2 The teacher tells the students what they are going to do that evening. He explains the procedure for the first activity and sets a time limit.	Any new learning experience can be threatening. When students have an idea of what will happen in each activity, they often feel more secure. People learn nondefensively when they feel secure.
3 Students have a conversation.	Language is for communication.
4 The teacher stands behind the students.	The superior knowledge and power of the teacher can be threatening. If the teacher does not remain in the front of the classroom, the threat is reduced and the students' learning is facilitated. Also this fosters interaction among students, rather than only from student to teacher.
5 The teacher translates what the students want to say in chunks.	The teacher should be sensitive to students' level of confidence and give them just what they need to be successful.
6 The teacher tells them that they have only a few minutes remaining for the conversation.	Students feel more secure when they know the limits of an activity.
7 Students are invited to talk about how they felt during the conversation.	Teacher and students are whole persons. Sharing their feelings about their learning experience allows learners to get to know one another and to build community.

8 The teacher accepts what each student says.	Guided by the knowledge that each learner is unique, the teacher creates an accepting atmosphere. Learners feel free to lower their defenses, and the learning experience becomes less threatening.
9 The teacher understands what the students say.	The teacher 'counsels' the students. He does not offer advice, but rather shows them that he is really listening to them and understands what they are saying. By understanding how students feel, the teacher can help students gain insights into their own learning process as well as transform their negative feelings, which might otherwise block their learning.
10 The students listen to the tape and give the Indonesian translation.	The students' native language is used to make the meaning clear and to build a bridge from the known to the unknown. Students feel more secure when they understand everything.
11 The teacher asks the students to form a semicircle in front of the whiteboard so they can see easily.	The teacher should take the responsibility for structuring activities clearly in the most appropriate way possible for successful completion of an activity.
12 The teacher reassures the students that they will have time later on to copy the sentences.	Learning at the beginning stages is facilitated if students attend to one task at a time.
13 The teacher asks the students to give the Indonesian equivalents as he points to different phrases in the transcript. He points to the first phrase and pauses; if no one volunteers the meaning, he writes it himself.	The teacher encourages student initiative and independence, but does not let students flounder in uncomfortable silences.
14 The teacher reads the transcript three times. The students relax and listen.	Students need quiet reflection time in order to learn.

15 In the Human Computer™ activity, the students choose which phrase they want to practice pronouncing; the teacher, following the student's lead, repeats the phrase until the learner is satisfied and stops.	Students learn best when they have a choice in what they practice. Students develop an inner wisdom about where they need to work. If students feel in control, they can take more responsibility for their own learning.
16 The students learn to listen carefully to see if what they say matches what the teacher is saying.	Students need to learn to discriminate, for example, in perceiving the similarities and differences among the target language forms.
17 Students work together in groups of three.	In groups, students can begin to feel a sense of community and can learn from each other as well as the teacher. Cooperation, not competition, is encouraged.
18 The teacher corrects by repeating correctly the sentence the students have created.	The teacher should work in a non-threatening way with what the learner has produced.
19 The students read their sentences to the other members of the class.	Developing a community among the class members builds trust and can help to reduce the threat of the new learning situation.
20 The teacher plays the tape two more times while the students listen.	Learning tends not to take place when the material is too new or, conversely, too familiar. Retention will best take place somewhere in between novelty and familiarity.
21 The students are once again invited to talk about the experience they have had that evening.	In addition to reflecting on the language, students reflect on what they have experienced. In this way, they have an opportunity to learn about the language, their own learning, and how to learn from one another in community.
22 Other activities with the transcript of the first conversation occur. Then the learners have a new conversation.	In the beginning stages, the 'syllabus' is generated primarily by the students. Students are more willing to learn when they have created the material themselves.

Reviewing the Principles

Let us now review the principles of the Community Language Learning Method (CLL). In answering our 10 questions, some additional information about the method will also be provided.

1 What are the goals of teachers who use the Community Language Learning Method?

Teachers who use CLL want their students to learn how to use the target language communicatively. In addition, they want their students to learn about their own learning, to take increasing responsibility for it, and to learn how to learn from one another. All of these objectives can be accomplished in a nondefensive manner if the teacher and learner(s) treat each other as whole persons, valuing both thoughts and feelings.

2 What is the role of the teacher? What is the role of the students?

The teacher's initial role is primarily that of a counselor. This does not mean that the teacher is a therapist, or that the teacher does no teaching. Rather, it means that the teacher recognizes how threatening a new learning situation can be for adult learners, so he skillfully understands and supports his students in their struggle to master the target language.

Initially, the learners are very dependent upon the teacher. It is recognized, however, that as the learners continue to study, they become increasingly independent. Community Language Learning methodologists have identified five stages in this movement from dependency to mutual interdependency with the teacher. In Stages I, II, and III, the teacher focuses not only on the language but also on being supportive of learners in their learning process. In Stage IV, because of the students' greater security in the language and readiness to benefit from corrections, the teacher can focus more on accuracy. It should be noted that accuracy is always a focus even in the first three stages; however, it is subordinated to fluency. The reverse is true in Stages IV and V.

3 What are some characteristics of the teaching/learning process?

In a beginning class, which is what we observed, students typically have a conversation using their native language. The teacher helps them express what they want to say by giving them the target language translation in chunks. These chunks are recorded, and when they are replayed, it sounds like a fairly fluid conversation. Later, a transcript is made of the conversation, and native language equivalents are written beneath the target language words. The transcription of the conversation becomes a 'text' with which students work. Various activities are conducted (for example, examination of a grammar point, working on pronunciation of a particular phrase, or creating new sentences with words from the transcript) that allow students to further explore the language they have generated. During the course of the lesson, students are invited to say how they feel, and in return the teacher understands them.

According to Curran, there are six elements necessary for nondefensive learning. The first of these is security. Next is aggression, by which Curran means that students should be given an opportunity to assert themselves, be actively involved, and invest themselves in the learning experience. One way of allowing for this in the lesson we observed was for students to conduct their own conversation. The third element is attention. One of the skills necessary in learning a second or foreign language is to be able to attend to many factors simultaneously. To facilitate this, especially at the beginning of the learning process, the teacher helps to narrow the scope of attention. Recall that the teacher in our lesson asked the students not to copy the transcript while he was writing it on the board. Instead, he wanted them to attend to what he was writing and to add what translation they may have recalled in order to complete the transcript.

The fourth element, reflection, occurred in two different ways in our lesson. The first was when the students reflected on the language as the teacher read the transcript three times. The second was when students were invited to stop and consider the active experience they were having. Retention is the fifth element, the integration of the new material that takes place within the whole self. The last element is discrimination, sorting out the differences among target language forms. We saw this element when the students were asked to listen to the Human Computer™ and attempt to match their pronunciation to the computer's.

4 What is the nature of student–teacher interaction? What is the nature of student–student interaction?

The nature of student-teacher interaction in CLL changes within the lesson and over time. Sometimes the students are assertive, as when they are having a conversation. At these times, the teacher facilitates their ability to express themselves in the target language. He physically removes himself from the circle, thereby encouraging students to interact with one another. At other times in the lesson, the teacher is very obviously in charge and providing direction. At all times initially, the teacher structures the class; at later stages, the students may assume more responsibility for this. As Rardin (1988) has observed, the Community Language Learning Method is neither student-centered, nor teacher-centered, but rather teacher–student centered, with both being decision-makers in the class.

Building a relationship with and among students is very important. In a trusting relationship, any debilitating anxiety that students feel can be reduced, thereby helping students to stay open to the learning process. Students can learn from their interaction with each other as well as their interaction with the teacher. A spirit of cooperation, not competition, can prevail.

5 How are the feelings of the students dealt with?

Responding to the students' feelings is considered very important in CLL. One regular activity is inviting students to comment on how they feel. The teacher listens and responds to each comment carefully. By showing students he understands how they feel, the teacher can help them overcome negative feelings that might otherwise block their learning.

Student security in this lesson was provided for in a number of ways. Some of these were the teacher's use of the students' native language, telling students precisely what they would be doing during the lesson, respecting established time limits, giving students only as much language at a time as they could handle, and taking responsibility for structuring activities clearly in the most appropriate way. While security is a basic element of the learning process, the way in which it is provided will change depending upon the stage of the learner.

6 How is the language viewed? How is culture viewed?

Language is for communication. Curran writes that 'learning is persons,' meaning that both teacher and students work at building trust in one another and the learning process. At the beginning of the process, the focus is on 'sharing and belonging between persons through the language tasks.' Then the focus shifts more to the target language which becomes the group's individual and shared identity. Curran also believes that in this kind of supportive learning process, language becomes the means for developing creative and critical thinking. Culture is an integral part of language learning.

7 What areas of language are emphasized? What language skills are emphasized?

In the early stages, typically the students generate the material since they decide what they want to be able to say in the target language. Later on, after students feel more secure, the teacher might prepare specific materials or work with published textbooks.

Particular grammar points, pronunciation patterns, and vocabulary are worked with, based on the language the students have generated. The most important skills are understanding and speaking the language at the beginning, with reinforcement through reading and writing.

8 What is the role of the students' native language?

Students' security is initially enhanced by using their native language. The purpose of using the native language is to provide a bridge from the familiar to the unfamiliar. Where possible, literal native language equivalents are given to the target language words that have been transcribed. This makes their meaning clear and allows students to combine the target language words in different ways to create new sentences. Directions in class and sessions during which students express their feelings and are understood are conducted in the native language. In later stages, of course, more and more of the target language can be used. By the time students are in Stages III and IV, their conversations have few native language words and phrases. In a class where the students speak a variety of native languages, conversations take place right from the start in the target language. Meaning is made clear in other ways, with pantomime, pictures, and the use of target language synonyms, for example.

9 How is evaluation accomplished?

Although no particular mode of evaluation is prescribed in the Community Language Learning Method, whatever evaluation is conducted should be in keeping with the principles of the method. If, for example, the school requires that the students take a test at the end of a course, then the teacher would see to it that the students are adequately prepared for taking it.

Also, a teacher-made classroom test would likely be more of an integrative test than a discrete-point one. Students would be asked to write a paragraph or be given an oral interview, rather than being asked to answer a question which deals with only one point of language at a time. (Compare this with the evaluation procedures for the Audio-Lingual Method.)

Finally, it is likely that teachers would encourage their students to self-evaluate—to look at their own learning and to become aware of their own progress.

10 How does the teacher respond to student errors?

Teachers should work with what the learner has produced in a nonthreatening way. One way of doing this is for the teacher to recast the student's error, i.e. to repeat correctly what the student has said incorrectly, without calling further attention to the error. Techniques depend on where the students are in the five-stage learning process, but are consistent with sustaining a respectful, nondefensive relationship between teacher and students.

Reviewing the Techniques

We will review the techniques described in this CLL lesson and provide a little more detail. You may have agreed with some or all of the answers to our 10 questions and might like to try to incorporate some of these techniques into your own approach to language teaching. Of course, there may also be techniques you are currently using that can be adapted so that they are consistent with the whole-person approach we have explored here.

- **Recording Student Conversation**

   This is a technique used to record student-generated language as well as to give the opportunity for community learning to come about. By giving students the choice about what to say and when to say it, students are in a good position to take responsibility for their own learning. Students are asked to have a conversation using their native language or a language common to the group. In multilingual groups with no common language, other means will have to be employed. For instance, students can use gestures to get their meaning across. After each native language utterance or use of a gesture, the teacher translates what the student says or acts out into the target language. The teacher gives the students the target language translation in appropriate-sized chunks. Each chunk is recorded, giving students a final recording with only the target language on it. In the lesson we observed, a tape recorder was used; however, these days, other teachers might use a digital voice-recording device, such as an MP3 player, a cell phone, or a computer. Such recording technology allows for instant 'repeats' without rewinding. Also, a teacher can burn a CD or send an MP3 (or other) file to students electronically, which allows students to listen to the recording in their own time.

   After a conversation has been recorded, it can be replayed. Since the students have a choice in what they want to say in the original conversation, it is easier for them to associate meaning with a particular target language utterance. Being able to recall the meaning of almost everything said in a first conversation is motivating for learners. The recording can also be used to simply listen to their voices in the target language.

   Recording student conversation works best with 12 or fewer students. In a larger class, students can take turns being the ones to have the conversation.

- **Transcription**

   The teacher transcribes the students' recorded target language conversation. Each student is given the opportunity to translate his or her utterances and the teacher writes the native language equivalent beneath the target language words. Students can copy the transcript after it has been completely written up on the board or on large, poster-sized paper, or the teacher may provide them with a copy. The transcript provides a basis for future activities. If poster-sized paper is used, the transcript can be put up in the classroom for later reference and for the purpose of increasing student security.

Thinking about the Experience

The teacher takes time during and/or after the various activities to give the students the opportunity to reflect on how they feel about the language learning experience, themselves as learners, and their relationship with one another. As students give their reactions, the teacher understands them—shows that he has listened carefully by giving an appropriate **understanding response** to what the student has said. He does not repeat what the learner says, but rather shows that he understands its essence. You may wish to return to the lesson we observed where the teacher understood the students' reactions to their conversation. Such responses can encourage students to think about their unique engagement with the language, the activities, the teacher, and the other students, thus strengthening their independent learning.

- **Reflective Listening**
  The students relax and listen to their own voices speaking the target language on the recording. Another possible technique is for the teacher to read the transcript while the students simply listen, with their eyes open or shut. A third possibility is for the students to mouth the words as the teacher reads the transcript.

- **Human Computer™**
  A student chooses some part of the transcript to practice pronouncing. She is 'in control' of the teacher when she tries to say the word or phrase. The teacher, following the student's lead, repeats the phrase as often as the student wants to practice it. The teacher does not correct the student's mispronunciation in any way. It is through the teacher's consistent manner of repeating the word or phrase clearly that the student self-corrects as she tries to imitate the teacher's model.

- **Small Group Tasks**
  The small groups in the class we observed were asked to make new sentences with the words on the transcript. Afterward, the groups

shared the sentences they made with the rest of the class. Later in the week, students working in pairs made sentences with the different verb conjugations.

There are a lot of different activities that could take place with students working in small groups. Teachers who use small group activities believe students can learn from each other and get more practice with the target language by working in small groups. Also, small groups allow students to get to know each other better. This can lead to the development of a community among class members.

Conclusion

As indicated earlier in this chapter, the particular class that we observed represents the first lesson of what is considered a Stage I experience in the Community Language Learning Method. The principles we have drawn from it can also be seen in Stage II, III, IV, and V relationships, although they will be implemented in different ways in order to respond appropriately to learner growth.

The two most basic principles which underlie the kind of learning that can take place in CLL are summed up in the following phrases:

1   'Learning is persons,' which means that whole-person learning of another language takes place best in a relationship of trust, support, and cooperation between teacher and students and among students.
2   'Learning is dynamic and creative,' which means that learning is an ongoing developmental process.

Do you agree with these two basic principles? Do you believe that a teacher should adopt the role of a counselor, as Curran uses the term? Should the development of a community be encouraged? Do you think that students should be given the opportunity for, in effect, creating part of their own syllabus? Which of these or any other principles is compatible with your personal approach to teaching?

Do you think you could use the technique of recording your students' conversation? Should you give your students an opportunity to reflect on their experience? Can you use the Human Computer™? Which of the other techniques can you see adapting to your teaching style?

Activities

A Check your understanding of the Community Language Learning Method.

1   Curran says there are six elements of nondefensive learning: security, aggression, attention, reflection, retention, and discrimination (**SAARRD**). Some of the ways these were manifest in our lesson were pointed out in answer to questions 3 and 5. Can you find any other examples of these in the class we observed?

2   Curran claims learners pass through five stages of learning as they go from being a beginning language learner to an advanced language learner. As they experience these stages, they change from being dependent *on* the teacher to being mutually interdependent *with* the teacher. Can you see how these students are dependent on the teacher now? Can you find anything in the class we observed that encourages learner independence?

B Apply what you have understood about the Community Language Learning Method.

1   Have some students record a conversation with your help as the language counselor. Tell them to record only the target language. After you have completed the conversation, think of five different activities to help them process and review the target language conversation they have created while being consistent with the principles of CLL.

2   Try teaching a lesson as you normally do, but think of your students in a whole-person way, if this is a new idea to you. Does this change the way you work? If so, then how?

References/Additional Resources

Curran, C. 1976. *Counseling-Learning in Second Languages.* Cliffside Park, NJ: Counseling-Learning Institutes.

——. 1977. *Counseling-Learning: A Whole-person Approach for Education* (2nd edn.). Cliffside Park, NJ: Counseling-Learning Institutes.

Rardin, J. et al. 1988. *Education in a New Dimension.* Cliffside Park, NJ: Counseling-Learning Institutes.

Samimy, K. and **J. Rardin.** 1994. 'Adult language learners' affective reactions to community language learning: A descriptive study.' *Foreign Language Annals* 27/3.

Stevick, E. 1998. *Working with Teaching Methods: What's at Stake?* Boston, MA: Heinle & Heinle.

8

Total Physical Response

Introduction

Let us first consider a general approach to foreign language instruction which has been named the **Comprehension Approach**. It is called this because of the importance it gives to listening comprehension. Most of the other methods we have looked at have students speaking the target language from the first day. In the 1960s, James Asher's research gave rise to the hypothesis that language learning starts first with understanding and ends with production. After the learner internalizes an extensive map of how the target language works, speaking will appear spontaneously. Of course, the students' speech will not be perfect, but gradually speech will become more target-like. Notice that this is exactly how an infant acquires its native language. A baby spends many months listening to the people around it long before it ever says a word. The child has the time to try to make sense out of the sounds it hears. No one tells the baby that it must speak. The child chooses to speak when it is ready to do so.

There are several methods being practiced today that have in common an attempt to apply these observations to language instruction. One such method is Krashen and Terrell's Natural Approach. The Natural Approach shares certain features with the Direct Method, which we examined in Chapter 3. Emphasis is placed on students' developing basic communication skills through receiving meaningful exposure to the target language (**comprehensible input**). Meaning is given priority over form and thus vocabulary acquisition is stressed. The students listen to the teacher using the target language communicatively from the first day of instruction. They do not speak at first. The teacher helps her students to understand her by using pictures and occasional words in the students' native language and by being as expressive as possible. It is thought that if the teacher uses language that is just in advance of students' current level of proficiency (**i+1**), while making sure that her input is comprehensible, acquisition will proceed 'naturally.' Unconscious acquisition, then, is favored over more conscious learning. Creating a low **affective filter** is also a condition for acquisition that is met when the classroom atmosphere is one in which anxiety is reduced and students' self-confidence is boosted. The filter is kept low as well by the fact that students are not put on the spot to speak; they speak when they are ready to do so.

Another method that fits within the Comprehension Approach is Winitz and Reed's self-instructional program and Winitz' *The Learnables*. In this method, students listen to tape-recorded words, phrases, and sentences while they look at accompanying pictures. The meaning of the utterance is clear from the context the picture provides. The students are asked to respond in some way, such as pointing to each picture as it is described, to show that they understand the language to which they are listening; however, they do not speak. Stories illustrated by pictures are also used as a device to convey abstract meaning.

A third method that fits here is the Lexical Approach. Although its originator, Michael Lewis, claims that the Lexical Approach is an approach, not a method, it really belongs under the category of the Comprehension Approach, we feel. This is because the Lexical Approach is less concerned with student production and more concerned that students receive and comprehend abundant input. Particularly at lower levels, teachers talk extensively to their students in the target language, while requiring little or no verbal response from them. Students are also given exercises and activities that raise their awareness about multi-word lexical items, such as 'I see what you mean,' and 'Take your time.' Like Krashen and Terrell, Lewis emphasizes acquisition over learning, assuming that 'It is exposure to enough suitable input, not formal teaching, which is key to increasing the learner's lexicon (Lewis 1997: 197).

A fourth method, James Asher's Total Physical Response (TPR), is the one we will examine in detail here in order to see how the principles of the Comprehension Approach are put into practice. Based on his research cited above, Asher reasoned that the fastest, least stressful way to achieve understanding of any target language is to follow directions uttered by the instructor (without native language translation). We will learn about Total Physical Response through our usual way of observing a class in which it is being used. The class is located in Sweden. It is a beginning class for 30 Grade 5 students. They study English for one class period three times a week.

Experience[1]

We follow the teacher as she enters the room, and we take a seat in the back of the room. It is the first class of the year, so after the teacher takes attendance,

[1] This lesson is based upon the one in Asher (1982).

she introduces the method they will use to study English. She explains in Swedish, 'You will be studying English in a way that is similar to the way you learned Swedish. You will not speak at first. Rather, you will just listen to me and do as I do. I will give you a command to do something in English, and you will do the actions along with me. I will need four volunteers to help me with the lesson.'

Hands go up, and the teacher calls on four students to come to the front of the room and sit with her on chairs that are lined up facing the other students. She tells the other students to listen and to watch.

In English the teacher says, 'Stand up.' As she says it, she stands up and she signals for the four volunteers to rise with her. They all stand up. 'Sit down,' she says, and they all sit. The teacher and the students stand up and sit down together several times according to the teacher's command; the students say nothing. The next time that they stand up together, the teacher issues a new command, 'Turn around.' The students follow the teacher's example and turn so that they are facing their chairs. 'Turn around,' the teacher says again and this time they turn to face the other students as before. 'Sit down. Stand up. Turn around. Sit down.' She says, 'Walk,' and they all begin walking towards the front row of the students' seats. 'Stop. Jump. Stop. Turn around. Walk. Stop. Jump. Stop. Turn around. Sit down.' The teacher gives the commands and they all perform the actions together. The teacher gives these commands again, changing their order and saying them quite quickly. 'Stand up. Jump. Sit down. Stand up. Turn around. Jump. Stop. Turn around. Walk. Stop. Turn around. Walk. Jump. Turn around. Sit down.'

Once again the teacher gives the commands; this time, however, she remains seated. The four volunteers respond to her commands. 'Stand up. Sit down. Walk. Stop. Jump. Turn around. Turn around. Walk. Turn around. Sit down.' The students respond perfectly. Next, the teacher signals that she would like one of the volunteers to follow her commands alone. One student raises his hand and performs the actions the teacher commands.

Finally, the teacher approaches the other students who have been sitting observing her and their four classmates. 'Stand up,' she says and the class responds. 'Sit down. Stand up. Jump. Stop. Sit down. Stand up. Turn around. Turn around. Jump. Sit down.' Even though they have not done the actions before, the students are able to perform according to the teacher's commands.

The teacher is satisfied that the class has mastered these six commands. She begins to introduce some new ones. 'Point to the door,' she orders. She extends her right arm and right index finger in the direction of the door at the side of the classroom. The volunteers point with her. 'Point to the desk.' She points to her own big teacher's desk at the front of the room. 'Point to the chair.' She points to the chair behind her desk and the students follow.

Figure 8.1   Students and teacher acting out the teacher's command

'Stand up.' The students stand up. 'Point to the door.' The students point. 'Walk to the door.' They walk together. 'Touch the door.' The students touch it with her. The teacher continues to command the students as follows: 'Point to the desk. Walk to the desk. Touch the desk. Point to the door. Walk to the door. Touch the door. Point to the chair. Walk to the chair. Touch the chair.' She continues to perform the actions with the students, but changes the order of the commands. After practicing these new commands with the students several times, the teacher remains seated, and the four volunteers carry out the commands by themselves. Only once do the students seem confused, at which point the teacher repeats the command which has caused difficulty and performs the action with them.

Next the teacher turns to the rest of the class and gives the following commands to the students sitting in the back row: 'Stand up. Sit down. Stand up. Point to the desk. Point to the door. Walk to the door. Walk to the chair. Touch the chair. Walk. Stop. Jump. Walk. Turn around. Sit down.' Although she varies the sequence of commands, the students do not seem to have any trouble following the order.

Next, the teacher turns to the four volunteers and says, 'Stand up. Jump to the desk.' The students have never heard this command before. They hesitate a second and then jump to the desk just as they have been told. Everyone laughs at this sight. 'Touch the desk. Sit on the desk.' Again, the teacher uses a novel command, one they have not practiced before. The teacher then issues two commands in the form of a compound sentence, 'Point to the door, and walk to the door.' Again, the group performs as it has been commanded.

As the last step of the lesson, the teacher writes the new commands on the board. Each time she writes a command, she acts it out. The students copy the sentences into their notebooks.

The class is over. No one except the teacher has spoken a word. However, a few weeks later when we walk by the room we hear a different voice. We stop to listen for moment. One of the students is speaking. We hear her say, 'Raise your hands. Show me your hands. Close your eyes. Put your hands behind you. Open your eyes. Shake hand with your neighbor. Raise your left foot.' We look in and see that the student is directing the other students and the teacher with these commands. They are not saying anything; they are just following the student's orders.

Thinking about the Experience

Now that we have observed the Total Physical Response Method being used in a class, let us examine what we have seen. We will list our observations and then try to understand the principles upon which the teacher's behavior is based.

Observations	Principles
1 The teacher gives a command in the target language and performs the action with the students.	Meaning in the target language can often be conveyed through actions. Memory is activated through learner response. Beginning language instruction should address the right hemisphere of the brain, the part which controls nonverbal behavior. The target language should be presented in chunks, not just word by word.
2 The students say nothing.	The students' understanding of the target language should be developed before speaking.
3 The teacher gives the commands quite quickly.	Students can initially learn one part of the language rapidly by moving their bodies.

4 The teacher sits down and issues commands to the volunteers.	The imperative is a powerful linguistic device through which the teacher can direct student behavior.
5 The teacher directs students other than the volunteers.	Students can learn through observing actions as well as by performing the actions themselves.
6 The teacher introduces new commands after she is satisfied that the first six have been mastered.	It is very important that students feel successful. Feelings of success and low anxiety facilitate learning.
7 The teacher changes the order of the commands.	Students should not be made to memorize fixed routines.
8 When the students make an error, the teacher repeats the command while acting it out.	Correction should be carried out in an unobtrusive manner.
9 The teacher gives the students commands they have not heard before.	Students must develop flexibility in understanding novel combinations of target language chunks. They need to understand more than the exact sentences used in training. Novelty is also motivating.
10 The teacher says, 'Jump to the desk.' Everyone laughs.	Language learning is more effective when it is fun.
11 The teacher writes the new commands on the board.	Spoken language should be emphasized over written language.
12 A few weeks later, a student who has not spoken before gives commands.	Students will begin to speak when they are ready.
13 A student says, 'Shake *hand with your neighbor.'	Students are expected to make errors when they first begin speaking. Teachers should be tolerant of them. Work on the fine details of the language should be postponed until students have become somewhat proficient.

Reviewing the Principles

We will next turn to our 10 questions in order to increase our understanding of Total Physical Response.

1 What are the goals of teachers who use TPR?

Teachers who use TPR believe in the importance of having their students enjoy their experience of learning to communicate in another language. In fact, TPR was developed in order to reduce the stress people feel when they are studying other languages and thereby encourage students to persist in their study beyond a beginning level of proficiency.

The way to do this, Asher believes, is to base foreign language learning upon the way children learn their native language.

2 What is the role of the teacher? What is the role of the students?

Initially, the teacher is the director of all student behavior. The students are imitators of her nonverbal model. At some point (usually after 10–20 hours of instruction), some students will be 'ready to speak.' At that point, there will be a role reversal with individual students directing the teacher and the other students.

3 What are some characteristics of the teaching/learning process?

The first phase of a lesson is one of modeling. The teacher issues commands to a few students, then performs the actions with them. In the second phase, these same students demonstrate that they can understand the commands by performing them alone. The observers also have an opportunity to demonstrate their understanding.

The teacher next recombines elements of the commands to have students develop flexibility in understanding unfamiliar utterances. These commands, which students perform, are often humorous.

After learning to respond to some oral commands, the students learn to read and write them. When students are ready to speak, they become the ones who issue the commands. After students begin speaking, activities expand to include skits and games.

4 What is the nature of student–teacher interaction? What is the nature of student–student interaction?

The teacher interacts with the whole group of students and with individual students. Initially, the interaction is characterized by the teacher speaking and the students responding nonverbally. Later on, the students become more verbal and the teacher responds nonverbally.

Students perform the actions together. Students can learn by watching each other. At some point, however, Asher believes observers must demonstrate their understanding of the commands in order to retain them.

As students begin to speak, they issue commands to one another as well as to the teacher.

5 How are the feelings of the students dealt with?

One of the main reasons TPR was developed was to reduce the stress people feel when studying other languages. One of the primary ways this is accomplished is to allow learners to speak when they are ready. Forcing them to speak before then will only create anxiety. Also, when students do begin to speak, perfection should not be expected.

Another way to relieve anxiety is to make language learning as enjoyable as possible. The use of zany commands and humorous skits are two ways of showing that language learning can be fun.

Finally, it is important that there not be too much modeling, but that students not be too rushed either. Feelings of success and low anxiety facilitate learning.

6 How is the language viewed? How is culture viewed?

Just as with the acquisition of the native language, the oral modality is primary. Culture is the lifestyle of people who speak the language natively.

7 What areas of language are emphasized? What language skills are emphasized?

Vocabulary and grammatical structures are emphasized over other language areas. These are embedded within imperatives. The imperatives are single words and multi-word chunks. One reason for the use of imperatives is their frequency of occurrence in the speech directed at young children learning their native language.

Understanding the spoken word should precede its production. The spoken language is emphasized over written language. Students often do not learn to read the commands they have already learned to perform until after 10 hours of instruction.

8 What is the role of the students' native language?

TPR is usually introduced in the student's native language. After the introduction, rarely would the native language be used. Meaning is made clear through body movements.

9 How is evaluation accomplished?

Teachers will know immediately whether or not students understand by observing their students' actions. Formal evaluations can be conducted simply by commanding individual students to perform a series of actions. As students become more advanced, their performance of skits they have created can become the basis for evaluation.

10 How does the teacher respond to student errors?

It is expected that students will make errors when they first begin speaking. Teachers should be tolerant of them and only correct major errors. Even these should be corrected unobtrusively. As students get more advanced, teachers can 'fine tune'—correct more minor errors.

Reviewing the Techniques

The major technique, as we saw in the lesson we observed, is the use of commands to direct behavior. Asher acknowledges that, although this technique is powerful, a variety of activities is preferred for maintaining student interest. A detailed description of using commands is provided below. If you find some of the principles of Total Physical Response to be of interest, you may wish to devise your own techniques to supplement this one.

- **Using Commands to Direct Behavior**

  It should be clear from the class we observed that the use of commands is the major teaching technique of TPR. The commands are given to get students to perform an action; the action makes the meaning of the command clear. Since Asher suggests keeping the pace lively, it is necessary for a teacher to plan in advance just which commands she will introduce in a lesson. If the teacher tries to think them up as the lesson progresses, the pace will be too slow.

  At first, to clarify meaning, the teacher performs the actions with the students. Later the teacher directs the students alone. The students' actions tell the teacher whether or not the students understand.

  As we saw in the lesson we observed, Asher advises teachers to vary the sequence of the commands so that students do not simply memorize the action sequence without ever connecting the actions with the language.

  Asher believes it is very important that the students feel successful. Therefore, the teacher should not introduce new commands too fast. It is recommended that a teacher present three commands at a time. After students feel successful with these, three more can be taught.

Although we were only able to observe one beginning class, people always ask just how much of a language can be taught through the use of imperatives. Asher claims that all grammar features can be communicated through imperatives. To give an example of a more advanced lesson, one might teach the past tense as follows:

TEACHER: Ingrid, walk to the blackboard.
(Ingrid gets up and walks to the blackboard.)
TEACHER: Class, if Ingrid walked to the blackboard, stand up.
(The class stands up.)
TEACHER: Ingrid, write your name on the blackboard.
(Ingrid writes her name on the blackboard.)
TEACHER: Class, if Ingrid wrote her name on the blackboard,
            sit down.
(The class sits down.)

- **Role Reversal**

Students command their teacher and classmates to perform some actions. Asher says that students will want to speak after 10–20 hours of instruction, although some students may take longer. Students should not be encouraged to speak until they are ready.

- **Action Sequence**

At one point we saw the teacher give three connected commands. For example, the teacher told the students to point to the door, walk to the door, and touch the door. As the students learn more and more of the target language, a longer series of connected commands can be given, which together comprise a whole procedure. While we did not see a long action sequence in this very first class, a little later on students might receive the following instructions, which they act out:

Take out a pen.
Take out a piece of paper.
Write a letter. (imaginary)
Fold the letter.
Put it in an envelope.
Seal the envelope.
Write the address on the envelope.
Put a stamp on the envelope.
Mail the letter.

This series of commands is called an action sequence, or an 'operation.' Many everyday activities, like writing a letter, can be broken down into an action sequence that students can be asked to perform.

Conclusion

Now that we have had a chance to experience a Total Physical Response class and to examine its principles and techniques, you should try to think about how any of this will be of use to you in your own teaching. The teacher we observed was using TPR with Grade 5 children; however, this same method has been used with adult learners and younger children as well.

Ask yourself: Does it make any sense to delay the teaching of speaking the target language? Do you believe that students should not be encouraged to speak until they are ready to do so? Should a teacher overlook certain student errors in the beginning? Which, if any, of the other principles do you agree with?

Would you use the imperative to present the grammatical structures and vocabulary of the target language? Do you believe it is possible to teach all grammatical features through the imperative? Do you think that accompanying language with action aids recall? Would you teach reading and writing in the manner described in this lesson? Would you want to adapt any of the techniques of TPR to your teaching situation? Can you think of any others you would create that would be consistent with the principles presented here?

Activities

A **Check your understanding of Total Physical Response.**

1   Asher believes that additional language instruction can and should be modeled on native language acquisition. What are some characteristics of his method that are similar to the way children acquire their native language?
2   One of the principles of TPR is that when student anxiety is low, language learning is enhanced. How does this method lower student anxiety?

B **Apply what you have understood about Total Physical Response.**

1   Although the teacher uses imperatives, she does so in a gentle, pleasant way, the way a parent would (usually) do with a child. Her voice, facial expression, and manner are kind. Practice giving the commands in this chapter in this way.
2   A lot of target language structures and vocabulary can be taught through the imperative. Plan part of a TPR lesson in which the present continuous tense, or another structure in the target language, is introduced.

3   In the action sequence (operation) that we looked at, the teacher had the students pretend to write and mail a letter. Think of three other common activities which could be used as action sequences in the classroom. Make a list of commands for each one.

References/Additional Resources

Asher, J. 2009. *Learning Another Language Through Actions: The Complete Teacher's Guidebook* (7th edn.). Los Gatos, CA: Sky Oaks Productions.

Garcia, R. 1996. *Instructor's Notebook: How to Apply TPR for Best Results* (4th edn.). Los Gatos, CA: Sky Oaks Productions.

Krashen, S. and T. Terrell. 1983. *The Natural Approach: Language Acquisition in the Classroom.* Hayward, CA: The Alemany Press.

——. 1987. *Principles and Practice in Second Language Acquisition.* Englewood Cliffs, NJ: Prentice-Hall.

Lewis, M. 1993. *The Lexical Approach.* Boston: Heinle/Cengage.

——. 1997. *Implementing the Lexical Approach.* Boston: Heinle/Cengage.

Nelson, G., T. Winters, and R. Clark. 2004. *Do as I Say: Operations, Procedures and Rituals for Language Acquisition* (3rd edn.). Brattleboro, VT: Pro Lingua Associates, Publishers.

Richards, J. and T. Rodgers. 1986. *Approaches and Methods in Language Teaching.* Cambridge: Cambridge University Press.

Romijn, E. and C. Seely. 2000. *Live Action English.* Berkley, CA: Command Performance Language Institute. (Also available in Spanish, French, German, Italian, and Japanese.)

Seeley, C. and E. Romijn. 2006. *TPR is More than Commands at All Levels* (3rd edn.). Los Gatos, CA: Sky Oaks Productions.

Winitz, H. 1978. *The Learnables.* Kansas City, MO: International Linguistics. (Cassette program series.)

—— (ed.). 1981. *The Comprehension Approach to Foreign Language Instruction.* Rowley, MA: Newbury House.

9

Communicative Language Teaching

Introduction

You may have noticed that the goal of most of the methods we have looked at so far is for students to learn to communicate in the target language. In the 1970s, though, educators began to question if they were going about meeting the goal in the right way. Some observed that students could produce sentences accurately in a lesson, but could not use them appropriately when genuinely communicating outside of the classroom. Others noted that being able to communicate required more than mastering linguistic structure, due to the fact that language was fundamentally social (Halliday 1973). Within a social context, language users needed to perform certain **functions**, such as promising, inviting, and declining invitations (Wilkins 1976). Students may know the rules of linguistic usage, but be unable to use the language (Widdowson 1978). In short, being able to communicate required more than **linguistic competence**; it required **communicative competence** (Hymes 1971)—knowing when and how to say what to whom. Such observations contributed to a shift in the field in the late 1970s and early 1980s from a linguistic structure-centered approach to a **Communicative Approach** (Widdowson 1990; Savignon 1997).

Applying the theoretical perspective of the Communicative Approach, Communicative Language Teaching (CLT) aims broadly to make communicative competence the goal of language teaching. What this looks like in the classroom may depend on how the principles are interpreted and applied. Indeed, Klapper (2003) makes the point that because CLT lacks closely prescribed classroom techniques, as compared with some of the other methods we have just looked at, CLT is 'fuzzy' in teachers' understanding. This fuzziness has given CLT a flexibility which has allowed it to endure for thirty years. However, its flexibility also means that classroom practices differ widely even when teachers report that they are practicing CLT. It is probably fair to say that there is no one single agreed upon version of CLT. Nevertheless, we will follow our usual way of understanding the theory and associated practices by visiting a class in which a form of Communicative Language Teaching is being practiced.

The class we will visit is one being conducted for immigrants to Canada. These twenty people have lived in Canada for two years and are at a high-intermediate level of English proficiency. They meet two evenings a week for two hours each class.

Experience

The teacher greets the class and distributes a handout. There is writing on both sides. On one side is a copy of a sports column from a recent newspaper. The reporter is discussing the last World Cup competition. The teacher asks the students to read it and then to underline the predictions the reporter makes about the next World Cup. He gives them these directions in the target language. When the students have finished, they read what they have underlined. The teacher writes what they have found on the board. Then he and the students discuss which predictions the reporter feels more certain about and which predictions he feels less certain about:

> France is very likely to win the next World Cup.
> Spain can win if they play as well as they have lately.
> Germany probably won't be a contender next time.
> Argentina may have an outside chance.

Then he asks the students to look at the first sentence and to tell the class another way to express this same prediction. One student says, 'France probably will win the next World Cup.' 'Yes,' says the teacher. 'Any others?' No one responds. The teacher offers, 'France is almost certain to win the World Cup.' 'What about the next?' he asks the class. One student replies, 'It is possible that Spain will win the World Cup.' Another student offers, 'There's a possibility that Spain will win the World Cup.' Each of the reporter's predictions is discussed in this manner. All the paraphrases the students suggest are evaluated by the teacher and the other students to make sure they convey the same degree of certainty as the reporter's original prediction.

Next, the teacher asks the students to turn to the other side of the handout. On it are all the sentences of the article that they have been working on. They are, however, out of order. For example, the first two sentences on this side of the handout are:

> Argentina may have an outside chance.
> In the final analysis, the winning team may simply be the one with the most experience.

The first sentence was in the middle of the original sports column. The second was the last sentence of the original column. The teacher tells the students to unscramble the sentences, to put them in their proper order by numbering them. When they finish, the students compare what they have done with the original on the other side of the handout.

The teacher then asks the students if they agree with the reporter's predictions. He also asks them to get into pairs and to write their own prediction about who will be the next World Cup champion.

The teacher then announces that the students will be playing a game. He divides the class into small groups of five people each. He hands each group a deck of 13 cards. Each card has a picture of a piece of sports equipment. As the students identify the items, the teacher writes each name on the board: basketball, soccer ball, volleyball, tennis racket, skis, ice skates, roller skates, football, baseball bat, golf clubs, bowling ball, badminton racket, and hockey stick.

The cards are shuffled and four of the students in a group are dealt three cards each. They do not show their cards to anyone else. The extra card is placed face down in the middle of the group. The fifth person in each group receives no cards. She is told that she should try to predict what it is that Dumduan (one of the students in the class) will be doing the following weekend. The fifth student is to make statements like, 'Dumduan may go skiing this weekend.' If one of the members of her group has a card showing skis, the group member would reply, for example, 'Dumduan can't go skiing because I have her skis.' If, on the other hand, no one has the picture of the skis, then the fifth student can make a strong statement about the likelihood of Dumduan going skiing. She can say, for example, 'Dumduan will go skiing.' She can check her prediction by turning over the card that was placed face down. If it is the picture of the skis, then she knows she is correct.

The students seem to really enjoy playing the game. They take turns so that each person has a chance to make the predictions about how a classmate will spend his or her time.

For the next activity, the teacher reads a number of predictions like the following:

By 2030, solar energy will replace the world's reliance on fossil fuels.

By 2050, people will be living on the moon.

The students are told to make statements about how probable they think the predictions are and why they believe so. They are also asked how they feel about the prediction. In discussing one of the predictions, a student says he does not think it is *like that a world government will be in place by the twenty-second century. The teacher and students ignore his error and the discussion continues.

Next, the teacher has the students divide into groups of three. Since there are 20 students, there are six groups of three students and one group of two. One member of each group is given a picture strip story. There are six pictures in a column on a piece of paper, but no words. The pictures tell a story. The student with the story shows the first picture to the other members of her group, while covering the remaining five pictures.

Figure 9.1   Students making predictions about a strip story

The other students try to predict what they think will happen in the second picture. The first student tells them whether they are correct or not. She then shows them the second picture and asks them to predict what the third picture will look like. After the entire series of pictures has been shown, the group gets a new strip story and they change roles, giving the first student an opportunity to work with a partner in making predictions.

For the final activity of the class, the students are told that they will do a role-play. The teacher tells them to get into groups of four. They are to imagine that they are all employees of the same company. One of them is the others' boss. They are having a meeting to discuss what will possibly occur as a result of their company merging with another company. Before they begin, they discuss some possibilities together. They decide that they can talk about topics such as whether or not some of the people in their company will lose their jobs, whether or not they will have to move, whether or not certain policies will change, whether or not they will earn more money. 'Remember,' says the teacher, 'that one of you in each group is the boss. You should think about this relationship if, for example, she makes a prediction that you don't agree with.'

For 10 minutes the students perform their role-play. The teacher moves from group to group to answer questions and offer any advice on what the groups can discuss. After it is over, the students have an opportunity to pose any questions. In this way, they elicit some relevant vocabulary words. They then discuss what language forms are appropriate in dealing with one's boss. 'For example,' the teacher explains, 'what if you know that your boss doesn't think that the vacation policy will change, but you think it will. How will you state your prediction? You are more likely to say something like "I think the vacation policy might change," than "The vacation policy will change." '

'What if, however,' the teacher continues, 'it is your colleague with whom you disagree and you are certain that you are right. How will you express your prediction then?' One student offers, 'I know that the vacation policy will change.' Another student says, 'I am sure that the vacation policy will change.' A third student says simply, 'The vacation policy will change.'

The class is almost over. The teacher uses the last few minutes to give the homework assignment. The students are to find out what they can about two political candidates running against each other in the upcoming election. The students are then to write their prediction of who they think will win the election and why they think so. They will read these to their classmates at the start of the next class.

Thinking about the Experience

As we have seen before, there are important principles underlying the behavior we have observed. Let us now investigate these by compiling our two lists: our observations and the underlying principles.

Observations	Principles
1 The teacher distributes a handout that has a copy of a sports column from a recent newspaper.	Whenever possible, **authentic language**—language as it is used in a real context—should be introduced.
2 The teacher tells the students to underline the reporter's predictions and to say which ones they think the reporter feels most certain of and which he feels least certain of.	Being able to figure out the speaker's or writer's intentions is part of being communicatively competent.

3	The teacher gives the students the directions for the activity in the target language.	The target language is a vehicle for classroom communication, not just the object of study.
4	The students try to state the reporter's predictions in different words.	One function can have many different linguistic forms. Since the focus of the course is on real language use, a variety of linguistic forms are presented together. The emphasis is on the process of communication rather than just mastery of language forms.
5	The students unscramble the sentences of the newspaper article.	Students should work with language at the discourse or suprasentential (above the sentence) level. They must learn about **cohesion** and **coherence**, those properties of language which bind the sentences together.
6	The students play a language game.	Games are important because they have certain features in common with real communicative events—there is a purpose to the exchange. Also, the speaker receives immediate feedback from the listener on whether or not she has successfully communicated. Having students work in small groups maximizes the amount of communicative practice they receive.
7	The students are asked how they feel about the reporter's predictions.	Students should be given an opportunity to express their ideas and opinions.
8	A student makes an error. The teacher and other students ignore it.	Errors are tolerated and seen as a natural outcome of the development of communication skills. Since this activity was working on fluency, the teacher did not correct the student, but simply noted the error, which he will return to at a later point.
9	The teacher gives each group of students a strip story and a task to perform.	One of the teacher's major responsibilities is to establish situations likely to promote communication.

10 The students work with a partner or partners to predict what the next picture in the strip story will look like.	Communicative interaction encourages cooperative relationships among students. It gives students an opportunity to work on negotiating meaning.
11 The students do a role-play. They are to imagine that they are all employees of the same company.	The social context of the communicative event is essential in giving meaning to the utterances.
12 The teacher reminds the students that one of them is playing the role of the boss and that they should remember this when speaking to her.	Learning to use language forms appropriately is an important part of communicative competence.
13 The teacher moves from group to group offering advice and answering questions.	The teacher acts as a facilitator in setting up communicative activities and as an advisor during the activities.
14 The students suggest alternative forms they would use to state a prediction to a colleague.	In communicating, a speaker has a choice not only about what to say, but also how to say it.
15 After the role-play is finished, the students elicit relevant vocabulary.	The grammar and vocabulary that the students learn follow from the function, situational context, and the roles of the interlocutors.
16 For their homework, the students are to find out about political candidates and to make a prediction about which one will be successful in the forthcoming election.	Students should be given opportunities to work on language as it is used in authentic communication. They may be coached on strategies for how to improve their comprehension.

Reviewing the Principles

The answers to our 10 questions will help us come to a better understanding of Communicative Language Teaching. In some answers new information has been provided to clarify certain concepts.

1 What are the goals of teachers who use Communicative Language Teaching (CLT)?

The goal is to enable students to communicate in the target language. To do this, students need knowledge of the linguistic forms, meanings, and functions. They need to know that many different forms can be used to perform a function and also that a single form can often serve a variety of functions. They must be able to choose from among these the most appropriate form, given the social context and the roles of the interlocutors. They must also be able to manage the process of negotiating meaning with their interlocutors. Communication is a process; knowledge of the forms of language is insufficient.

2 What is the role of the teacher? What is the role of the students?

The teacher facilitates communication in the classroom. In this role, one of his major responsibilities is to establish situations likely to promote communication. During the activities he acts as an advisor, answering students' questions and monitoring their performance. He might make a note of their errors to be worked on at a later time during more accuracy-based activities. At other times he might be a 'co-communicator' engaging in the communicative activity along with students (Littlewood 1981).

Students are, above all, communicators. They are actively engaged in negotiating meaning—in trying to make themselves understood—even when their knowledge of the target language is incomplete.

Also, since the teacher's role is less dominant than in a teacher-centered method, students are seen as more responsible for their own learning.

3 What are some characteristics of the teaching/learning process?

The most obvious characteristic of CLT is that almost everything that is done is done with a communicative intent. Students use the language a great deal through communicative activities such as games, role-plays, and problem-solving tasks (see discussion of these in the review of the techniques).

Activities that are truly communicative, according to Morrow (Johnson and Morrow 1981), have three features in common: **information gap**, choice, and feedback.

An information gap exists when one person in an exchange knows something the other person does not. If we both know today is Tuesday, and I ask you, 'What is today?' and you answer, 'Tuesday,' our exchange is not really communicative. My question is called a **display question**, a question teachers use to ask students to display what they know, but it is not a question that asks you to give me information that I do not know.

In communication, the speaker has a choice of what she will say and how she will say it. If the exercise is tightly controlled, so that students can only say something in one way, the speaker has no choice and the exchange, therefore, is not communicative. In a chain drill, for example, if a student must reply to her neighbor's question in the same way as her neighbor replied to someone else's question, then she has no choice of form and content, and real communication does not occur.

True communication is purposeful. A speaker can thus evaluate whether or not her purpose has been achieved based upon the information she receives from her listener. If the listener does not have an opportunity to provide the speaker with such feedback, then the exchange is not really communicative. Forming questions through a transformation drill may be a worthwhile activity, but it is not in keeping with CLT since a speaker will receive no response from a listener. She is thus unable to assess whether her question has been understood or not.

Another characteristic of CLT is the use of authentic materials. It is considered desirable to give students an opportunity to develop strategies for understanding language as it is actually used.

Finally, we noted that activities in CLT are often carried out by students in small groups. Small numbers of students interacting are favored in order to maximize the time allotted to each student for communicating. While there is no explicit theory of learning connected with CLT, the implicit assumption seems to be that students will learn to communicate by practicing functional and socially appropriate language.

4 What is the nature of student–teacher interaction? What is the nature of student–student interaction?

The teacher may present some part of the lesson. At other times, he is the facilitator of the activities, but he does not always himself interact with the students. Sometimes he is a co-communicator, but more often he establishes situations that prompt communication between and among the students.

Students interact a great deal with one another. They do this in various configurations: pairs, triads, small groups, and whole group.

5 How are the feelings of the students dealt with?

One of the basic assumptions of CLT is that by learning to communicate students will be more motivated to study another language since they will feel they are learning to do something useful. Also, teachers give students an opportunity to express their individuality by having them share their ideas and opinions on a regular basis. Finally, student security is enhanced by the many opportunities for cooperative interactions with their fellow students and the teacher.

6 How is the language viewed? How is culture viewed?

Language is for communication. Linguistic competence, the knowledge of forms and their meanings, is only one part of communicative competence. Another aspect of communicative competence is knowledge of the functions that language is used for. As we have seen in this lesson, a variety of forms can be used to accomplish a single function. A speaker can make a prediction by saying, for example, 'It may rain,' or 'Perhaps it will rain.' Conversely, the same form of the language can be used for a variety of functions. 'May,' for instance, can be used to make a prediction or to give permission ('You may leave now.').

Thus, the learner needs knowledge of forms and meanings and functions. However, to be communicatively competent, she must also use this knowledge and take into consideration the social situation in order to convey her intended meaning appropriately (Canale and Swain 1980). A speaker can seek permission using 'may' ('May I have a piece of fruit?'); however, if the speaker perceives his listener as being more of a social equal or the situation as being informal, he would more likely use 'can' to seek permission ('Can I have a piece of fruit?').

Culture is the everyday lifestyle of people who use the language. There are certain aspects of it that are especially important to communication—the use of nonverbal behavior, for example, which might receive greater attention in CLT.

7 What areas of language are emphasized? What language skills are emphasized?

Language functions might be emphasized over forms. Typically, although not always, a functional syllabus is used. A variety of forms are introduced for each function. Only the simpler forms would be presented at first, but as students get more proficient in the target language, the functions are reintroduced and more complex forms are learned. Thus, for example, in learning to make requests, beginning students might practice 'Would you ...?' and 'Could you ...?' Highly proficient students might learn 'I wonder if you would mind ...'

Students work with language at the **discourse or suprasentential level**. They learn about cohesion and coherence. For example, in our lesson the students recognized that the second sentence of the scrambled order was the last sentence of the original sports column because of its introductory adverbial phrase, 'In the final analysis …'. This adverbial phrase is a cohesive device that binds and orders this sentence to the other sentences. The students also recognized the lack of coherence between the first two sentences of the scrambled order, which did not appear connected in any meaningful way.

Students work on all four skills from the beginning. Just as oral communication is seen to take place through negotiation between speaker and listener, so too is meaning thought to be derived from the written word through an interaction between the reader and the writer. The writer is not present to receive immediate feedback from the reader, of course, but the reader tries to understand the writer's intentions and the writer writes with the reader's perspective in mind. Meaning does not, therefore, reside exclusively in the text, but rather arises through negotiation between the reader and writer.

8 What is the role of the students' native language?

Judicious use of the students' native language is permitted in CLT. However, whenever possible, the target language should be used not only during communicative activities, but also for explaining the activities to the students or in assigning homework. The students learn from these classroom management exchanges, too, and realize that the target language is a vehicle for communication, not just an object to be studied.

9 How is evaluation accomplished?

A teacher evaluates not only his students' accuracy, but also their fluency. The student who has the most control of the structures and vocabulary is not always the best communicator.

A teacher can evaluate his students' performance informally in his role as advisor or co-communicator. For more formal evaluation, a teacher is likely to use an integrative test which has a real communicative function. In order to assess students' writing skill, for instance, a teacher might ask them to write a letter to a friend.

10 How does the teacher respond to student errors?

Errors of form are tolerated during fluency-based activities and are seen as a natural outcome of the development of communication skills. Students can have limited linguistic knowledge and still be successful communicators. The teacher may note the errors during fluency activities and return to them later with an accuracy-based activity.

Reviewing the Techniques

There may be aspects of CLT that you find appealing. This review has been provided in the event you wish to try to use any of the techniques or materials associated with CLT.

- **Authentic Materials**

  To overcome the typical problem that students cannot transfer what they learn in the classroom to the outside world, and to expose students to natural language in a variety of situations, adherents of CLT advocate the use of authentic language materials.[1] In this lesson we see that the teacher uses a newspaper article. He also assigns the students homework, requiring that they learn about two political candidates who are running for election.

  Of course, the class that we observed was at the high-intermediate level of proficiency. For students with lower proficiency in the target language, it may not be possible to use authentic language materials such as these. Simpler authentic materials (for example, the use of a weather forecast when working on predictions), or at least ones that are realistic, are most desirable. It is not so important that the materials be genuine as it is that they be used authentically, with a communicative intent.

  Another possibility for the use of authentic materials with a lower-level class is to use items of realia that do not contain a lot of language, but about which a lot of discussion could be generated. Menus in the target language are an example; timetables are another.

- **Scrambled Sentences**

  The students are given a passage (a text) in which the sentences are in a scrambled order. This may be a passage they have worked with or one they have not seen before. They are told to unscramble the sentences so that the sentences are restored to their original order. This type of exercise teaches students about the cohesion and coherence properties of language. They learn how sentences are bound together at the suprasentential level through formal linguistic devices such as pronouns, which make a text cohesive, and semantic propositions, which unify a text and make it coherent.

  In addition to written passages, students might also be asked to unscramble the lines of a mixed-up dialogue. Or they might be asked to put the

---

[1] Of course, what is authentic and natural to native speakers of the target language is not so to learners in the classroom. What is important is that these materials are used in a way that is real for learners (Widdowson 1998).

pictures of a picture strip story in order and write lines to accompany the pictures.

- **Language Games**

  Games are used frequently in CLT. The students find them enjoyable, and if they are properly designed, they give students valuable communicative practice. Games that are truly communicative, according to Morrow (ibid. 1981), have the three features of communication: information gap, choice, and feedback.

  These three features were manifest in the card game we observed in the following way: An information gap existed because the speaker did not know what her classmate was going to do the following weekend. The speaker had a choice as to what she would predict (which sport) and how she would predict it (which form her prediction would take). The speaker received feedback from the members of her group. If her prediction was incomprehensible, then none of the members of her group would respond. If she got a meaningful response, she could presume her prediction was understood.

- **Picture Strip Story**

  Many activities can be done with picture strip stories. We suggested one in our discussion of scrambled sentences.

  In the activity we observed, one student in a small group was given a strip story. She showed the first picture of the story to the other members of her group and asked them to predict what the second picture would look like. An information gap existed—the students in the groups did not know what the picture contained. They had a choice as to what their prediction would be and how they would word it. They received feedback, not on the form but on the content of the prediction, by being able to view the picture and compare it with their prediction.

  The activity just described is an example of using a problem-solving task as a communicative technique. Problem-solving tasks work well in CLT because they usually include the three features of communication. What is more, they can be structured so that students share information or work together to arrive at a solution. This gives students practice in negotiating meaning.

- **Role-play**

  We already encountered the use of role-plays as a technique when we looked at Desuggestopedia. Role-plays are very important in CLT because they give students an opportunity to practice communicating in different social contexts and in different social roles. Role-plays can be set up so that they are very structured (for example, the teacher tells the students who they are and what they should say) or in a less structured way (for example, the teacher tells the students who they are, what the situation is, and what they are talking about, but the students determine what they will say). The latter is more in keeping with CLT, of course, because it gives the students more of a choice. Notice that role-plays structured like this also provide information gaps since students cannot be sure (as with most forms of communication) what the other person or people will say (there is a natural unpredictability). Students also receive feedback on whether or not they have communicated effectively.

Conclusion

Perhaps the greatest contribution of CLT is asking teachers to look closely at what is involved in communication. If teachers intend students to use the target language, then they must truly understand more than grammar rules and target language vocabulary.

Is achieving communicative competence a goal for which you should prepare your students? Would you adopt a functional syllabus? Should a variety of language forms be presented at one time? Are there times when you would emphasize fluency over accuracy? Do these or any other principles of CLT make sense to you?

Would you ever use language games, problem-solving tasks, or role-plays? Should all your activities include the three features of communication? Should authentic language be used? Are there any other techniques or materials of CLT that you would find useful?

Activities

Ⓐ Check your understanding of Communicative Language Teaching.

1   Explain in your own words Morrow's three features of communication: information gap, choice, and feedback. Choose one of the activities in the lesson we observed and say whether or not these three features are present.
2   Why do we say that communication is a process?
3   What does it mean to say that the linguistic forms a speaker uses should be appropriate to the social context?

B **Apply what you have understood about Communicative Language Teaching.**

1   If you wanted to introduce your friend Paula to Roger, you might say:

Roger, this is (my friend) Paula.
I would like you to meet Paula.
Let me present Paula to you.
Roger, meet Paula.
Allow me to introduce Paula.

In other words, there are a variety of forms for this one function. Which would you teach to a beginning class, an intermediate class, an advanced class? Why?

List linguistic forms you can use for the function of inviting. Which would you teach to beginners? To intermediates? To an advanced class?

2   Imagine that you are working with your students on the function of requesting information. The authentic material you have selected is a railroad timetable. Design a communicative game or problem-solving task in which the timetable is used to give your students practice in requesting information.

3   Plan a role-play to work on the same function as in 2 above.

References/Additional Resources

Breen, M. and **C. Candlin.** 1980. 'The essentials of a communicative curriculum in language teaching.' *Applied Linguistics* 1/2: 89–112.

Brumfit, C. and **K. Johnson** (eds.). 1979. *The Communicative Approach to Language Teaching*. Oxford: Oxford University Press.

Canale, M. and **M. Swain.** 1980. 'Theoretical bases of communicative approaches to second language teaching and testing.' *Applied Linguistics* 1: 1–47.

Halliday, M. A. K. 1973. *Explorations in the Functions of Language*. London: Edward Arnold.

Hymes, D. 1971. 'Competence and performance in linguistic theory' in R. Huxley and E. Ingram (eds.). *Language Acquisition: Models and Methods*, 3–28. London: Academic Press.

Johnson, K. and **K. Morrow** (eds.). 1981. *Communication in the Classroom*. Essex: Longman.

Klapper, J. 2003. 'Taking communication to task? A critical review of recent trends in language teaching.' *Language Learning Journal* 27: 33–42.

Lee, J. and **B. van Patten.** 1995. *Making Communicative Language Teaching Happen*. New York: McGraw-Hill.

Littlewood, W. 1981. *Communicative Language Teaching*. Cambridge: Cambridge University Press.

Savignon, S. 1997. *Communicative Competence: Theory and Classroom Practice* (2nd edn.). New York: McGraw-Hill.

Widdowson, H. G. 1978. *Teaching Language as Communication*. Oxford: Oxford University Press.

——. 1990. *Aspects of Language Teaching*. Oxford: Oxford University Press.

——. 1998. 'Context, community, and authentic language.' *TESOL Quarterly* 32/4: 705–15.

Wilkins, D. 1976. *Notional Syllabuses*. Oxford: Oxford University Press.

Yalden, J. 1987. *The Communicative Syllabus: Evolution, Design, and Implementation*. Englewood Cliffs, NJ: Prentice-Hall.

10

Content-based Instruction

Introduction

Howatt (1984) notes that there are two versions of the Communicative Approach: a strong version and a weak version. The weak version, which we illustrated in the previous chapter, recognizes the importance of providing learners with opportunities to practice English for communicative purposes. For instance, we saw in the CLT lesson we observed that students were provided with a great deal of practice in learning the forms for a particular function, i.e. predicting. The **strong version** of the Communicative Approach goes beyond giving students opportunities to practice communication. The strong version asserts that language is acquired through communication. The **weak version** could be described as 'learning to use' English; the strong version entails 'using English to learn it' (Howatt 1984: 279). Content-based instruction, which we explore in this chapter, and task-based and participatory approaches, which we will look at in the next two chapters, belong in the strong-version category. While the three may seem different at first glance, what they have in common is that they give priority to communicating, over predetermined linguistic content, teaching through communication rather than for it.

Before we examine the three approaches in detail, two points need to be made. First, some language educators might object to the inclusion of content-based, task-based, and participatory approaches in a methods book, for they might be more comfortable calling these 'syllabus types'. Nevertheless, others feel that a 'method' designation is very appropriate. Snow (1991), for instance, characterizes content-based instruction as a 'method with many faces'— both to make the case for content-based instruction as a method of language teaching and to portray the great variety of forms and settings in which it takes place. In addition, Kumaravadivelu (1993) observes that the term 'task' is often used with reference to both content and methodology of language teaching. Indeed, within the strong version of a communicative approach, the traditional separation of syllabus design and methodology is blurred. If students learn to communicate by communicating (Breen 1984), then the destination and the route become one and the same (Nunan 1989).

Second, some might question whether the three are different enough to be treated separately. For example, Skehan (1998) makes the point that one could regard much content-based instruction (as well as project work, which we will briefly discuss in the next chapter) as particular examples of a task-based approach. And others have suggested that task-based and participatory approaches are a form of content-based instruction. In any case, although it should be acknowledged that these methods are unified by the assumption that students learn to communicate by communicating, their scope and their particular foci seem distinctive enough to warrant independent treatment, which we do, starting in this chapter with content-based instruction.

Rationale for Content-based Instruction

Using content from other disciplines in language courses is not a new idea. For years, specialized language courses have treated content relevant to a particular profession or academic discipline. So, for example, the content of a language course for airline pilots is different from one for computer technicians. This is usually thought of as teaching a **language for specific purposes**. In an academic setting, it might be called teaching **language for academic purposes**. Other examples of language programs that use specific content to teach language to adults are programs that teach workplace literacy for adult immigrants and competency-based programs, which serve the same population. In the former, adult learners learn at their workplace to read and write about content that relates to what they need in their work environment, for example, being able to read technical manuals. In **competency-based instruction**, adults learn language skills by studying vital 'life-coping' or 'survival' skills, such as filling out job applications or using the telephone.

The special contribution of content-based instruction (CBI)[1] is that it is not exclusively a language program, but instead it integrates the learning of language with the learning of some other content. The content can be themes, i.e. some topic such as popular music or sports in which students are interested. Often, the content is academic subject matter (Brinton, Snow, and Wesche 2003). It has been observed that academic subjects provide natural content for language study. Such observations motivated the 'language across the curriculum' movement for native English speakers in England, which was

---

[1] For the sake of simplicity, for the remainder of this chapter, we will use CBI to mean the integration of language and content in instruction.

launched in the 1970s to integrate the teaching of reading and writing into all other subject areas. In Canada, second language immersion programs, in which Anglophone children learn their academic subjects in French, have existed for many years. In the United States, CBI instruction was begun to help English language learners in public schools.[2] It had been found that when English language learners (ELLs) were put in regular school classes with native speakers of English, some ELLs did not master either content or English. On the other hand, when these students studied English first, their study of academic content was delayed. In order to prevent both problems, instructors teach academic subjects, such as history or science, while also teaching the language that is related to that content. Language thus becomes the medium for learning content (Mohan 1986).

In the European context, the name for the same instructional approach is content and language integrated learning (CLIL). Marsh defines CLIL as:

> … any dual-focused educational context in which an additional language, thus not usually the first language of the learners involved, is used as a medium in the teaching and learning of non-language content.
> (Marsh 2002: 15)

'This approach can be viewed as being neither language learning, nor subject learning, but rather an amalgam of both' (Marsh 2008: 233). In recent years, a number of countries (Estonia, Finland, Latvia, the Netherlands, and Spain) have implemented a widespread CLIL approach to language and content learning.

Since CBI and CLIL are growing rapidly, it would be good to interject a note of caution here. The teaching of language to younger and younger learners has taken place around the world, partly because governments are not satisfied with what is achieved in language study, and partly because the young learners' parents naturally want their children to have the opportunities in life that knowledge of another language potentially affords. However, this drive to teach young learners an additional language needs to be carefully considered with regard to two important factors. First, it is important for children to establish literacy in their native language before learning to read and write another language. Second, it is important to draw on what is known about how children learn in order to develop a program that meets their needs (Cameron 2003; California State Department of Education 2010). It is not simply the case that the earlier the better when it comes to language instruction.

---

[2] Although it has since been used with other populations, such as university students (see Byrnes 2005).

Naturally, when students do study academic subjects in another language, they will need a great deal of assistance in understanding subject matter texts and in learning to use the academic language associated with the subject. Therefore, teachers must have clear language objectives as well as content learning objectives for their lessons. Sherris underscores this point by using the language of mathematics as an example:

> For instance, in planning to teach the concept of quadratic equations, a teacher might construct the following possible outcome statement: 'Students will be able to solve quadratic equations, discuss different methods of solving the same quadratic equations, and write a summary of each method.' Solve, discuss, and write are the descriptive verbs that determine whether a particular outcome addresses the knowledge and skill of a content area or specific language functions. Solving a quadratic equation describes a content outcome, whereas discussing and writing about the methods used to solve a quadratic equation describe language outcomes related to the content.
> (Sherris 2008: 1)

Of course, considering the verbs in the objectives is only the first step. Teachers of CBI have to be concerned with language objectives that include vocabulary, structure, and discourse organization. We will see how these are implemented by observing the following lesson.

Experience

Let us step into the classroom, where a sixth grade class in an international school in Taipei is studying both geography and English through content-based instruction.[3] Most of the students are Chinese speakers, but there are several who speak Japanese natively and a few who speak Korean. Their English proficiency is at a low intermediate level. The teacher asks the students in English what a globe is. A few call out 'world.' Others make a circle with their arms. Others are silent. The teacher then reaches under her desk and takes out a globe. She puts the globe on the desk and asks the students what they know about it.

---

[3] This lesson is based partly on Cristelli (1994) 'An Integrated, Content-based Curriculum for Beginning Level English as a Second Language Learners of Middle School Age: Four Pilot Units,' an Independent Professional Project, School for International Training.

Figure 10.1   Teaching a geography lesson through the medium of English

They call out answers enthusiastically as she records their answers on the board. When they have trouble explaining a concept, the teacher supplies the missing language. Next, she distributes a handout that she has prepared, based on a video, 'Understanding Globes.' The top section on the handout is entitled 'Some Vocabulary to Know.' Listed are some key geographical terms used in the video. The teacher asks the students to listen as she reads the 10 words: 'degree,' 'distance,' 'equator,' 'globe,' 'hemisphere,' 'imaginary,' 'latitude,' 'longitude,' 'model,' 'parallel.'

Below this list is a modified cloze passage. The teacher tells the students to read the passage. They should fill in the blanks in the passage with the new vocabulary where they are able to do so. After they are finished, she shows them the video. As they watch the video, they fill in the remaining blanks with certain of the vocabulary words that the teacher has read aloud.

The passage begins:

A _____ is a three-dimensional _____ of the earth. Points of interest are located on a globe by using a system of_____ lines. For instance, the equator is an imaginary line that divides the earth in half. Lines that are parallel to the equator are called lines of _____ . Latitude is used to measure _____on the earth north and south of the equator …

After the video is over, the students pair up to check their answers.

Next, the teacher calls attention to a particular verb pattern in the cloze passage: *are located, are called, is used*, etc. She tells students that these are examples of the present passive, which they will be studying in this lesson and later in the week. She explains that the passive is used to 'defocus' the agent or doer of an action. In fact, in descriptions of the sort that they have just read, the agent of the action is not mentioned at all because the agent is not relevant.

The teacher then explains how latitude and longitude can be used to locate any place in the world. She gives them several examples. She has the students use latitude and longitude coordinates to locate cities in other countries. By stating 'This city is located at 60° north latitude and 11° east longitude,' the teacher integrates the present passive and the content focus at the same time. Hands go up. She calls on one girl to come to the front of the room to find the city. She correctly points to Oslo, Norway, on the globe. The teacher provides a number of other examples.

Later, the students play a guessing game. In small groups, they think of the names of five cities. They then locate the city on the globe and write down the latitude and longitude coordinates. When they are finished, they read the coordinates out loud and see if the other students can guess the name of the city. The first group says: 'This city is located at 5° north latitude and 74° west longitude.' After several misses by their classmates, group 4 gets the correct answer: 'Bogotá.' Group 4 then give the others new coordinates: 'This city is located at 34° south latitude and 151° east longitude.' The answer: 'Sydney!'

Next, the teacher tells the students that they will do a dictogloss. The teacher reads to the students two paragraphs about Australia. The first time she reads them, the students are supposed to listen for the main ideas. The second time she reads them, she tells the students to listen for details. Following the second reading, she explains to the students that they should reconstruct what she has read as much as they can from memory. The students are hard at work. After 10 minutes, she tells them to discuss their drafts with a partner and that the two partners should combine and edit their drafts into one, making it as close as possible to the original. She then has each pair of students read their draft to the other students, and the class votes on which version is the closest to the original. The teacher points out how the paragraphs are organized, with a general opening sentence followed by specific examples.

For homework, the students are given a description of Australia and a **graphic organizer** to help them organize and recall the new information. They have to read the description and label the major cities and points of interest on the map and complete the items in the graphic organizer.

AUSTRALIA

Australia is the 6th largest country in the world. With an area of 7,692,000 sq km, it has a relatively small population of around 22.5 million people. Its largest city is Sydney, home of the famous Opera House and Harbour Bridge, and is located on the east coast to the north-east of the capital city, Canberra. Other major cities include Melbourne, in the south, and Perth, which is situated on the west coast, over 3,500 km from the capital.

Australia's highest peak, Mount Kosciuszko, is relatively small at 2,228 metres and is situated in Kosciuszko National Park. Australia has many national parks including Kakadu, the largest national park in Australia, which covers almost 2,000 sq km, and Karijini, which features spectacular waterfalls and gorges. Other places of interest include Alice Springs, in the heart of the Australian outback and situated in the centre of the country. To the south-west of Alice Springs is Uluru (Ayers Rock), a huge sandstone rock and an Aboriginal sacred site situated in the Uluru-Kata Tjuta National Park.

There are many other famous attractions. Situated off the north-east coast, visitors can marvel at the Great Barrier Reef – the world's largest coral reef. Further south, beach lovers may wish to visit The Gold Coast, a 70 km stretch of golden sand running along Australia's east coast.

Label the map with the following:

Sydney	Alice Springs
Melbourne	The Gold Coast
Perth	Uluru
Canberra	The Great Barrier Reef

Facts

Capital City: _____

Largest City: _____

Area: _____

Population: _____

Highest Point: _____

National Parks: _____

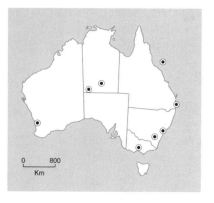

Figure 10.2 An example of a graphic organizer

Thinking about the Experience

Let us follow our customary procedure by listing our observations and the principles that underlie them.

Observations	Principles
1 The class is studying geography through the target language.	Both the content and the language are targets for learning.
2 The teacher asks the students what they know about a globe.	Teaching should build on students' previous experience.
3 The teacher supplies the missing language when the students have trouble in explaining a concept in the target language.	The teacher scaffolds the linguistic content, i.e. helps learners say what it is they want to say by building a complete utterance together with the students.
4 The students call out their answers enthusiastically as the teacher writes them on the blackboard.	When learners perceive the relevance of their language use, they are motivated to learn. They know that it is a means to an end, rather than an end in itself.
5 The teacher reads the new vocabulary and then the students watch a video entitled 'Understanding Globes.'	Language is learned most effectively when it is used as a medium to convey content of interest to the students.
6 The students fill in the vocabulary words in the blanks in the modified cloze passage as they watch the video.	Vocabulary is easier to acquire when there are contextual clues to help convey meaning. It is important to integrate all the skills, as well as vocabulary and grammar in an authentic context.
7 The teacher provides a number of examples using the present passive with latitude and longitude coordinates.	When they work with authentic subject matter, students need language support. For instance, the teacher may provide a number of examples, build in some redundancy, use comprehension checks, etc.
8 The students are given the latitude and longitude coordinates, and they have to come to the front of the classroom to find the city on the globe.	Learners work with meaningful, cognitively demanding language and content within the context of authentic material and tasks.

9 The teacher uses a dictogloss. She discusses its organization.	It is important for students to learn the discourse organization of academic texts.
10 For homework, the students are given a graphic organizer, which they are to label based on a descriptive reading they have been given.	Graphic organizers help students develop the skills that they need to learn academic content.

Reviewing the Principles

Let us now see what principles underlie content-based instruction by answering our usual 10 questions and considering a number of additional principles.

1 What are the goals of teachers who use CBI?

In a CBI class, teachers want the students to master both language and content. The content can be themes of general interest to students, such as current events or their hobbies, or it can be an academic subject, which provides natural content for the study of language. Teachers do not want to delay students' academic study or language study, so teachers encourage the development of both simultaneously.

2 What is the role of the teacher? What is the role of the students?

The teacher needs to set clear learning objectives for both content and language. The teacher then creates activities to teach both, **scaffolding** the language needed for study of the content. The students' role is to engage actively with both content and language, using each to learn the other.

3 What are some characteristics of the teaching/learning process?

Teachers must help learners understand authentic texts. Teachers make meaning clear through the use of visuals, realia, repeating, and by giving a lot of examples, building on students' previous experiences. Teachers also design activities that address both language and content, and the discourse organization of the content, with specific language activities highlighting how language is used in a particular subject—the language of mathematics (Ball and Goffney 2006) differs from the language for history (Schleppegrell, Achugar, and Oteiza 2004), for example. Students are actively involved in learning language and content, often through interaction with other students. Thinking skills are also taught in order to help students undertake academic tasks. Graphic organizers are one tool used to assist this process.

4 What is the nature of student–teacher interaction? What is the nature of student–student interaction?

The teacher guides student learning. She supports them by having students pay attention to how language is used to deliver content and by scaffolding their language development. Students often work collaboratively to understand content while actively using the language they are studying.

5 How are the feelings of the students dealt with?

It is assumed that learning content and language together keeps students interested and motivated. They understand the relevance of what they are studying and that language is a means to an end.

6 How is the language viewed? How is culture viewed?

Language is meaningful and a medium through which content is conveyed. Culture is addressed in teaching to the extent that it is present in the content area being studied.

7 What areas of language are emphasized? What language skills are emphasized?

The content determines what language is worked on. The language includes not only vocabulary items and grammar structures, but also how these contribute to the discourse organization of texts. All four skills are integrated in authentic contexts.

8 What is the role of the students' native language?

There is no overt role for the students' native language.

9 How is evaluation accomplished?

Students are evaluated on their knowledge of content and their language ability.

10 How does the teacher respond to student errors?

The teacher corrects student errors by giving students the correct form or allowing students to self-correct. She notes the errors, and recycles content to ensure that students are learning to use language they will need in a school context.

● **Teacher Preparation**

CBI inspires questions about appropriate teacher preparation. Clearly teachers need to have content and language knowledge and teaching skills. Teacher preparation can also help teachers to understand the rationale for integrated instruction and give them practice designing lessons with language and content objectives, and interesting, stimulating content material. One well-known resource is the **Sheltered Instruction Observation Protocol (SIOP)** (Short and Echevarria 1999), which helps teachers by describing effective practices. **Sheltered-language instruction**, such as in the lesson we observed, supports students through the use of particular instructional techniques and materials such as specialized vocabulary-building activities, graphic organizers, and cloze activities.

In some settings, team teaching has been adopted, with one teacher in the class focusing on content and another on language support. At the university level, sometimes an **adjunct model** is used. In the adjunct model for university students, students enroll in a regular academic course. In addition, they take a language course that is linked to the academic course. During the language class, the language teacher's focus is on helping students process the language in order to understand the academic content presented by the content teacher. The language teacher also helps students to complete academic tasks such as writing term papers, improving their note-taking abilities, and reading academic textbooks assigned by the content teacher.

What all CBI models have in common is learning both specific content and related language skills. 'In content-based language teaching, the claim in a sense is that students get 'two for one'—both content knowledge and increased language proficiency' (Wesche 1993).

Whole Language

Before moving on, it would be worthwhile to touch briefly upon one more approach here since its philosophy has much in common with CBI. Although it originated in classes for children who speak English as a native language, the Whole Language Approach has often been used with second language learners as well. The Whole Language (WL) approach, as the name suggests, calls for language to be regarded holistically, rather than as pieces, i.e. the vocabulary words, grammar structures, and pronunciation points. In other words, students work from the **top-down**, attempting first to understand the meaning of the overall text before they work on the linguistic forms comprising it. This contrasts with the **bottom-up** approach we have seen in other methods in this book, where students learn a language piece by piece and then work to put the pieces in place, constructing whole meaningful texts out of the pieces. It is thought that the top-down process will work best when students are engaged in purposeful use of language, and not learning linguistic forms for their own sake. 'Therefore WL [Whole Language] educators provide content-rich curriculum where language and thinking can be about interesting and significant content' (Edelsky, Altwerger, and Flores 1991: 11). WL educators see errors as part of learning and they encourage students to experiment with reading and writing to promote both their enjoyment and ownership.

WL and CBI educators embrace the ideas of Vygotsky (1978) about the social nature of learning. As a social process, it is assumed that learning is best served by collaboration between teacher and students and among students. According to Vygotsky, it is through social interaction that higher order thinking emerges. The 'place' where this is most likely to be facilitated is in the **zone of proximal development (ZPD)**:

> … the distance between the actual developmental level [of the learner] as determined by independent problem-solving and the level of potential development as determined through problem solving under adult guidance or in collaboration with more capable peers.
> (Vygotsky 1978: 86)

One example of such a technique to teach WL is the Language Experience Approach. Two writing techniques that are consonant with WL philosophy are process writing and journal keeping. All three of these techniques are described in the next section.

Reviewing the Techniques

- **Dictogloss**

In a dictogloss (Wajnryb 1990), students listen twice to a short talk or a reading on appropriate content. The first time through, students listen for the main idea, and then the second time they listen for details. Next, students write down what they have remembered from the talk or reading. Some teachers have their students take notes while listening. The students then use their notes to reformulate what has been read. Students get practice in note-taking in this way. Next, they work with a partner or in a small group to construct together the best version of what they have heard. What they write is shared with the whole class for a peer-editing session. Through these processes, students become familiar with the organization of a variety of texts within a content area.

- **Graphic Organizers**

Graphic organizers are visual displays that help students to organize and remember new information. They involve drawing or writing down ideas and making connections. They combine words and phrases, symbols, and arrows to map knowledge. They include diagrams, tables, columns, and webs. Through the use of graphic organizers, students can understand text organization, which helps them learn to read academic texts and to complete academic tasks, such as writing a summary of what they have read. A key rationale for the use of graphic organizers in CBI is that they facilitate recall of cognitively demanding content, enabling students to process the content material at a deeper level and then be able to use it for language practice.

- **Language Experience Approach**
Students take turns dictating a story about their life experiences to the teacher who writes it down in the target language. Each student then practices reading his or her story with the teacher's assistance. The Language Experience Approach applies the principles of WL: The text is about content that is significant to the students, it is collaboratively produced, it is whole, and since it is the student's story, the link between text and meaning is facilitated.

- **Process Writing**
Traditionally, when teachers teach writing, they assign topics for students to write on; perhaps they do a bit of brainstorming about the topic during a pre-writing phase, and then have students write about the topic without interruption. Subsequently, teachers collect and evaluate what students have written. Such instruction is very 'product-oriented;' there is no involvement of the teacher in the act or 'process' of writing. In process writing, on the other hand, students may initially brainstorm ideas about a topic and begin writing, but then they have repeated conferences with the teacher and the other students, during which they receive feedback on their writing up to that point, make revisions, based on the feedback they receive, and carry on writing. In this way, students learn to view their writing as someone else's reading and to improve both the expression of meaning and the form of their writing as they draft and redraft. Process writing shifts the emphasis in teaching writing from evaluation to revision.

- **Dialogue Journals**
Another way to work on literacy skills is to have students keep dialogue journals. The particular way that journals are used varies, but it essentially involves students writing in their journals in class or for homework regularly, perhaps after each class or once a week. There may be a particular focus for the writing, such as the students' expressing their feelings toward how and what they are learning, or the writing focus could be on anything that the student wishes to communicate to the teacher. Usually it is the teacher who 'dialogues' with the student, i.e. is the audience for the journal. The teacher reads the student's journal entry and writes a response to it, but does not correct its form.

Conclusion

Content-based instruction, with all its many faces, offers teachers a way of addressing issues of language and content learning and allows students to make ongoing progress in both. This can provide an efficient manner of learning, ensuring that students are not left behind while learning language or while learning content. For this reason, CBI can also be an effective way for students to learn language in the language class, using themes that students find of interest. Such themes provide sustained motivation beyond intermediate levels of proficiency and prepare students, if they choose, for the transition to content area classes in school, college, or university. Some questions for your consideration: What do you see as the benefits to learners of integrating content and language? Are there situations that would not be appropriate for the use of content-based instruction? Do you think that content-based instruction lends itself to certain age groups more than others? Why or why not?

Activities

A Check your understanding of Content-based Instruction.

1 In your own words describe the difference between the approach to teaching communication taken in the previous chapter and this one.
2 Why do you think that CBI has been called a method with many faces (Snow 1991)?
3 What type(s) of preparation might be useful for a teacher who will teach content along with language?

B Apply what you have understood about Content-based Instruction.

1 Even if you do not teach in a program that regularly uses CBI, try incorporating the teaching of content into your language class. Teach a poem or adopt a theme of interest to your students, for instance. See what you learn from that experience.
2 How are process writing and journal keeping consistent with the Whole Language Approach? Can you think of any other writing techniques which are?

References/Additional Resources

Ball, D. and **I. Goffney.** 2006. The role of mathematical language in learning and succeeding in mathematics. A presentation at the Association of State Supervisors of Mathematics. 2006 Annual Meeting, St. Louis, MO.

Breen, M. 1984. 'Process syllabuses for the language classroom' in C. Brumfit, (ed.). *General English Syllabus Design—Curriculum and Syllabus Design for the General English Classroom* (EFL Documents 118). Oxford: Pergamon Press for the British Council.

Brinton, D., A. Snow, and **M. Wesche.** 1989. *Content-based Second Language Instruction.* Boston, MA: Heinle & Heinle.

———. 2003. *Content-based Second Language Instruction.* Michigan Classics Edition. Ann Arbor, MI: University of Michigan Press.

Byrnes, H. 2005. 'Content-based foreign language instruction' in C. Sanz (ed.). *Mind and Context in Adult Second Language Acquisition,* 282–302. Washington, DC: Georgetown University Press.

California State Department of Education. 2010. *Improving Education for English Learners: Research-based Approaches.* Sacramento, CA: CDE Press.

Cameron, L. 2003. 'Challenges for ELT from the expansion in teaching children.' *ELT Journal* 57/2: 105–12.

Cantoni-Harvey, G. 1987. *Content-area Language Instruction: Approaches and Strategies.* Reading, MA: Addison-Wesley.

Coyle, D., P. Hood, and **D. Marsh.** 2007. *Content and Language Integrated Learning.* Cambridge: Cambridge University Press.

Crandall, J-A. (ed.). 1987. *ESL through Content-area Instruction.* Englewood Cliffs, NJ: Prentice Hall Regents.

DeGraaff, R., G. Koopman, Y. Anikina, and **G. Westhoff.** 2007. 'An observation tool for effective L2 pedagogy in content and language integrated learning (CLIL).' *International Journal of Bilingual Education and Bilingualism* 10/5: 603–24.

Echevarria, J., M-E. Vogt, and **D. Short.** 2008. *Making Content Comprehensible to English Learners: The SIOP Model.* Boston, MA: Pearson/ Allyn and Bacon.

Edelsky, C., B. Altwerger, and **B. Flores.** 1991. *Whole Language: What's the Difference?* Portsmouth, NH: Heinemann.

Freeman, Y. and **D. Freeman.** 1992. *Whole Language for Second Language Learners.* Portsmouth, NH: Heinemann.

Gibbons, P. 2003. 'Mediating language learning: Teacher interactions with ESL students in a content-based classroom.' *TESOL Quarterly* 37/2: 247–73.

Goodman, K. 1986. *What's Whole in Whole Language?* Portsmouth, NH: Heinemann.

Heald-Taylor, G. 1989. *Whole Language Strategies for ESL students*. San Diego, CA: Dormac, Inc.

Howatt, A. P. R. 1984. *A History of English Language Teaching*. Oxford: Oxford University Press.

Kumaravadivelu, B. 1993. 'The name of the task and the task of naming: Methodological aspects of task-based pedagogy' in G. Crookes and S. Gass (eds.). *Tasks in a Pedagogical Context*. Clevedon: Multilingual Matters Ltd.

Marsh, D. (ed.). 2002. CLIL/EMILE European Dimension: Actions, Trends and Foresight Potential. European Commission, Public Services Contract DG 3406/001–001.

——. 2008 in J. Cenoz and N. Hornberger (eds.). *Encyclopedia of Language and Education* (2nd edn.) Volume 6: 'Knowledge about Language,' 233–46. New York: Springer.

Mehisto, P., M-J. Frigols, and D. Marsh. 2008. *Uncovering CLIL: Content and Language Integrated Learning and Multilingual Education*. Oxford: Macmillan.

Met, M. 1999. *Content-based Instruction: Defining Terms, Making Decisions*. Washington, DC: The National Foreign Language Center, Washington, DC.

Mohan, B. 1986. *Language and Content*. Reading, MA: Addison-Wesley.

Nordmeyer, J. and S. Barduhn (eds.). 2010. *Integrating Language and Content*. Alexandria, VA: TESOL, Inc.

Nunan, D. 1989. *Designing Tasks for the Communicative Classroom*. Cambridge: Cambridge University Press.

Riggs, P. 1991. 'Whole language in TESOL.' *TESOL Quarterly* 25/3: 521–42.

Schleppegrell, M., M. Achugar, and T. Oteiza. 2004. 'The grammar of history: Enhancing content-based instruction through a functional focus on language.' *TESOL Quarterly* 38/1: 67–93.

Sherris, A. 2008. 'Integrated language and content instruction.' *CAL Digest*. Washington, DC: Center for Applied Linguistics.

Short, D. and J. Echevarria. 1999. *The Sheltered Instruction Observation Protocol: A Tool for Teacher–Researcher Collaboration and Professional Development*. Educational Practice Report, Santa Cruz, CA and Washington, DC: Center for Research on Education, Diversity & Excellence.

Skehan, P. 1998. 'Task-based instruction.' *Annual Review of Applied Linguistics: Foundations of Second Language Teaching*. Volume 18.

Snow, M. 1991. 'Content-based instruction: A method with many faces' in J. Alatis. (ed.). Georgetown University Round Table on Languages and Linguistics 1991: *Linguistics and Language Pedagogy*, 461–70. Washington, DC: Georgetown University Press.

——, and **D. Brinton**. 1997. *The Content-based Classroom: Perspectives on Integrating Language and Content*. White Plains, New York: Addison Wesley Longman Publishing Company.

Staton, J., **R. Shuy**, **J. Peyton**, and **L. Reed**. 1988. *Dialogue Journal Communication: Classroom, Linguistic, Social, and Cognitive Views*. Norwood, NJ: Ablex.

Stryker, S. and **B. Weaver**. 1997. *Content-based Instruction in Foreign Language Education: Methods and Models*. Washington, DC: Georgetown University Press.

Vygotsky, L. 1978. *Mind in Society*. Cambridge, MA: Harvard University Press.

Wajnryb, R. 1990. *Grammar Dictation*. Oxford: Oxford University Press.

Wesche, M. 1993. 'Discipline-based approaches to language study: Research issues and outcomes' in M. Krueger and F. Ryan (eds.). *Language and Content: Discipline and Content-based Approaches to Language Study*. Lexington, MA: D. C. Heath.

Zamel, V. 1982. 'Writing: The process of discovering meaning.' *TESOL Quarterly* 16/2: 195–209.

11

Task-based Language Teaching

Introduction

In 1976, Wilkins distinguished between two types of syllabi—**synthetic syllabi** and **analytic syllabi**. Synthetic syllabi comprise linguistic units: grammar structures, vocabulary items, functions, etc. The units are usually ordered logically, in a sequence from linguistic simplicity to linguistic complexity. It is the learners' responsibility to synthesize the linguistic units for the purpose of communication. Analytic syllabi, on the other hand, '… are organised in terms of the purposes for which people are learning language and the kinds of language performance that are necessary to meet those purposes' (Wilkins 1976: 13). Content-based instruction, which we looked at in the previous chapter, employs an analytic syllabus. Rather than learning language items one by one in a specific sequence, learners work on relevant content texts and the language of the texts. Second language acquisition (SLA) research supports the use of analytic syllabi because such research shows that learners do not learn linguistic items one at a time. Instead, they induce linguistic information from the language samples they work on, and they acquire language items only when they are ready to do so. A task-based syllabus, which we take up in this chapter, falls into the category of an analytic syllabus. The syllabus is composed of tasks, not a sequence of linguistic items.

Tasks are meaningful, and in doing them, students need to communicate. Tasks have a clear outcome so that the teacher and students know whether or not the communication has been successful. An example of a task in a task-based syllabus is for students to plan an itinerary for a trip. Students work in small groups with a train schedule. They are given certain destinations to include, and they have to decide on the most direct route to travel by train—the one that will take the least amount of travel time. As the students seek to complete the task, they have to work to understand each other and to express their own thoughts. By so doing, they have to check to see if they have comprehended correctly and, at times, they have to seek clarification.

This interaction and checking is thought to facilitate language acquisition (Long 1996; Gass 1997). As Candlin and Murphy note:

> The central purpose we are concerned with is language learning, and tasks present this in the form of a problem-solving negotiation between knowledge that the learner holds and new knowledge.
> (Candlin and Murphy 1987:1)

Task-based Language Teaching is another example of the 'strong version' of the communicative approach, where language is acquired through use. In other words, students acquire the language they need when they need it in order to accomplish the task that has been set before them.

Before proceeding to the lesson, following Ellis (2009) we should point out that there is a difference between task-based syllabi and task-based language teaching or TBLT. Task-based syllabi have been criticized for the absence of grammatical items (Sheen 2003; Swan 2005). While it may be true that task-based syllabi, being analytic in nature, do not expressly feature grammar structures, task-based teaching or **task-supported teaching** (Ellis 2003), in the minds of some methodologists, does not exclude it. For instance, Loschky and Bley-Vroman (1993) see value in engaging students in structure-based communicative tasks, which are designed to have students automatize the use of a structure that they have already internalized. A structure-based communicative task might involve making inferences about the identity of someone whose briefcase has been left in the back of a taxi (Riggenbach, Samuda, and Wisniewska 2007). Completing such a task by identifying the owner is likely to necessitate the use of certain modal verbs and/or adverbs of probability ('It might be a woman.' 'She is probably a businesswoman.').

Other methodologists claim that along with communicative tasks, there can be focused tasks that do not call for speaking, but instead, are designed to raise learners' consciousness with regard to specific linguistic items (Ellis 2009). For instance, students might be asked to trace a path on a map of a town, following directions given by the teacher. In this way, students would receive comprehensible input involving imperatives, prepositions of location and direction, and the names of different buildings. Other communicative tasks can be designed in such a way that they encourage students to notice a particular target language feature, possibly by means of **input enhancement**, such as using boldface type for a particular structure in a reading passage or **input flooding**, which means using particular vocabulary items or grammar structures with great frequency in the input. Such input enhancement techniques are thought to work well for structures that are not easily perceived, such as grammatical morphemes.

Then, too, Ellis (2003) suggests that there are a number of ways in which grammar can be addressed as a follow-up to a communicative task, including direct explicit instruction and traditional practice-type exercises. Willis (1996) has also proposed a variety of such options for the post-task phase. Still others, while rejecting a role for such direct explicit instruction, claim that even within communicative tasks, some attention should be paid to linguistic form, through a **focus on form**, not a return to grammar drills and exercises, which is termed a focus on forms (Long 1991). A focus on form might involve a teacher's reformulating or recasting a student's error or providing a brief grammar explanation. It is said that focusing student attention on grammatical form in these ways can have a positive effect, provided that such attention is brief and reactive, in that it takes place when problems of grammatical inaccuracy arise (Long 2009).

Samuda and Bygate (2008) reach back into history even further than SLA research to find theoretical support for task-based language teaching. They do so citing the work of John Dewey (1913), who emphasized the need for experience, relevance, and 'intelligent effort' for effective learning. Dewey is generally considered to be the founder of **constructivism**. He rejected approaches that viewed learners as receptacles of the teacher's knowledge and favored ones where students are actively involved in constructing their own knowledge through experience and problem solving. Let us see how this plays out in our lesson.

Experience

The following lesson is one that has been adapted and expanded from Prabhu (1987). It takes place in southern India. The class consists of forty 10-year-old children, who are advanced beginners in English. As we enter the classroom, the teacher is speaking:

'We are going to do a lesson today on timetables. OK?'

The teacher draws the columns and rows of a class timetable on the whiteboard. At the head of the first column, he writes 9:30–10:15. The students understand that the teacher has written the duration of the first class period of the day.

'What should I write here?' asks the teacher, pointing to the head of the second column. The students respond, 'Ten fifteen.' And then 'Eleven o'clock,' as the teacher moves his finger across the top row. The teacher points in turn to the top of each column, and the students chorus the time that each class period begins and ends.

Then the teacher asks: 'Who will write the names for the days of the week here?' Several students raise their hands. The teacher calls on one. 'Come,' he says. The student he has called on comes to the front of the room, takes the marker, and writes the names of each weekday beside each row, Monday to Friday, correctly, as the rest of the class helps with the spelling.

'Is that correct?' the teacher asks. 'Correct!' the students chorus back.

'What about Saturday? Do we have school on Saturday?'

The students reply in unison, 'No … weekend.'

The teacher responds, 'Yes. Saturday is on the weekend. Saturday's a weekend day.'

Next, the teacher has the students copy the blank schedule from the board. As he talks, each student fills in the schedule. He tells them, 'On Monday, you study English during the first period. How many of you like to study English?' Most hands go up in response. Then, he says, 'I guess that English is your favorite period, second only to lunch.' The students laugh. The teacher goes on, 'You also study English on Wednesday and Friday, first period. During the second period on these days, you study math.' The teacher continues until the schedules are completed. Students check each other's work.

The teacher then divides the class into eight groups of five students. Each student in a group receives the schedule for one day of the school week. The students' task is to complete the week's schedule by sharing the information on their cards with each other. There is much discussion as each group works to draw up a full schedule.

As he circulates among the groups, the teacher hears students making errors. He does not say anything, but he notes them and continues around the classroom. As he moves about the room listening to the groups, the teacher reminds the students to speak in English.

The first group that is finished comes up to the board and writes up the schedule. After the students have checked their work, the teacher collects each group's schedule so he can read it and return it to them the next day. He checks their schedules mainly to see that the content is correct.

Next, still working in their groups, the students are told that they are to find a way to determine their classmates' favorite school subjects. They must find out from class members which are the three most popular subjects and the three least popular. Each group is to discuss ways it might gather the information. The group might design a survey, for instance, or go around the room interviewing other students. After they have completed their survey or interviews, the groups have to summarize and report the results. They have to decide how to do this. For example, they may use percentages, a bar graph, a pie chart, or some other visual display. Once again, much conversation takes place. Students are busily talking about how they will obtain the information they need to complete the task and later to report their findings.

Figure 11.1 Students completing a schedule on the board

These will have to wait for another day to report, though, because there is no time left today. In the following period, the teacher will give them another task, where he will do the talking and the students will listen and do something. The input task the teacher has chosen takes into account what errors he has noted and written down in today's class.

Thinking about the Experience

We have seen that tasks are also used in Communicative Language Teaching (CLT), so at first glance this short lesson may not seem so different. But notice that while the task in our CLT lesson in Chapter 9 was designed to get students to practice making predictions (a communicative function), the task-based lesson we have just observed did not focus on a particular function, or even a particular form of the language. In fact, the teacher used a wide variety of linguistic forms, the meaning of which was made clear by the context. The 'departure from CLT [in such lessons] … lay not in the tasks themselves, but in the accompanying pedagogic focus on task completion instead of on the language used in the process' (Long and Crookes 1993: 31). This is a major shift of perspective.

Let us compile the principles underlying the task-based method shown in the lesson from Prabhu (1987) by making some observations and then attempting to infer the underlying principles from them.

Observations	Principles
1 The teacher tells the class that they are going to complete a timetable.	The class activities have a perceived purpose and a clear outcome.
2 The teacher begins by having the class help him to fill out a class schedule. This is done through whole class interaction in the form of teacher question and student response.	A pre-task, in which students work through a task that they will later do individually, is a helpful way to have students see the logic involved in what they are being asked to do. It will also allow the language necessary to complete the task to come into play.
3 The teacher first has the students label the time periods and then the days.	The teacher breaks down into smaller steps the logical thinking process necessary to complete the task. The demand on thinking made by the activity should be just above the level which learners can meet without help.
4 The teacher asks the students if a particular answer is right.	The teacher needs to seek ways of knowing how involved the students are in the process, so he can make adjustments in light of the learners' perceptions of relevance and their readiness to learn. Such teacher–class negotiation ensures that as many students as possible in a mixed-ability class grasp the nature of the activity.
5 The teacher asks, 'What about Saturday? Do we have school on Saturday?'	The teacher doesn't consciously simplify his language; he uses whatever language is necessary to have students comprehend the current step in the pre-task. Here he switched from an abbreviated *Wh*-question to a *yes/no* question. This switch is a natural strategy that proficient speakers use when interacting with less proficient speakers inside and outside of the classroom.

6 The students reply, 'Weekend.' The teacher responds, 'Yes. Saturday is on the weekend. Saturday's a weekend day.'	The teacher supplies the correct target form by reformulating or recasting what the students have said.
7 The teacher talks about the schedule.	The teacher provides good models of the target language.
8 The students then do the task in groups, following the teacher's instructions. They are each given some of the information they need to complete the task.	This jigsaw task, where students have to piece together information they need to complete a task, gives them an opportunity for interaction.
9 They make errors. The teacher notes them.	The teacher should not necessarily interrupt the students when they are focused on meaning.
10 The students' papers were marked for content.	Students should receive feedback on their level of success in completing the task. The need to achieve an outcome makes students pay attention.
11 Students are asked to design a way to survey the other students about their favorite and least favorite subjects. They are to figure out a way to report their findings to the rest of the class.	Students have input into the design and the way that they carry out the task. This gives them more opportunity for interaction.
12 Students report in the next class.	A public presentation encourages students to work on accuracy and organization, as well as meaning.
13 In their reports, students use the language they have been working on.	Repeating the language that they have been working on shows learners what they can and what they cannot yet do.
14 The teacher prepares a new task based on the errors he has noted.	'Listen-and-do' tasks promote acquisition of new vocabulary and provide a good model for grammatical form. This task follow-up can enhance the learning that has taken place earlier.

Reviewing the Principles

We will now follow our customary procedure and review the answers to our 10 questions.

1 What are the goals of teachers who use TBLT?

The goal of teachers is to facilitate students' language learning by engaging them in a variety of tasks that have a clear outcome.

2 What is the role of the teacher? What is the role of the students?

The teacher's role is to choose tasks, based on an analysis of students' needs, that are appropriate to the level of the students and to create pre-task and task follow-up phases that are in line with the abilities and needs of the students. The teacher also monitors the students' performance, and intervenes as necessary. The role of the students is to communicate with their peers to complete a task.

3 What are some characteristics of the teaching/learning process?

A pre-task phase typically begins a task sequence. During this phase, a teacher can introduce the students to the language they will need to complete the task. The tasks are meaningful and relevant so that the students see the reason for doing the task and can see how the task relates to possible situations in their lives outside the classroom. Students are actively engaged with the task, with the teacher monitoring their performance and intervening when necessary. The task has clear outcomes so that both students and teachers can tell if the task has been successfully completed. A post-task phase takes place to reinforce students' learning or to address any problems that may have arisen.

4 What is the nature of student–teacher interaction? What is the nature of student–student interaction?

The teacher is the input provider during the initial phase of the lesson. He also sets the task for students to perform. The teacher pays attention during the task, making note of language that should be focused on. He provides feedback such as recasts. Students often work closely together to help each other accomplish the task and to problem-solve.

5 How are the feelings of the students dealt with?

Students are motivated by doing tasks that prepare them for the real world.

6 How is the language viewed? How is culture viewed?

Language is for communicating and for 'doing.' Culture is not explicitly dealt with although certain tasks might have a cultural focus, such as when students prepare different ethnic foods to share.

7 What areas of language are emphasized? What language skills are emphasized?

The meaning dimension of language is emphasized. Depending on the nature of the task, any of the four skills can be utilized.

8 What is the role of the students' native language?

There is no explicit role for the students' native language.

9 How is evaluation accomplished?

The teacher constantly evaluates students in light of task outcomes and the language they use.

10 How does the teacher respond to student errors?

Focus on form is essential to students' learning. Error correction is done through recasts or modeling or by giving brief grammar explanations.

As we saw in the lesson we have just observed, in Prabhu's approach the teacher designs which tasks are to be worked on. Alternatively, Breen (1987) suggests that the choice of task should be negotiated between the teacher and students. A third way to decide on which tasks to include in a course is to conduct a needs analysis to determine which real-world tasks students will need to perform (Long, cited in Skehan 1998).

● **Project Work**

Another approach, which is also concerned with real-world language use, but is distinctive enough to merit special consideration, is project work. As with a task-based approach, the language practiced in the classroom is not predetermined, but rather derives from the nature of a particular project that students elect to do. For example, students might decide to take on a project such as publishing a school newspaper in the target language. This project would follow the same three stages of all projects (based on Fried-Booth 2002):

During the first stage, the students would work in their class, collaborating with their teacher, to plan the content and scope of the project and specific language needs they might have. They might also devise some strategies for how they would carry out the tasks, such as assigning each other specific roles to fulfill.

The second stage typically takes place outside the classroom and involves the gathering of any necessary information. For example, if the students have decided to publish a school newspaper, then this stage might involve their conducting interviews, taking photographs, and gathering printed or visual material. It would also include writing up their interviews and laying out, printing, and distributing the first edition of their newspaper. During this stage, students may well use all four skills in a natural, integrated fashion.

In the third and final stage, students review their project. They monitor their own work and receive feedback from the teacher on their performance. At each of these three stages, the teacher will be working with the students, acting as counselor and consultant, not as the project director.

By encouraging students to move out of the classroom and into the world, project work helps to bridge the gap between language study and language use. Project work also appeals to both the social and cognitive aspects of learning, which many teachers find important.

Reviewing the Techniques

Prabhu identified three types of tasks, all of which were represented in the lesson we have just observed: an information-gap, an opinion-gap, and a reasoning-gap task.

- **Information-gap Task**

  An information-gap activity, which we saw used previously in CLT and now in TBLT, involves the exchange of information among participants in order to complete a task. In the TBLT lesson, students had to exchange information within their groups in order to complete the schedule. Other examples might be where one student is given a picture and describes the picture for another student to draw, or where students draw each other's family trees.

- **Opinion-gap Task**

  An opinion-gap task requires that students express their personal preferences, feelings, or attitudes in order to complete the task. For instance, students might be given a social problem, such as high unemployment, and be asked to come up with a series of possible solutions, or they might be asked to compose a letter of advice to a friend who has sought their counsel about a dilemma. In our lesson, the students were only at the advanced-beginning level. Their opinion-gap task was a rather simple one, which involved students' surveying their classmates about their most and least favorite subjects.[1]

- **Reasoning-gap Task**

A reasoning-gap activity requires that students derive some new information by inferring it from information they have already been given. For example, students might be given a railroad schedule and asked to work out the best route to get from one particular city to another, or they might be asked to solve a riddle. In the lesson we observed, students were asked to use the results of their surveys or interviews to find out which were the three most popular and the least popular subjects. Prabhu (1987) feels that reasoning-gap tasks work best since information-gap tasks often require a single step transfer of information, rather than sustained negotiation, and opinion-gap tasks tend to be rather open-ended. Reasoning-gap tasks, on the other hand, encourage a more sustained engagement with meaning, though they are still characterized by a some-what predictable use of language.

According to Ellis (2009), TBLT tasks can be unfocused or focused:

- **Unfocused Tasks**

Unfocused tasks are tasks designed to provide learners with opportunities for communicating generally. The task described in the introduction to this chapter, where students have to plan an itinerary for a train trip, is an example. Students draw on their own language resources to fulfill the task.

- **Focused Tasks**

Focused tasks are tasks designed to provide opportunities for communicating using some specific linguistic item, typically a grammar structure. The task of trying to identify the owner of a briefcase left in a taxi is an example. Of course, there is no guarantee that the task will elicit the grammar structure that the task designers intended (Loschky and Bley-Vroman 1993). As with all tasks, focused tasks should be meaningful. For this reason, the target linguistic feature of a focused task is 'hidden' (the learners are not told explicitly what the feature is) (Ellis 2009).[2]

One other distinction that Ellis (2009) makes is between input-providing and output-prompting tasks:

---

[1] See Cohen (2009) for another example of using surveys in TBLT.
[2] For further examples, see the series *Grammar Dimensions,* directed by Larsen-Freeman (2007).

- **Input-providing Tasks**

  Input-providing tasks engage learners with the receptive skills of listening and reading. We saw in the lesson in this chapter that the students completed a schedule with the content that the teacher provided.

  Input-providing (e.g. 'listen and do' tasks) not only work on the receptive skills, but also give teachers an opportunity to introduce new language.

- **Output-prompting Tasks**

  Output-prompting tasks stimulate the students to write or speak meaningfully. In our lesson, there was an output-prompting task when students had to share the information on their cards so that their group members could complete a schedule.

Conclusion

Task-based language teaching challenges mainstream views about language teaching in that it is based on the principle that language learning will progress most successfully if teaching aims simply to create contexts in which the learner's natural language learning capacity can be nurtured rather than making a systematic attempt to teach the language bit by bit (Ellis 2009: 222).

For some methodologists, there is no contradiction in saying this and at the same time saying that TBLT can also be complemented by explicit instruction in grammar and vocabulary; for others, focusing on forms is an unacceptable compromise. In any case, it is probably fair to say that TBLT is the one method that has support from SLA researchers.

Still, the question must always be asked if TBLT is appropriate for all teaching contexts (Andon and Eckerth 2009). While learners may well learn effectively using analytic syllabi, the adoption of such syllabi may be particularly difficult in situations where the success of language instruction is judged by examinations containing grammar and vocabulary items and questions.

Nevertheless, we have seen that task-based instruction can help to encourage students to use the target language actively and meaningfully. Therefore, if you decide that TBLT is appropriate in your teaching context, what appeals to you about task-based instruction? What reservations do you have? How would you go about choosing tasks? Can you imagine challenges in managing your task-based class? If so, how would you address them, or plan to make the most of the opportunities in task-based teaching while working effectively with the challenges?

Activities

A Check your understanding of Task-based Language Teaching.

1 Explain how TBLT is consistent with the use of an analytic syllabus.
2 What is input enhancement? Give an example. Why would you do it?

B Apply what you have understood about Task-based Language Teaching.

1 Think of one example of each of Prahbu's three types of task: information-gap, opinion-gap, and reasoning-gap. Try them out in the classroom and see what you can learn.
2 Draw up a list of projects that might be undertaken by your students. Remember that the project is not designed to suit a particular syllabus unit. Also remember the crucial fact that students want to be involved. On your list could be something like publishing a school newspaper as described in this chapter. Other ideas might be planning a field trip, conducting a survey, or researching a topic such as an environmental concern. If you do decide to have your students go ahead and work on a project, you may wish to consult Fried-Booth (2002).

References/Additional Resources

Adams, R. 2009. 'Recent publications on task-based language teaching: A review.' *International Journal of Applied Linguistics* 19/3: 339–55.

Andon, N. and J. Eckerth. 2009. 'Chacun à son goût? Task-based L2 pedagogy from the teacher's point of view.' *International Journal of Applied Linguistics* 19/3: 286–310.

Breen, M. 1987. 'Learner contributions to task design' in C. Candlin and D. Murphy (eds.). *Language Learning Tasks*, 23–46: Englewood Cliffs, NJ: Prentice Hall.

Candlin, C. and D. Murphy (eds.). 1987. *Language Learning Tasks*. Englewood Cliffs, NJ: Prentice Hall.

Cohen, J. 2009. 'Using student-generated surveys to enhance communication.' *Essential Teacher* 6/3–4: 42–4.

Dewey, J. 1913. *Interest and Effort in Education*. Boston: Houghton-Mifflin.

Eckerth, J. and S. Siekmann. 2008. *Task-based Language Learning and Teaching: Theoretical, Methodological, and Pedagogical Perspectives*. Frankfurt: Peter Lang.

Ellis, R. 2003. *Task-based Language Learning and Teaching.* Oxford: Oxford University Press.

——. 2009. 'Task-based language teaching: Sorting out the misunderstandings.' *International Journal of Applied Linguistics* 19/3: 221–46.

Fried-Booth, D. 2002. *Project Work* (2nd edn.). Oxford: Oxford University Press.

García Mayo, M. (ed.). 2007. *Investigating Tasks in Formal Language Learning.* Clevedon: Multilingual Matters.

Gass, S. 1997. *Input, Interaction, and the Second Language Learner.* Mahwah, NJ: Lawrence Erlbaum.

Haines, S. 1989. *Projects for the EFL Classroom.* London: Nelson.

Larsen-Freeman, D. (Series Director) 2007. *Grammar Dimensions: Form, Meaning, and Use* (4th edn.). Boston: Heinle/Cengage.

Long, M. 1991. 'Focus on form: A design feature in language teaching methodology' in K. de Bot, R. Ginsberg, and C. Kramsch (eds.). *Foreign Language Research in Cross-cultural Perspective,* 39–52. Amsterdam: John Benjamins.

——. 1996. 'The role of the linguistic environment in second language acquisition' in W. Ritchie, and T. Bahtia (eds.). *Handbook of Second Language Acquisition,* 413–68. New York: Academic Press.

——. 2009. 'Methodological principles for language teaching' in M. Long, and C. Doughty (eds.). *The Handbook of Language Teaching,* 373–94. Malden, MA: Wiley-Blackwell.

——. and **G. Crookes.** 1993. 'Units of analysis in syllabus design: The case for task' in G. Crookes and S. Gass (eds.). *Tasks in a Pedagogical Context,* 9–54. Clevedon: Multilingual Matters.

Loschky, L. and **R. Bley-Vroman.** 1993. 'Grammar and task-based methodology' in G. Crookes and S. Gass (eds.). *Tasks in Language Learning,* 123–67. Clevedon: Multilingual Matters.

Norris, J. 2009. 'Task-based teaching and testing' in M. Long and C. Doughty (eds.). *The Handbook of Language Teaching,* 578–94. Malden, MA: Wiley-Blackwell.

Nunan, D. 2004. *Task-based Language Teaching.* Cambridge: Cambridge University Press.

Prabhu, N. S. 1987. *Second Language Pedagogy.* Oxford: Oxford University Press.

Riggenbach, H., V. Samuda, and **I. Wisniewska.** 2007. *Grammar Dimensions* (Book 2, 4th edn.). Boston: Heinle/Cengage.

Rott, S. 2000. 'Teaching German grammar through communicative tasks: Some suggestions.' *Die Unterrichtspraxis* 33/2: 125–33.

Samuda, V. and M. Bygate. 2008. *Tasks in Second Language Learning.*
Basingstoke: Palgrave Macmillan.

Sheen, R. 2003. 'Focus-on-form: A myth in the making.' *ELT Journal* 57:
225–33.

Skehan, P. 1998. 'Task-based instruction.' *Annual Review of Applied
Linguistics: Foundations of Second Language Teaching* 18.

Swan, M. 2005. 'Legislating by hypothesis: The case of task-based instruction.'
Applied Linguistics 26/3: 376–401.

van den Branden, K. 2006. *Task-based Language Teaching: From Theory to
Practice.* Cambridge: Cambridge University Press.

——. 2009. 'Mediating between predetermined order and chaos: The role
of the teacher in task-based language education.' *International Journal of
Applied Linguistics* 19/3: 264–85.

——, M. Bygate, and J. Norris. 2009. *Task-based Language Teaching: A
Reader.* Amsterdam: John Benjamins.

Wilkins, D. 1976. *Notional Syllabuses.* Oxford: Oxford University Press.

Willis, D. and J. Willis. 2007. *Doing Task-based Teaching.* Oxford: Oxford
University Press.

Willis, J. 1996. *A Framework for Task-based Learning.* London: Longman.

12

The Political Dimensions of Language Teaching and the Participatory Approach

Introduction

In this chapter, we look at the politics of language use and language teaching. We also discuss one language teaching method, the Participatory Approach, which pays particular attention to the political dimensions of education.

The Politics of Language

Learning a language is a political act. Those that know a language are empowered in a way that those who do not know the language are not. These days, because of its status as an international language, it is English that is seen to be the language of power.[1] Many people around the world want to learn English because they believe that it will help them to get a good education or job. They feel that knowing English gives them a greater chance for economic advancement. 'On the one hand,' Graddol (2006: 22) notes, 'the availability of English as a global language is accelerating globalisation. On the other, the globalisation is accelerating the use of English.'

This view sees English as a tool that benefits the individual who learns it. Other people, however, express concern about what is lost when an individual learns English or 'adds' an English-speaking identity. They worry that learning English might mean losing some ability in another language—even an individual's native language—or that a new identity as an English speaker might cause another identity to fade or to die. They are also concerned about the educational inequality that results. After all, not everyone has the opportunity to study English. More generally, some worry about English dominance leading to the loss of **endangered languages**, such as those spoken by indigenous people and immigrants living in countries where English use predominates, especially when 'English only' policies are adopted.

[1] Although Graddol (2006) suggests that other languages such as Arabic, Chinese, and Spanish may increasingly play a role as international languages.

Whose English Should be Taught?

Related to these issues is the political question of whose English is to be the language of instruction. Should it be native-speaker English as spoken in the United Kingdom? The United States? Or what Kachru (1992) calls other 'inner circle' countries (Anglophone Canada, Australia, Ireland, Malta, New Zealand, South Africa, and certain countries in the Caribbean)?[2] There are clear differences within and among these varieties, so a choice must be made. Then, what about the variety of English spoken in other countries where English is commonly used and is often an official language—countries such as India, Nigeria, and Singapore—which Kachru refers to as the 'outer circle' countries? These former British colonies have evolved their own varieties of native-speaker English, which have become established, among others, as **World Englishes**. Should these varieties be the target of instruction as well? The truth is that there are many different forms of English, which are mutually intelligible for the most part, but which also have unique characteristics. Even within a country, this is the case. For example, in Singapore, there is Standard Singaporean English used for education, and there is 'Singlish', often used for communication within families and among friends.

English as a Lingua Franca

Then there is the fact that there are millions of users of English in Kachru's third circle, 'the expanding circle', who have learned English as an additional language. They use it primarily to communicate in multilingual contexts, sometimes even those within the same country. In other words, English is used primarily as a contact language (Canagarajah 2006). This variety has been called **English as a Lingua Franca**, 'English as an International Language', or 'Global English'. English as a Lingua Franca or ELF has features that are different from the English spoken in countries belonging to the inner or the outer circles, whose norms are controlled by native speakers.

It might be asked who 'owns' the English language? (Widdowson 1994) One answer to this question (Cummins and Davison 2007) is that English 'belongs' to those for whom it is a mother tongue, those who speak it from childhood. Another answer is that English is owned by whoever uses it regularly, for whatever purpose. This second answer is the answer that Seidlhofer, Breitender, and Pitzl (2006) give. They recognize that a common language like English is needed for a sense of community, but they also recognize that a common language can be a threat to multilingualism. In order to have both

---

[2] Languages other than English are spoken in these countries, of course, and sometimes English is only spoken as a native language by a minority of the citizens. For example, Crystal (2003) estimates that only about 10 percent of South Africans are native speakers of English.

a unified community and at the same time protect the rights for speakers of all languages, their answer is to consider English as no longer a possession of native speakers of English. As with all languages, then, the norms for English as a Lingua Franca are determined by its users (Walker 2010).

Of course, as it is widely spoken around the world, ELF is not a homogenous language, and there is certainly no single culture with which it is associated. Scholars who accept the second answer to the question about the ownership of English have identified features of ELF that would not be considered accurate by inner circle native speaker standards, but they are ones that are regular in ELF. One example is that ELF speakers frequently omit the 's' on the end of third person singular present tense verbs. They say 'He walk to school every day,' rather than 'He walks to school every day.' Omitting the 's' would not be seen as an 'error' if comprehensibility is more important than conformity to native-speaker norms. The fact is that few learners aspire to be or need to be native-like speakers of English.

Because ELF is a natural language, it is variable just like other natural languages. Therefore, not all ELF speakers omit the 's.' Nevertheless, the recognition of ELF has prompted teachers to ask questions about which form of English is correct. Some teachers point out that while the omission of the 's' does not seem to affect the substance of a message, it may affect how the speaker is perceived (Ur 2010). Others (Kuo 2006; see also Bruthiaux 2010) argue that one of the 'dominant models' should be the starting point, including one of the World Englishes, if that is the dominant model in a particular place. Indeed:

> ELF does not at all discourage speakers from learning and using their local variety in local communicative contexts, regardless of whether this is an inner, outer, or expanding circle English.
> (Jenkins 2006: 161)

Of course, no one outside of the local educational context can really answer the question of which English should be taught in a particular place at a particular time.

Critical Discourse Analysis

Critical discourse analysis is the study of how identity and power relations are constructed in language. Critical discourse analysts (such as Fairclough 2001) observe and comment on how language is linked to social practice and the implicit message that is sometimes conveyed. For instance, Stubbs (in Batstone 1995) cites the example of a headline from an apartheid-era South African newspaper. Upon the release of Nelson Mandela from prison, the headline read: 'Jubilant Blacks Clashed with Police.' It would have been possible for this headline to have had a different word order: 'Police Clashed with Jubilant Blacks,' but this would have assigned responsibility for initiating the confrontation to the police not to the Blacks. In other words, texts are not ideologically neutral. The lack of neutrality extends to other aspects of identity besides race. Gender discrimination occurs, for example, when language teaching materials present women as always being subservient to men.

Of course, these issues can apply to languages other than English as well. We would find that in most countries that have been at one time dominated by another world power, questions and issues about language use and power dynamics would be present, be that language Dutch, English, French, German, Portuguese, Russian, Spanish, or another. No one is suggesting that teachers not teach the language that their students want to learn. What, then, can teachers do about the politics of language?

Critical Approaches to Pedagogy

A minimal answer to this question is that it is important for teachers to develop an awareness of political issues around the use of language. Language teachers are not merely teaching language as a neutral vehicle for the expression of meaning. **Critical pedagogy** is an approach to teaching that aims to create a more egalitarian society by raising awareness of social injustice as a necessary part of the curriculum. What you should do about critical pedagogy should not be determined by someone else, who may be unfamiliar with your teaching context or your own political orientation. However, if you wish to become more 'critical' in your teaching, here are a few ideas that have been discussed.

Literacies

Some educators (Gee 1996, Luke 2004) have explored **literacies** as a plural rather than singular concept, stressing the fact that participation in a literate English culture means more than being able to read English—learners need to gain access to the specific English language norms, grammar, and vocabulary used by those in power. So students are not just learning to read in English; they would also be learning the discourse of politics, or education, or business. Learning the unique forms, vocabulary, and norms of different discourses is empowering. Teachers who embrace this idea will find themselves examining their teaching practice, choice of texts, activities, and assessment tools, looking for when and how power is explicitly and implicitly expressed. In addition, they may decide to work with students on a sample of language, looking at the author's word choices, what grammar structures are used, and other aspects of language use. This activity might increase students' ability to make vocabulary and grammar choices within the range available to them.

Plurilingualism and Multicompetence

To keep one language from complete domination, teachers can foster positive attitudes towards all languages. All language learning should be additive, not subtractive. In other words, the language being studied should not replace any other language, but should rather enrich the learners' language capacity. Many learners of English are plurilingual, which refers to an individual's ability to speak more than one language to the extent that they need to, without sacrificing any language they have acquired (see Council of Europe document, 2007). Teachers need to respect their students' identities as plurilinguals. In addition, according to Cook (2002), the goal of language teaching should be successful language use and **multicompetence**, not trying to get students to imitate monolingual native-speaker use.

Non-native Speakers as Teachers

Another political issue is the one regarding the speaker status of a teacher (whether native speaker or non-native speaker). Many language education programs prefer to hire native speakers, presumably for the model they provide and the access they have to intuitions about what is correct and how the language works. However, in actual fact, non-native speakers bring a great number of strengths to language teaching, not the least of which is that they are role models of successful learning themselves. Besides, if they speak the language of their students, they know the obstacles to acquisition and how to surmount them. The teacher's status is a political issue, then, not an issue of competence. It is not whether or not they are native speakers of the language they are teaching that makes for a good teacher.

Hidden Curriculum

Another topic has to do with a teacher's awareness of the hidden curriculum of a language class—what is being taught and learned that is not explicit. What do teachers indicate, for example, when they move their students' desks into a circle formation rather than leaving them in rows? When a teacher asks the students what they want to learn in the class, what message is sent? How is this message different from a teacher presenting a carefully-planned syllabus on the first day of class? What if a teacher does not choose to do certain activities in the coursebook and instead replaces them with activities with students' backgrounds and interests in mind? What meaning might be attributed to these actions by the students (and potentially those concerned observers such as parents and administrators) and is that meaning something positive or negative? In order to answer these questions, you may need to think differently about both what you teach and how.

As we have seen, the politics of teaching and learning English has become a conversation—and often a debate—in English programs as well as English teacher education programs worldwide. To conclude this introductory discussion, here is a question and some suggestions to consider. First the question:

Do you see English as something helpful in allowing people from around the world to communicate with each other or as something that is potentially a problem—the problem of English taking over the world (Phillipson 2008)? You might want to find out what your students think about this question. You might also want to explore which form(s) of English and English literacies to include in your classroom, especially ones that are not included in the curriculum or textbook you have been given. Finally, you might think about the extent to which your students' lives, issues, and struggles related to learning English could be discussed in your language classrooms. It is this last point that our lesson in this chapter addresses.

The Participatory Approach: One Response to the Politics of Language Teaching

Although it originated in the late 1950s with the work of Paulo Freire (perhaps the most famous of all critical educators), it was not until the 1980s that the Participatory Approach started being widely discussed in the language teaching literature. In some ways the Participatory Approach is similar to content-based instruction in that it begins with content that is meaningful to the students. The language that is worked upon emerges from it. What is strikingly different, though, is the nature of the content. It is not the content of subject-matter texts, but rather it is content that comes from issues of concern to students. The Participatory Approach is based on a growing awareness of the role that education, in general, and language education, specifically, have in creating and perpetuating power dynamics in society. As Ann Berthoff has written:

> Education does not substitute for political action, but it is indispensable to it because of the role it plays in the development of critical consciousness. That, in turn, is dependent on the transforming power of language.
> (Berthoff 1987: xix)

In the late 1950s, Freire, a Brazilian, developed a Portuguese literacy program for illiterate adults living in slums and rural areas. Members of Freire's literacy team spent time in the communities engaging adults in dialogues about the problems in their lives. From these dialogues, members of the team developed vocabulary lists of words that were important to the people in the communities. Certain of these words became **generative words** that were used to teach basic decoding and encoding skills, the first steps in becoming literate.

Since then, Freire's ideas have been adopted by adult literacy programs around the world. The central premise of Freire's approach is that education and knowledge have value only insofar as they help people liberate themselves from the social conditions that oppress them. The dialogues, therefore, not only have become the basis for literacy development, but also for reflection and action to improve students' lives. Education is not value-free—it occurs within a particular context. The goal of a Participatory Approach is to help students to understand the social, historical, or cultural forces that shaped a particular context, and then to help empower students to take action and make decisions in order to gain control over their lives in that context (Wallerstein 1983).

Like John Dewey, Freire (1970) criticized what he called the **banking method** of teaching in which the teacher 'deposits' information in the students, making the assumption that the teacher knows what the students need to learn. Instead, he advocated educational processes where students' lives, local cultural norms, and issues become the content for learning. He encouraged teachers to use these topics to create the basis for all teaching and learning. In this way, the teacher is no longer depositing information but is rather allowing learning to emerge from within the students. A core practice of the Participatory Approach is problem posing. Problem posing involves the selection of real-life issues from the students' lives and engages the students in an open-ended process of problem solving.

Experience

Let us now see a lesson in which the Participatory Approach is being practiced.[3] The students are recent immigrants to the United States from Central Europe. They are adults who work part-time during the day and study English at night. Although attendance fluctuates somewhat due to family and work demands placed on the students, tonight there are 10 adults present as the class gets underway.

The teacher begins, 'Good evening everyone. How are you tonight?' The students return the greeting warmly and interact with the teacher and each other, only interrupting to greet latecomers. They know from previous expe-

---

[3] This lesson is based on Elsa Auerbach's presentation at the School for International Training (SIT) on October 18, 1993, entitled "Participatory Approaches: Problem-Posing and Beyond." We have also drawn from Carolyn Layzer and Bill Perry's workshop at SIT on May 28, 1993 and Auerbach (1992).

rience that this is a time to catch up on anything of significance that has happened in their lives since last week's class. One student discusses the fact that one of her children is struggling at school. He never wants to go to school. She does not know what the problem is, but she is worried. Much of this conversation takes place in halting English and gesture since the students are still of low-intermediate English proficiency. Another student discusses the problem she has been having with her landlord. She can never get enough heat to make her comfortable. When she tries to communicate with the landlord, he tells her that it has always been that way. One bit of good news is that one of the student's brothers has just gotten word that he will be permitted entry into the United States soon and so will be able to join the rest of the family.

Having dialogued with the students and having taken note of their issues, the teacher continues, 'Last week, we were talking about why it is difficult for some of you to come to class regularly. Now I know that most of you work during the day and you have your family to take care of in the evening. In addition, several of the women were speaking about choosing not to come to class a few times because of not wanting to be out alone in the city after dark. I would like us to look at this situation a little more in depth tonight.'

The teacher shows the students a picture. It is a drawing of an apartment building.

Figure 12.1   A teacher using a picture to understand the problem and elicit solutions

In one of the windows of the building, there is a woman looking out. On the street below, three young men are standing around. The teacher tells the students that the woman has an English class that she does not want to miss, starting in an hour. Then she begins a discussion:

'What do you see?' The students reply, 'A woman.' And one student adds, 'Men.' 'Who is the woman? What is she doing?' the teacher queries. The students decide that the woman is Lina, one of the women who expressed her fear of being out in the city by herself after dark. The teacher continues with the questions. 'Who are the men? What are they doing?' 'Where are they?' The students reply as well as they can using the English they know.

Next the teacher asks the students to imagine how the people in the picture feel. 'How does the woman feel? Is she happy? Sad? Afraid?' 'Why?' 'How do the men feel?' 'Do they like standing in the street?'

The teacher then pursues a line of questioning that attempts to get students to relate the problem to their own experience. 'Has this ever happened to you?' she asks. 'How did you feel?' 'Did you leave the house?'

'In your country or culture are people alone much?' the teacher asks in an attempt to contextualize the problem. 'Do women walk in the streets alone?' Finally, to end this segment of the class, the teacher invites the students to discuss what they can do about this problem. She does this by posing a series of questions: 'What can Lina do about this?' 'What do you think will happen if she does?' 'What would *you* do about this?' and so forth.

Since one of the suggestions for a solution to Lina's problem was to have more street lighting installed in her neighborhood, the teacher asks the class if they would like to write a group letter to the mayor's office to request better lighting. The students think that this is a good idea, and they take out their notebooks. The teacher elicits content for the letter with questions such as 'What's important in this letter?' 'How do you want it to start?' 'What do you want me to write?' 'What comes next?' The teacher faithfully records the students' answers on the board, making sure not to change their words. She reads the text aloud as she writes it and she invites students to read along. When they are through, the teacher asks them if they want to change anything, pointing to each word as it is read. She then points out some changes that need to be made. When they are finished with their changes, each student reads one line. They do this several times with students reading different lines each time.

The students next copy their group letter into their notebooks. Since they actually intend to send the letter out, they want to make sure that the English is good. She asks them to reread and edit the letter for homework. They will read each other's letters in the following class and incorporate any necessary revisions in the group letter before sending it out. The class concludes with the students talking about what they liked in that evening's class and what they didn't like. They also respond to the teacher's questions about what they have learned and what they want to learn in the future.

Thinking about the Experience

Let us now examine the practices and principles of the Participatory Approach.

Observations	Principles
1 The teacher dialogues with students in order to learn what is happening in their lives.	What happens in the classroom should be connected with what happens outside. The teacher listens for themes in what students say that will provide the content for future lessons.
2 The teacher poses a problem that was voiced by several women during a discussion from a previous class.	The curriculum is not a predetermined product, but the result of an ongoing context-specific problem-posing process.
3 The teacher asks a number of questions and leads the class in discussing the problem.	Education is most effective when it is experience-centered—when it relates to students' real needs. Students are motivated by their personal involvement. Teachers are co-learners, asking questions of the students, who are the experts on their own lives.
4 The teacher asks the students if they want to write a group letter. She elicits the content of the letter from the students by asking leading questions.	When knowledge is jointly constructed, it becomes a tool to help students find a voice; and by finding their voices, students can act in the world. Students learn to see themselves as social and political beings.

5 The teacher writes down what the students tell her. She reads the text aloud, and the students do, too. She asks them if they want to make any changes. She offers feedback as well. After the changes have been made, the teacher has the students read the letter out loud several times.	Language teaching occurs with texts that the students have co-constructed.
6 Afterwards, the students copy the letter in their notebooks. They work on editing it for homework.	Focus on linguistic form occurs within a focus on content. Language skills are taught in service of action for change, rather than in isolation.
7 The students are asked to bring their revised versions of the letters to the next class for others to read.	Students can create their own materials, which, in turn, can become texts for other students.
8 The students discuss what they have learned in the class and what they want to learn in the future.	A goal of the Participatory Approach is for students to evaluate their own learning and to increasingly direct it themselves. This is one way that they can feel empowered.

Reviewing the Principles

As you can see, the language focus in the Participatory Approach is not established in advance. Rather, it follows from content, which itself emerges from ongoing, collaborative investigations of critical themes in students' lives. As Auerbach (1992: 14) puts it, 'Real communication, accompanied by appropriate feedback that subordinates form to the elaboration of meaning, is key for language learning.' Let us now examine the principles more specifically.

1 **What are the goals of teachers who use the Participatory Approach?**
   The teachers' goals are to teach language that is meaningful and to raise the political consciousness of her students. Teachers want their students to be empowered to use the language they are learning in order to solve political problems in their lives.

2 **What is the role of the teacher? What is the role of the students?**
   The teacher dialogues with the students in order to identify problems they are having. She then looks for ways to incorporate these problems into the

lessons. These problems become the content she focuses on in language instruction. The students are encouraged to share the daily concerns of their lives with the teacher and the class.

3 What are some characteristics of the teaching/learning process?

The teacher leads the students in a discussion about their lives. From this discussion, she identifies problems that the class can work on as a whole. She then poses these problems to the students. Students learn how to use language in real-world situations in order to address their problems. Knowledge is jointly constructed with the teacher asking questions and the students responding. Collaboration among students is also encouraged. Focusing on language form occurs within a focus on content relevant to students' lives. Students are encouraged to evaluate their own learning.

4 What is the nature of student–teacher interaction? What is the nature of student–student interaction?

The teacher is supportive of her students. She helps them advocate for themselves. She helps the students find solutions to problems while also teaching them the necessary language to understand, discuss and, address these problems. Students work supportively with one another.

5 How are the feelings of the students dealt with?

The students learn that their feelings are important and that their study of language is relevant to their lives. The students are invited to express their feelings. They are also empowered by directing and evaluating their own learning.

6 How is the language viewed? How is culture viewed?

Language is an instrument of power necessary for active and equal participation in society. Language is not a neutral subject. Culture relates to students' daily experiences.

7 What areas of language are emphasized? What language skills are emphasized?

Language is used meaningfully, with a focus on form subordinate to communication initially. Ultimately, correctness of form is taught and valued so that students can be successful in using language with authorities. Literacy is thought to be very important, although no skill is neglected.

8 What is the role of the students' native language?

The students' native language is valued. It should not be lost when students learn a new language.

9 How is evaluation accomplished?

As much as possible the students are encouraged to direct and to evaluate their own learning so that it is connected with their lives.

10 How does the teacher respond to student errors?

Students are encouraged to self-correct. The teacher also points out student errors and provides feedback on how to correct errors.

Reviewing the Techniques

The Participatory Approach is another example of a 'strong version' of the Communicative Approach. An analytic syllabus is adopted, and the use of meaningful language predominates over learning linguistic items one by one.

Here are the two special techniques associated with the Participatory Approach:

- **Dialoguing**

  In the Participatory Approach, teacher and students dialogue about issues in the students' lives that relate to their power and the power of others. Students are encouraged 'to perceive critically the way they exist in the world with which and in which they find themselves' (Freire 1970: 64).

- **Problem Posing**

  The teacher poses a problem that she has identified from dialoguing with students. Students are encouraged to examine their own practices and beliefs and to engage in collaborative planning and problem solving around the problem that has been posed. Problem posing helps students to understand the social, historical, and cultural forces that shaped the context in which they live, and then helps empower them to take action and make decisions in order to gain control over their lives in that context.

Conclusion

In this chapter we have investigated the political dimensions of language teaching and learning, and we have had an experience with the Participatory Approach as one way to address these issues through classroom practice. In her Introduction to *Participatory Practices in Adult Education*, Campbell (2001) defines the goal of participatory practices as 'building a just society through individual and socioeconomic transformation and ending domination through changing power relations.'

While this is an ambitious goal, teachers can contribute to meeting it. As North American teacher educators Hawkins and Norton have written:

> Because language, culture, and identity are integrally related, language teachers are in a key position to address educational inequality, both because of the particular learners they serve, many of whom are marginalized members of the wider community, and because of the subject matter they teach—language—which can serve itself to both empower and marginalize …
>
> (Hawkins and Norton 2009: 31)

Of course, in some settings even to suggest that there are social problems is to implicitly criticize the government, which can be seen as threatening. Clearly, whether or not to address the political dimensions of language teaching will have to be determined by each teacher. Whatever you believe about the political dimensions of language teaching, do you see the value of working on issues, if not problems, that are relevant to your students' lives so that your teaching can be a vehicle for their personal empowerment as well as their language experience? If so, you should ask yourself which, if any, of the techniques presented here you can adapt to your own teaching context.

Activities

Ⓐ Check your understanding of the political dimensions of language teaching and the Participatory Approach.

1 Proponents of ELF suggest that the target language model not be the native speaker of English, but a fluent bilingual speaker, who can negotiate meaning with other non-native speakers. What do you think about this proposal?

2 How is the Participatory Approach an example of a method that takes the politics of language teaching seriously?

Ⓑ Apply what you have understood about the political dimensions of language teaching and the Participatory Approach.

1 Much has been written in this chapter about politics in terms of national identity. But educational inequality arises due to other issues as well. One example mentioned in this chapter is gender discrimination. Can you think of others? What should you do about such issues?

2 Speak with your students about what is happening in their lives. Are there themes that emerge around which you can plan lessons?

References/Additional Resources

Auerbach, E. 1992. *Making Meaning, Making Change: A Guide to Participatory Curriculum Development for Adult ESL and Family Literacy.* McHenry, IL: Center for Applied Linguistics and Delta Systems, Inc.

———. and N. Wallerstein. 1987. *ESL for Action: Problem Posing at Work.* Reading, MA: Addison-Wesley.

Batstone, R. 1995. 'Grammar in discourse: Attitudes and deniability' in G. Cook and B. Seidlhofer (eds.). *Principles and Practice in Applied Linguistics*, 197–213. Oxford: Oxford University Press.

Berlin, L. 2005. *Contextualizing College ESL Classroom Practice: A Participatory Approach to Effective Instruction.* Mahwah, NJ: Lawrence Erlbaum Associates.

Berthoff, A. 1987. 'Foreword' in P. Freire and D. Macedo. 1987.

Bruthiaux, P. 2010. 'World Englishes and the classroom: An EFL perspective.' *TESOL Quarterly* 44/2: 365–9.

Campbell, P. and B. Burnaby (eds.). 2001. *Participatory Practices in Adult Education.* Mahwah, NJ: Lawrence Erlbaum Associates.

Canagarajah, A. 1999. *Resisting Linguistic Imperialism in English Teaching.* Oxford: Oxford University Press.

———. 2006. 'TESOL at forty: What are the issues?' *TESOL Quarterly* 40, 9–34.

Cook, V. (ed.). 2002. *Portraits of the L2 User.* Clevedon: Multilingual Matters.

Council of Europe. 2007. *From Linguistic Diversity to Plurilingual Education: Guide for the Development of Language Education Policies in Europe.* Strasbourg: Council of Europe.

Crystal, D. 2003. *English as a Global Language.* Cambridge: Cambridge University Press.

Cummins, J. and C. Davison (eds.). 2007. *International Handbook of English Language Teaching.* New York: Springer International.

Fairclough, N. 2001. *Language and Power: Language in Social Life* (2nd edn.). London: Pearson.

Freire, P. 1970. *Pedagogy of the Oppressed.* New York: Continuum.

——— and D. Macedo. 1987. *Literacy: Reading the Word and the World.* South Hadley, MA: Bergin and Garvey.

Gee, J. 1996. *Social Linguistics and Literacies: Ideology in Discourses.* London: Taylor and Francis.

Graddol, D. 2006. *English Next.* London: The British Council.

Hawkins, M. and B. Norton. 2009. 'Critical language teacher education' in A. Burns and J. Richards (eds.). *Second Language Teacher Education*, 310–39. Cambridge: Cambridge University Press.

Holliday, A. 2005. *The Struggle to Teach English as an International Language.* Oxford: Oxford University Press.

Jenkins, J. 2006. 'Current perspectives on teaching World Englishes and English as a lingua franca.' *TESOL Quarterly* 40/1: 157–81.

———. 2007. *English as a Lingua Franca: Attitude and Identity*. Oxford: Oxford University Press.

Kachru, B. 1992. *The Other Tongue: English across Cultures* (2nd edn.). Urbana IL: University of Illinois Press.

Kirkpatrick, A. 2007. *World Englishes: Implications for International Communication and English Language Teaching*. Cambridge: Cambridge University Press.

Kuo, I-C. 2006. 'Addressing the issue of teaching English as a lingua franca.' *ELT Journal* 60/3: 213–21.

Luke, A. 2004. 'Two takes on the critical' in B. Norton, and K. Toohey (eds.). *Critical Pedagogy and Language Learning*, 21–9. Cambridge: Cambridge University Press.

McKay, S. 2002. *Teaching English as an International Language: Rethinking Goals and Approaches*. Oxford: Oxford University Press.

McLaren, P. and P. Leonard. 1993. *Paulo Freire: A Critical Encounter*. New York: Routledge.

Morgan, B. 1998. *The ESL Classroom: Teaching, Critical Practice and Community Development*. Toronto: University of Toronto Press.

Nash, A. 1992. *Talking Shop: A Curriculum Sourcebook for Participatory ESL*. McHenry, IL: Center for Applied Linguistics and Delta Systems, Inc.

Phillipson, R. 2008. 'English, Panacea or Pandemic?' Keynote lecture. International conference 'Language issues in English-medium universities.' University of Hong Kong, June.

Roberts, P. 2000. *Education, Literacy and Humanization*. Westport, CT: Bergin and Garvey.

Seidlhofer, B. 2011. *Understanding English as a Lingua Franca*. Oxford: Oxford University Press.

———, A. Breiteneder, and M-L. Pitzl. 2006. 'English as a lingua franca in Europe: Challenges for applied linguistics.' *Annual Review of Applied Linguistics* 26, 3–34.

Ur, Penny. 2010. Teacher, is it OK to say 'she come'? Paper presented at the Third International Conference of English as a Lingua Franca. Vienna, May 22.

Walker, R. 2010. *Teaching the Pronunciation of English as a Lingua Franca*. Oxford: Oxford University Press.

Wallerstein, N. 1983. *Language and Culture in Conflict: Problem-posing in the ESL Classroom*. Reading, MA: Addison Wesley.

Widdowson, H. G. 1994. 'The ownership of English.' *TESOL Quarterly* 28/2: 377–89.

13

Learning Strategy Training, Cooperative Learning, and Multiple Intelligences

Introduction

In this chapter, we discuss three methodological innovations: learning strategy training, **cooperative learning**, and multiple intelligences. What these three have in common differs from the approaches in the previous chapters in that they are not full-blown methods, and their main concern is the language learner. Because of their different focus, they complement, rather than challenge, language teaching methods. While these innovations are not comprehensive methods of language teaching, they reflect interesting and enduring methodological practices, and thus are presented here.

Learning Strategy Training

It was noted in Chapter 5, when discussing the Cognitive Approach, that beginning in the early 1970s, language learners were seen to be more actively responsible for their own learning. In keeping with this perception, in 1975 Rubin investigated what 'good language learners' did to facilitate their learning. From this investigation, she identified some of their learning strategies, 'the techniques or devices which a learner may use to acquire knowledge' (p.43). Good language learners, according to Rubin, are willing and accurate guessers who have a strong desire to communicate, and will attempt to do so even at the risk of appearing foolish. They attend to both the meaning and the form of their message. They also practice and monitor their own speech as well as the speech of others.

While early research went toward identifying just these kinds of learning strategies, it was not long before language educators realized that simply recognizing learners' contributions to the process was not sufficient. In order to maximize their potential and contribute to their autonomy, language learners—and especially those not among the group of so-called 'good' learners—

needed training in learning strategies. Indeed, Wenden (1985) observed that language teachers' time might be profitably spent in learner training, as much as in language training. Such suggestions led to the idea of learning strategy training—training students in the use of learning strategies in order to improve their learning effectiveness.

Experience[1]

Let us now see one model for such training. We enter a secondary school in Japan. There are 32 students in the class at intermediate-level target language proficiency. Prior to the lesson, the teacher has read the students' learning journals and has interviewed the students. One of the problems that students have been complaining about is that their reading assignments are lengthy. There is a lot of new vocabulary in the readings, and it takes a long time for them to look up all the new words in the dictionary. Based on these comments, the teacher has decided to teach the strategy of **advance organization**.

He begins the class with a presentation. He tells students that they are going to work on a learning strategy called advance organization. They will be working on improving their reading by learning to preview and to skim to get the gist of a reading passage. Learning this strategy will improve their comprehension and the speed at which they read, he explains. He begins by modeling. He uses the think-aloud technique, telling students what he is doing as he is modeling. He has distributed a reading passage. Let us listen in.

'What I do first is read the title. I try to figure out what the passage is about. I look at the subheadings and pictures, too, if there are any. I ask myself what I know about the topic and what questions I have. Next, I read the first paragraph. I don't read every word, however. I let my eyes skim it very quickly—just picking out what I think are the main ideas. I especially look at the content or meaning-bearing words—usually the nouns and verbs.'

The teacher calls out the words that he considers key in the first paragraph. 'From doing these things, I know that this passage is about wild horses. I do not know very much about the topic, but from skimming the first paragraph, I have gotten the impression that the passage is about the challenges of catching and taming wild horses.'

---

[1] The lesson outline, not content, is based on a presentation by Anna Chamot (1998), entitled 'Language Learning Strategies Instruction: Promises and Pitfalls' at the Twenty-third Annual Congress of the Applied Linguistics Association of Australia, Griffith University, Brisbane, Australia. Chamot and Michael O'Malley have developed the Cognitive Academic Language Learning Approach (CALLA), which integrates content, academic language development, and explicit instruction in learning strategies.

Figure 13.1   Teacher and class working on the learning strategy of advance organization

'I'd like you to practice just this much now. I am going to hand out a new reading passage for you to practice on. When you get it, keep it face down. Don't read it yet. Does everyone have one? Good. Now remember, before you turn the paper over, you are going to be practicing the strategy that I have just introduced. Ready? Turn over the paper. Take a look. Now quickly turn it face down again. What do you think that this passage is about? Who can guess?'

One student says he thinks that it is about whales. 'Why do you think so?' asks the teacher. The student says he has guessed from the title, which is *Rescuing the World's Largest Mammal.* 'What do you know about whales?' the teacher asks the class. One student replies that there are many different kinds of whales. Another adds that they travel long distances. A third says that they are very intelligent. 'What do you think is meant by "rescuing"?' the teacher asks. No one knows so the teacher asks them to keep this question in mind as they read.

'Turn your page over again. Read through the first paragraph quickly. Do not read every word. Skip those you don't know the meaning of. Don't use your dictionaries.' The teacher gives the students two minutes to read the first paragraph.

He then asks, 'Who can tell us what the main idea of the passage is—what is the gist?' A student replies that the passage is about certain types of whales being put on the endangered list. Another student immediately raises his hand. 'What does "endangered" mean?' he asks. The teacher encourages him to take a guess. 'Is there any part of the word "endangered" that you recognize? What do you think it might mean in the context of a passage about whales?' The student pauses, thinks for a minute, and then says, 'The whales, they are disappearing?'

'Yes,' replies the teacher; 'scientists are concerned that whales will disappear if conditions do not improve. Good. Do you know what "rescuing" means now?'

The students nod. One volunteers, 'saving.' 'OK,' says the teacher. 'Does anyone want to make a prediction about what the main idea is in the second paragraph?'

Several students venture that it may talk about the conditions that are not good for whales.

'That's a good guess,' says the teacher. 'Let's see if your predictions are correct. Skim the second paragraph now. This time, however, I am only going to give you one and a half minutes.'

The lesson proceeds like this until by the fourth paragraph, the students are given only a half a minute to skim for the main idea.

'Great. We are off to a good beginning. We will practice more with this tomorrow.'

Next the students evaluate how they have done. Some feel distressed because they still feel that they need to understand every word. However, others are feeling better because they realize that their reading assignments need not take as long as they have been taking. Some students discuss their implementation of the strategy and how they modified it.

The teacher encourages them to share any innovations they made. All of the students feel that they need a lot more practice with this new strategy.

'Yes,' responds the teacher, 'and you will begin tonight. For homework, I would like you to use your new strategy on something that you would like to read—a newspaper or magazine article, for example. Don't just begin by reading the first sentence. See what you can learn from reading the headline or title. See if there are any pictures with captions. Then when you do go to read, read the first paragraph first. When you come to a word you don't know, skip over it and continue. See what you can learn about the main idea of the article in this way. Then write about this experience in your learning journals. That's all for today.'

Thinking about the Experience

Let us examine this experience now in our usual manner—observations on the left, and the principles that might account for them on the right.

Observations	Principles
1 Prior to the lesson the teacher has been reading the students' learning journals, where the students regularly write about what and how they are learning. The teacher has also been interviewing the students.	The students' prior knowledge and learning experiences should be valued and built upon.
2 The teacher decides to have the students work on the strategy of advance organization.	Studying certain learning strategies will contribute to academic success.
3 The teacher models the use of the strategy using a think-aloud demonstration.	The teacher's job is not only to teach language, but to teach learning.
4 The students practice the new learning strategy.	For many students, strategies have to be learned. The best way to do this is with 'hands-on' experience.
5 The students evaluate their own success in learning the strategy. They modify the strategy to meet their own learning needs. They share their innovations with their classmates.	Students need to become independent, self-regulated learners. Self-assessment contributes to learner autonomy.
6 The teacher asks the students to try out the new strategy on a different reading they choose for homework that night.	An important part of learning a strategy is being able to transfer it, i.e. use it in a different situation.

It was pointed out at the beginning of this chapter that the methodological trends in this chapter complement the ones presented in previous chapters. It is easy to see how learning strategy training would fit with content-based instruction, for example. Indeed, research has shown that to be effective, strategies should not be taught in isolation, but rather as part of the content-area or language curriculum (Grabe and Stoller 1997). An added benefit of learning strategy training is that it can help learners to continue to learn after they have completed their formal study of the target language.

The strategy in the lesson we have just observed is an example of what Chamot and O'Malley (1994) call **metacognitive strategies**, strategies that are used to plan, monitor, and evaluate a learning task. Other examples of metacognitive strategies include arranging the conditions that help one learn (What conditions help you learn best?), setting long and short-term goals (What do you want to learn?), and checking one's comprehension during listening or reading (What have you understood?). Chamot and O'Malley identify two other categories. One is **cognitive strategies**, which involve learners interacting and manipulating what is to be learned. Examples include replaying a word or phrase mentally to 'listen' to it again, outlining and summarizing what has been learned from reading or listening, and using keywords (remembering a new target language word by associating it with a familiar word or by creating a visual image of it). The other category is **social/affective** strategies where learners interact with other persons or 'use affective control to assist learning.' Examples include creating situations to practice the target language with others, using self-talk, where one thinks positively and talks oneself through a difficult task, and cooperating or working with others to share information, obtain feedback, and complete a task. This last strategy, cooperation, gives us a convenient bridge to the next topic.

Cooperative Learning

Cooperative learning (sometimes called collaborative learning) essentially involves students learning from each other in groups. But it is not the group configuration that makes cooperative learning distinctive; it is the way that students and teachers work together that is important. As we have just seen, with learning strategy training, the teacher helps students learn how to learn more effectively. In cooperative learning, teachers teach students collaborative or social skills so that they can work together more effectively. Indeed, cooperation is not only a way of learning, but also a theme to be communicated about and studied (Jacobs 1998). Let us see how this is accomplished.

Experience[2]

As the 24 fifth grade ESL students in Alexandria, Virginia, USA settle down after lunch, the teacher asks for attention and announces that the day's vo-

---

[2] This lesson has been adapted from the one presented in Chapter 2 of Dishon and O'Leary 1984.

cabulary lesson will be done in cooperative groups. Several students ask, 'Which groups, teacher?'

'We'll stay in the same groups of six that you have been in so far this week,' he replies. 'I will give each group a different part of a story. There are four parts. Your group's job is to read the part of a story that I will give you and to discuss the meaning of any new vocabulary words. Use your dictionaries or ask me when you can't figure out the meaning of a word. In ten minutes, you will form new groups. Three of you will move to another group, and three of you will stay where you are and others will join you. In each new group you will tell your part of the story. You will teach your new group the meanings of any vocabulary words that the group members don't know. Listen to their part of the story. Learn the meaning of the new vocabulary in it. Then we will change groups again, and you will do the same thing. The third time you will return to your original group and tell the story from beginning to end. You will work together to learn the new vocabulary. After ten minutes of practice time, you will be asked to match each new vocabulary word with its definition on a worksheet that I will give you. Your group will help you during the practice time. During the test you're each on your own. Your score will depend on your results as a group, since your scores will be added together.' The teacher then writes the criteria on the board as he explains them:

90–100 percent = No one in your group has to take the test again.

89 percent or less = Everyone in your group takes the test again.

'Everyone in the class will get an extra five minutes of recess tomorrow if the room score is 90 percent or better.' There is a buzz of excitement about that possibility.

One student asks, 'What social skills, teacher?' In response, the teacher says, 'Today you are all to practice encouraging others while your group works on learning the vocabulary words.' He then asks, 'What can encouraging others sound like?'

One student responds, 'Nice job!' Another says, 'Way to go!' 'Clapping and cheering,' offers a third.

'Yes,' says the teacher. 'Now what can encouraging others look like?'

'A smile.'

'A nod.'

'A pat on the back.'

'All right. You've got the idea. Today I will observe each group. I will be looking for you to practice this social skill. Now, get into your groups.'

Figure 13.2   The teacher organizing cooperative learning groups

The teacher points out in which part of the room the groups are to sit. One group of students sits in a circle on the floor, two put chairs around two desks, and one group sits at a table in the back of the room.

The teacher distributes handouts with a different part of the story to each group. He then moves from group to group spending two or three minutes with each one.

The students appear to be busy working in their groups; there is much talking. After 10 minutes, the teacher tells the students to stop and asks for three students to leave their group and to join another group. After 10 more minutes, they do this again. Then the students return to their original groups and work on putting the parts of the story together and teaching each other the new vocabulary. It is then time for the individual vocabulary test. After the test, the students correct their own work. Students compare and combine scores. The students put their groups' scores on each of their papers.

The teacher picks up each group's paper and quickly figures the room score. There is much cheering and applauding when he announces that there will be five minutes of extra recess for everyone. He then tells the groups to look at how they did on the social skill of encouraging others and to complete two statements, which he has written on the board while they were taking the vocabulary test:

Our group did best on encouraging others by _____,
_____, and _____ (three specific
behaviors).

Goal setting: The social skill we will practice more often tomorrow is
_____.

He suggests that one of the students be the taskmaster to keep the group focused on the task of completing the statements, one be the recorder to write the group's answers, one be the timekeeper to keep track of the time, one be the checker to see that all of the work is done, and one be the reporter who will give the group report later. He tells them that they have 10 minutes for the discussion.

The teacher circulates among the groups, but does not say anything. After 10 minutes, he asks each group's reporter to share the group's responses. The teacher consults the notes that he has made during his observation and he offers his comments.

Thinking about the Experience

Let us list our observations and review the principles of cooperative learning.

Observations	Principles
1 The vocabulary lesson will be done in cooperative groups. Each student is to help the other students learn the new vocabulary words.	Students are encouraged to think in terms of 'positive interdependence,' which means that the students are not thinking competitively and individualistically, but rather cooperatively and in terms of the group.
2 The students ask which groups they should form. The teacher tells them to stay in the same groups they have been in this week.	In cooperative learning, students often stay together in the same groups for a period of time so they can learn how to work better together. The teacher usually assigns students to the groups so that the groups are mixed—males and females, different ethnic groups, different proficiency levels, etc. This allows students to learn from each other and also gives them practice in how to get along with people different from themselves.

3 The teacher gives the students the criteria for judging how well they have performed the task they have been given. There are consequences for the group and the whole class.	The efforts of an individual help not only the individual to be rewarded, but also others in the class.
4 The students are to work on the social skill of encouraging others.	Social skills such as acknowledging another's contribution, asking others to contribute, and keeping the conversation calm need to be explicitly taught.
5 The students appear to be busy working in their groups. There is much talking in the groups.	Language acquisition is facilitated by students' interacting in the target language.
6 Students take the test individually.	Although students work together, each student is individually accountable.
7 Students compare and combine scores. The students put their group's scores on each of their papers.	Responsibility and accountability for each other's learning is shared. Each group member should be encouraged to feel responsible for participating and for learning.
8 The group discusses how the target social skill has been practiced. Each student is given a role. The teacher gives feedback on how students did on the target social skill.	Leadership is 'distributed.' Teachers not only teach language; they teach cooperation as well. Of course, since social skills involve the use of language, cooperative learning teaches language for both academic and social purposes.

Once again note how cooperative learning complements methods presented in previous chapters. For instance, cooperative learning groups can easily work on tasks from a task-based approach to language instruction.

The same holds for the last methodological innovation we will consider in this chapter—multiple intelligences. Teachers who adopt this approach expand beyond language, learning strategy, and social skills training, to address other qualities of language learners.

Multiple Intelligences

Teachers have always known that their students have different strengths. In the language teaching field, some of the differences among students have been attributed to students' having different learning or cognitive styles. For instance, some students are better visual learners than aural learners. They learn better when they are able to read new material rather than simply listen to it. Of course, many learners can learn equally well either way; however, it has been estimated that for up to 25 percent of the population, the mode of instruction does make a difference in their success as learners (Levin et al. 1974, cited in Larsen-Freeman and Long 1991). Hatch (1974) further distinguishes between learners who are data-gatherers and those who are rule-formers. Data-gatherers are fluent but inaccurate; rule-formers are more accurate, but often speak haltingly.

Related work by psychologist Howard Gardner (1983, 1993, 1999, 2006) on multiple intelligences has been influential in language teaching circles. Teachers who recognize the multiple intelligences of their students acknowledge that students bring with them specific and unique strengths, which are often not taken into account in classroom situations. Gardner has theorized that individuals have at least eight[3] distinct intelligences that can be developed over a lifetime. The eight are:

1   Logical/mathematical—the ability to use numbers effectively, to see abstract patterns, and to reason well
2   Visual/spatial—the ability to orient oneself in the environment, to create mental images, and a sensitivity to shape, size, color
3   Body/kinesthetic—the ability to use one's body to express oneself and to solve problems
4   Musical/rhythmic—the ability to recognize tonal patterns and a sensitivity to rhythm, pitch, melody
5   Interpersonal—the ability to understand another person's moods, feelings, motivations, and intentions
6   Intrapersonal—the ability to understand oneself and to practice self-discipline
7   Verbal/linguistic—the ability to use language effectively and creatively
8   Naturalist—the ability to relate to nature and to classify what is observed.

[3] We have drawn on descriptions from Christison (1996) and Lazear (1997) to explain seven of the eight intelligences. Gardner added the eighth intelligence some years after he proposed the original seven. We have also learned from John Balbi's presentation on multiple intelligences at the New York State TESOL Conference, Saratoga Springs, New York, 24 November 1996.

While everyone might possess these eight intelligences, they are not equally developed in any one individual. Some teachers feel that they need to create activities that draw on all eight, not only to facilitate language acquisition among diverse students, but also to help them realize their full potential with all of the intelligences. One way of doing so is to think about the activities that are frequently used in the classroom and to categorize them according to intelligence type. By being aware of which type of intelligence is being tapped by a particular activity, teachers can keep track of which type they are emphasizing or neglecting in the classroom and aim for a different representation if they so choose. Christison (1996, 2005) and Armstrong (1994) give us examples of activities that fit each type of intelligence:

1 Logical/mathematical—puzzles and games, logical, sequential presentations, classifications and categorizations
2 Visual/spatial—charts and grids, videos, drawing
3 Body/kinesthetic—hands-on activities, field trips, pantomime
4 Musical/rhythmic—singing, playing music, jazz chants
5 Interpersonal—pairwork, project work, group problem solving
6 Intrapersonal—self-evaluation, journal keeping, options for homework
7 Verbal/linguistic—note-taking, storytelling, debates
8 Naturalist—collecting objects from the natural world; learning their names and about them.

A second way to teach from a multiple intelligence perspective is to deliberately plan lessons so that the different intelligences are represented. Here is one lesson plan, adapted and expanded from Emanuela Agostini,[4] which addresses all of the intelligences:

Step 1—Give students a riddle and ask them to solve it in pairs:
I have eyes, but I see nothing. I have ears, but I hear nothing. I have a mouth, but I cannot speak. If I am young, I stay young; if I am old, I stay old. What am I?
Answer: A person in a painting or photograph.
(Intelligences: interpersonal, verbal/linguistic)

Step 2—Guided imagery: Tell students to close their eyes and to relax; then describe a picture of a scene or a portrait. Ask them to imagine it. Play music while you are giving the students the description.
(Intelligences: spatial/visual intelligence, musical)

Step 3—Distribute to each person in a small group a written description of the same picture they have just heard described. Each description is

---

[4] Based on Emanuela Agostini's presentation 'Seven Easy Pieces,' at TESOL Italy on 6 December 1997.

incomplete, however, and no two in the group are quite the same. For example, one description has certain words missing; the others have different words missing. The students work together with the other members of their group to fill in the missing words so that they all end up with a complete description of the picture.
(Intelligences: interpersonal, verbal/linguistic)

Step 4—Ask the groups to create a tableau of the picture by acting out the description they have just completed.
(Intelligence: body/kinesthetic)

Figure 13.3   Forming a tableau representing a portrait to illustrate kinesthetic intelligence

Step 5—Show the students the picture. Ask them to find five things about it that differ from their tableau or from how they imagined the painting to look.
(Intelligence: logical/mathematical)

Step 6—Ask students to identify the tree in the painting.
(Intelligence: naturalist)

Step 7—Reflection: Ask students if they have learned anything about how to look at a picture. Ask them if they have learned anything new about the target language.
(Intelligence: intrapersonal)

Of course, not every intelligence has to be present in every lesson plan. The point is that, typically, linguistic and logical-mathematical intelligences are most prized in schools. In language classrooms, without any special attention, it is likely that verbal/linguistic intelligence and interpersonal intelligence will be regularly activated. The challenge for teachers who wish to honor the diversity of intelligences among their students is how to activate the other intelligences and enable each student to reach his or her full potential, while not losing sight of the teachers' purpose, which is to teach language.

More recently, Gardner (2007) has developed a related theory, focused on cognitive abilities that individuals need to develop in order to be successful in a changing world. Gardner proposes **five minds**, ways of thinking and acting in the world, which students need to develop. Of the five minds, three focus on intellectual development and two minds on character development.

1 The Disciplinary Mind is the first of the intellectual minds, in which students master a traditional body of information, such as important historical developments in a particular country or countries.

2 The second mind that deals with intellectual development is the Synthesizing Mind, where the focus shifts to bringing together, organizing, understanding, and articulating information from various disciplines in a unified and coherent whole. An example is comparing literature in Spanish, Arabic, and English to learn how the history of people speaking these languages has shaped literary styles.

3 The third mind is the Creating Mind, where students are encouraged to come up with new ideas, original solutions to problems, and creative questions. This could include creative writing or original historical or political analysis. We might consider use of the Creating Mind as an example of 'thinking outside the box', thinking in an unusual way.

The two minds focusing on character or moral development are the Respectful Mind and the Ethical Mind.

4 A well-developed Respectful Mind is reflected by an awareness of, appreciation for, and openness to the differences and individuality of others. This would naturally include fostering tolerance for people from other cultural backgrounds, religions, races, and identities within and beyond the classroom.

5 The Ethical Mind encourages students to cultivate a sense of responsibility for themselves and for the wellbeing of others.

Teaching students in a way that includes these five minds might encourage students to develop important skills for life and work in the world while also learning a language.

Conclusion

In this chapter we have considered methodological innovations that have revolved around language learners. Does it make sense to you that language teachers should think about teaching skills such as working cooperatively, in addition to skills that relate directly to language? Can you think of any learning strategies that you can introduce to your students to facilitate their language acquisition? Would you want to adopt any of the practices from cooperative learning when you ask your students to work in small groups? Does it make sense to diversify your instructional practices in order to accommodate your students' learning styles, multiple intelligences, or cultivate their five minds?

As teachers, it can be useful to be reminded about the unique qualities of each of our students. Keeping this in mind will provide a useful backdrop to Chapter 15, in which we address the question of methodological choice.

Activities

A **Check your understanding of Learning Strategy Training, Cooperative Learning, and Multiple Intelligences.**

1 State in your own words the difference between language training and learner training.
2 It has been said about cooperative learning that it attempts to teach students to 'think us, not me.' What do you think that this means?
3 Categorize each of the following eight activity types into the type of intelligence it likely taps. There is one intelligence for each: Listening to lectures, tapping out the stress patterns of sentences, cooperative tasks, goal setting, map reading, TPR, growing plants in a window box in the classroom, surveying students' likes and dislikes, and graphing the results.

B **Apply what you have understood about Learning Strategy Training, Cooperative Learning, and Multiple Intelligences.**

1 Interview a group of students about the learning strategies they use to facilitate their language acquisition. Are there any patterns? Are there strategies that might help your students if they knew how to use them? If so, plan a lesson to teach one. See what results.

2   Goodman (1998: 6) has written that 'one essential tenet of cooperative learning is the notion that any exercise, course material, or objective … may be reformulated into a cooperative experience.' With this in mind, think back to a recent exercise you asked your language students to do. How could you have reformulated it in such a way as to be consistent with cooperative learning principles?

3   Make a list of your most commonly used language teaching activities. Try to determine which intelligences or which of Gardner's five minds they work on. If there are intelligences/minds that are not included in your list, see if you can change the way you do the activities to include it/them. Alternatively, consider adding activities which work on the missing intelligence(s)/minds to your repertoire.

References/Additional Resources

Learning Strategy Training

Anderson, N. 2005. 'L2 learning strategies' in E. Hinkel (ed.). *Handbook of Research in Second Language Teaching and Learning*, 757–72. Mahwah, NJ: Lawrence Erlbaum.

Breen, M. (ed.). 2001. *Learner Contributions to Language Learning*. Essex: Pearson Education.

Brown, H. D. 2002. *Strategies for Success: A Practical Guide to Learning English*. White Plains, NY: Pearson Education.

Chamot, A. and **M. O'Malley.** 1994. *The CALLA Handbook: How to Implement the Cognitive–Academic Language Learning Approach*. White Plains, NY: Addison-Wesley Longman.

——, **S. Barnhardt**, **P. El-Dinary**, and **J. Robins.** 1999. *The Learning Strategies Handbook*. White Plains, NY: Addison-Wesley Longman.

Cohen, A. 1998. *Strategies in Learning and Using a Second Language*. New York: Longman.

Dickinson, L. 1987. *Self-instruction in Language Learning*. Cambridge: Cambridge University Press.

Ellis, G. and **B. Sinclair.** 1989. *Learning to Learn English: A Course in Learner Training*. Cambridge: Cambridge University Press.

Ehrman, M. 1996. *Understanding Second Language Learning Difficulties*. Thousand Oaks, CA: Sage Publications.

Grabe, W. and **F. Stoller.** 1997. 'A six-T's approach to content-based instruction' in M. Snow and D. Brinton (eds.). *The Content-based Classroom: Perspectives on Integrating Language and Content,*78–94. NY: Longman.

Grenfell, M. and **V. Harris.** 1999. *Modern Languages and Learning Strategies: In Theory and Practice*. London: Routledge.

O'Malley, M. and A. Chamot. 1990. *Learning Strategies in Second Language Acquisition*. Cambridge: Cambridge University Press.

Oxford, R. 1989. *Language Learning Strategies: What Every Teacher Should Know*. Boston, MA: Heinle/Cengage.

——. 2001. 'Language learning styles and strategies' in M. Celce-Murcia (ed.). *Teaching English as a Second or Foreign Language* (3rd edn.), 359–66. Boston: Heinle/Cengage.

Rubin, J. 1975. 'What the 'good language learner' can teach us.' *TESOL Quarterly* 9: 41–51.

Wenden, A. 1985. 'Learner Stategies'. *TESOL Newsletter* 19/1: 4–5, 7.

——. 1991. *Learner Strategies for Learner Autonomy*. London: Prentice-Hall International.

—— and J. Rubin. 1987. *Learner Strategies in Language Learning*. Englewood Cliffs, NJ: Prentice-Hall.

Cooperative Learning

Cohen, E., C. Brody, and M. Sapon-Shevin (eds.). 2004. *Teaching Cooperative Learning: The Challenge for Teacher Education*. Albany, NY: State University of New York Press.

Dishon, D. and P. O'Leary. 1984. *A Guidebook for Cooperative Learning*. Holmes Beach, FL: Learning Publications.

Gillies, R. 2007. *Cooperative Learning: Integrating Theory and Practice*. Thousand Oaks: Sage.

—— and A. Ashman (eds.). 2003. *Co-operative Learning: The Social and Intellectual Outcomes of Learning in Groups*. London: Routledge.

Goodman, M. 1998. 'Cooperative learning. The English Connection.' *The Newsletter of Korea Teachers of English to Speakers of Other Languages* 2/3: 1, 6–7.

Jacobs, G. 1998. 'Cooperative learning or just grouping students: The difference makes a difference' in W. Renandya and G. Jacobs (eds.). *Learners and Language Learning*. Singapore: SEAMEO Regional Language Centre.

Johnson, D., R. Johnson, and E. Johnson Holubec. 1988. *Cooperation in the Classroom*. Edina, MN: Interaction Books.

Kagan, S. 1990. *Cooperative Learning: Resources for Teachers*. San Juan Capistrano, CA: Resources for Teachers.

Kessler, C. (ed.). 1992. *Cooperative Language Learning: A Teacher's Resource Book*. Englewood Cliffs, NJ: Prentice Hall Regents.

McCafferty, S., G. Jacobs, and C. DaSilva Iddings (eds.). 2006. *Cooperative Learning and Second Language Teaching*. Cambridge: Cambridge University Press.

Slavin, R. 1995. *Cooperative Learning* (2nd edn.). Boston, MA: Allyn & Bacon.

Learning Styles

Hatch, E. 1974. 'Second Language Learners—Universals?' *Working Papers on Bilingualism* 3: 1–17.

Larsen-Freeman, D. and **M. Long.** 1991. *An Introduction to Second Language Acquisition Research.* London: Longman.

Levin, J., P. Divine-Hawkins, S. Kerst, and **J. Guttman.** 1974. 'Individual differences in learning from pictures and words: The development and application of an instrument.' *Journal of Educational Psychology* 66/3: 296–303.

Multiple Intelligences

Armstrong, T. 1993. *Seven Kinds of Smart: Discovering and Using your Natural Intelligences.* New York: Plume/Penguin.

———. 1994. *Multiple Intelligences in the Classroom.* Alexandria, VA: ASCD.

Berman, M. 2002. *A Multiple Intelligences Road to an ELT Classroom* (2nd edn.). Carmarthen: Crown House Publishing.

Chen, J-Q., S. Moran, and **H. Gardner** (eds.). 2009. *Multiple Intelligences Around the World.* San Francisco: Jossey-Bass.

Christison, M. 1996. 'Teaching and learning language through multiple intelligences.' *TESOL Journal*, Autumn: 10–14.

———. 2005. Multiple *Intelligences and Language Learning: A Guidebook of Theory, Activities, Inventories, and Resources.* San Francisco, CA: Alta Bank Center Publishers.

Gardner, H. 1983. *Frames of Mind: The Theory of Multiple Intelligences.* New York: Basic Books.

———. 1993. *Multiple Intelligences: The Theory in Practice.* New York: Basic Books.

———. 1999. *Intelligence Reframed. Multiple Intelligences for the 21st Century.* New York: Basic Books.

———. 2006. *Multiple Intelligences: New Horizons in Theory and Practice.* New York: Basic Books.

———. 2007. *Five Minds for the Future.* Cambridge, MA: Harvard Business School Press.

Lazear, D. 1997. *Seven Ways of Teaching: The Artistry of Teaching with Multiple Intelligences.* Arlington Heights, IL: Skylight Publishing.

Puchta, H. and **M. Rinvolucri.** 2007. *Multiple Intelligences in EFL: Exercises for Secondary and Adult Students.* Cambridge: Cambridge University Press.

14

Emerging Uses of Technology in Language Teaching and Learning

Introduction

There are two main ways to think about technology for language learning: technology as providing teaching resources and technology as providing enhanced learning experiences. On the one hand, if we think of technology as providing resources, then it is clear that technology has long been associated with language teaching. For years, the technology may have only been chalk and a blackboard. Later, film strips, audio, and video recording and playback equipment were additions to the technological tools available to many teachers. These days, of course, there are digital technological resources that teachers can draw on. The Internet, which connects millions of computers around the world, makes it possible to communicate from one computer to another. As a result, the **world wide web** (www or 'the web'), a way of accessing information over the Internet, has enabled teachers to find authentic written, audio, and visual texts on most any topic imaginable. There is a breadth and depth of material available for those who know how to surf the web, i.e. use online research tools known as 'search engines' to find it.[1]

Computers also provide the means to access online dictionaries, grammar and style checkers, and **concordances** (which we will discuss later in this chapter). On the other hand, if we think of technology as providing enhanced learning experiences, then the implications are even greater: Technology is no longer simply contributing machinery or making authentic material or more resources available that teachers can use; it also provides learners with greater access to the target language. As a result, it has the potential to change where and when learning takes place. Furthermore, it can even shape how we view the nature of what it is that we teach.

At first glance, neither definition of technology—providing teaching resources and providing enhanced learning experiences—would appear to

[1] For reference to one of the best-known and long-standing websites for teaching English, see page 218.

constitute a method. However, the use of technology for the latter is at least a significant methodological innovation and deserves a place in this book. As Kern has put it:

> Rapid evolution of communication technologies has changed language pedagogy and language use, enabling new forms of discourse, new forms of authorship, and new ways to create and participate in communities.
> (Kern 2006: 183)

A classroom setting with a teacher in front at the blackboard/whiteboard and with students at their desks reading from a textbook, while still the norm in much of the world, is giving way to the practice of students working independently or collaboratively at computers and using other technology, such as cell phones (mobile phones), inside and outside of classrooms. The new discourse, which students use to author and post messages online, has features of both written and oral language, and students participate in online or virtual communities that have no borders.

Even if all their language learning is done in formal learning contexts, learners who have access to computers have more autonomy in what they choose to focus on. With the use of technology, students are more likely to use language for:

> … ongoing identity formation and personally meaningful communication in the service of goals that extend beyond 'practice' or 'learning' in the restrictive senses associated with institutional settings.
> (Thorne 2006: 14)

Technology also allows teaching to be tailored to the individual to a greater extent than is normally possible. A few **Computer-assisted Language Learning (CALL)** programs can even adapt to diverse learners by analyzing their input and providing customized feedback and remedial exercises suited to their proficiency. There are also programs that feature computer adaptive testing so that students respond to test questions at an appropriate level.[2]

Complementing the greater individualization is the greater social interaction that can result from the ability to link students through networked computers. You may recall from our discussion in Chapter 10 the claim that learning takes place through social interaction (Vygotsky 1978). Social interaction helps students co-construct their knowledge by building on one another's experience. The fact that interaction in technology happens mainly through writing means that the interaction is available for later reflection and analysis. Here is how Eric, a student of French, describes learning from e-mail interactions with a native speaker of French:

---

[2] See Heift and Schulz (2003) for an example of a CALL program with this capacity, designed to teach German.

> ... e-mail is kind of like not a written thing ... when you read e-mail, you get conversation but in a written form so you can go back and look at them. ... I've had that experience where conversational constructions appear in an e-mail form from a native speaker of French, which is really neat. Because it doesn't fly by you ...
> (Kramsch and Thorne 2002: 97)

So technology makes possible greater individualization, social interaction, and reflection on language, and inferring from Eric's comments, greater student motivation.

At the same time as technology enhances language learning experiences, it also contributes to reshaping our understanding of the nature of language: Language is not a fixed system. Instead, it is always changing and being changed by those who use it (Larsen-Freeman and Cameron 2008). Because technology allows learners to explore language used in process (for example, Eric's comment above about language in use 'flying by'), it helps make visible the emergent, changing nature of language. In fact, this more dynamic view of language has even been applied to grammar in what Larsen-Freeman (2003) calls **grammaring**. Grammaring is not knowledge of grammar rules, but is rather the ability to use grammar structures accurately, meaningfully, appropriately, and creatively as well.

Despite what technology has to offer, we should always remember:

> ... that it is not technology per se that affects the learning of language and culture but the particular uses of technology. This emphasis on use highlights the central importance of pedagogy and the teacher.
> (Kern 2006: 200)

Technology should be integrated into the curriculum and not just added in because it is new.

Before observing a class, as we customarily do at this point, we are going to introduce a few of the terms that will be used in the lesson. We will elaborate on these terms later in this chapter.

A Blog

A blog (an abbreviation of web+log) is a personal online journal. The author of the journal can update it as often as he or she desires with personal reflections or by adding material from other sources.

A Social Networking Site

A social networking website such as Facebook is accessed via the web (for web address, see page 218). Participants have their own homepage on the site, to which they add personal information, links to other online sources, photos, etc. A participant has 'friends' who are other participants with whom they choose to be connected. If someone is your friend, you can see information and photos he or she has chosen to share.

YouTube

YouTube is a website where one can watch and share short videos (for web address, see page 218). Most YouTube videos are available to anyone who has a high-speed connection to the Internet. The range of topics is vast, including actual videos from language classrooms, lectures, and small vignettes from everyday life.

Wiki

A wiki is a quick way of being able to create and edit web-documents. Wikis are very useful in collaborative writing tasks, and they are very good for highlighting and observing the process of writing.

Electronic Text Corpus

An electronic text corpus is a collection of authentic spoken and written texts, often consisting of thousands, if not millions, of words. The corpus is computer-searchable. A teacher or a student can find many instances of a particular word or phrase as it is used in a sentence. The instances can then be analyzed for the form, meaning, and use of a word or expression, its frequency, and for what precedes and what follows it in a sentence.

Experience

Now, we turn to the experience. The following class takes place at an English language institute in Thailand. The class consists of 16 students between the ages of 16 and 30, who are high-intermediate learners of English. They meet for one and one-half hours two times a week. The classes are held in the evening because the students are also attending school or working at jobs. The institute has classrooms equipped with the following technology: a computer and a liquid crystal display (LCD) projector, an overhead projector, and a TV and VCR/DVD unit. There are two computer labs in the institute, each having 20 computers, offering high-speed Internet access and printers. In addition, the entire building is a wireless zone for Internet use. The class meets in one of the computer labs. The lab is set up with computer tables topped by computers around the edges of the room, facing the wall. This allows the teacher to have students turn their chairs to face inwards to form a circle for discussion and then easily turn back to work on the computers.

Prior to this lesson the students have been required to participate regularly in three online tasks. First, they have been asked to maintain an online blog, in which they regularly record their experiences in learning English. Some students have used this as a record of new vocabulary or to comment on a particular English language website they have found useful. Other students have chosen to use their blog for personal reflection. These students write about what is happening in the class or what they are learning. They also discuss experiences they are having in finding ways to use the language or reactions that others (such as tourists and visitors) have to their use of English. Each student has also been told to comment on at least three other classmates' blogs every week.

As a second ongoing task, the students have created a profile on a social networking site. Their teacher has chosen to use Facebook, where many of the students had a profile already. The students have to log on to Facebook a minimum of three times per week in order to read what their classmates have posted and to update their 'status'. They have also been encouraged to respond to the status updates of their classmates. In addition, as is the nature of social networking sites, the students each have their own set of 'friends', who are not members of the class and with whom they also exchange information and updates.

For the final ongoing task, the students are asked to do some research for the wiki that they have created with classmates. Earlier in the course, they chose a topic that they wanted the world to know about. They chose traditional Thai dance forms. On an ongoing basis they edit a wiki document on this topic, adding information and links to external websites and commenting on each other's contributions.

Some of the students have also chosen to correspond with 'e-pen pals', and some even chat electronically in real time with their pen pals. The teacher has helped match these students with Australians that she met when she was a student herself at the Australian National University in Canberra.

As the class begins, there is lively chatter about the assignments they have been working on, both in English and in Thai. The teacher greets the students, also in both languages. With each student now seated at his and her own computer, the teacher asks the students to check their language learning blogs and to read any new comments that have been made to their blog entries. The teacher peers over the shoulders of each student to look at the computer screen and to make sure that the assignment has been done. After giving the students a chance to check their blogs, the teacher asks the students to turn their chairs inwards to form a discussion circle. She begins the discussion by asking 'How many of you have received comments on your blogs?' All the students raise their hands. 'Did you receive any comments that were surprising?' 'Did you receive any comments from someone not in the class?' 'Who is willing to share a comment?'[3] One student, Tuk, says, 'I received a comment from an English language student in Jakarta, Indonesia, who wants to know if I use a word that I had written, "segue," in my everyday speaking. This Indonesian student, Dedi, said he had only seen this word written and never spoken.' The teacher asked for ideas from the class. 'How might Tuk respond to Dedi's comment? How have you heard the word "segue" used?' she asks. Many students have not heard the word before; those that are familiar with the word have only seen it in print. The teacher tells the class that later in the lesson they will use a computer corpus to see what they can learn about 'segue'.

A second student, Lek, says, 'I received a comment from an English student in Costa Rica, named Alejandro, that I don't understand.' The teacher asks, 'How can we help Lek understand what Alejandro was trying to tell her?' The class switches to a mixture of English and Thai for a few minutes as they brainstorm the best ways to respond to Alejandro. Lek thinks that she will be able to use the suggestions of her teacher and classmate to communicate with Alejandro.

Next, the teacher asks the students to form pairs at a computer. She tells them to take turns opening up their Facebook pages and reviewing together what has been posted there. There is a good deal of laughter as many posts are funny. One student in the class, Sunni, had written on his 'wall' (the location on Facebook where individuals can share their current status), 'I love coffee.' Other Facebook friends commented on the wall: 'If you love coffee, marry it.' and 'Aren't you getting enough sleep?' On his wall, Sunni also read an invitation to get coffee at a nearby café from a member of the class, Waew. He turned around and called over to her saying, 'Sure. Let's drink coffee. How about after class?'

After 10 minutes, the teacher asks the students again to turn their chairs to form a circle. She asks a few questions: 'What idioms or special use of English did you encounter or use on your Facebook page?' 'What do you think these idioms mean?' 'Did you try to use any new language on Facebook?'

Lam tells the class that she used the idiom 'get a grip' on Facebook. The students compare their ideas on the meaning of 'get a grip'. The teacher then suggests that they consult an online corpus, the British National Corpus (for web address, see page 218). (The British National Corpus (BNC) is a 100-million word collection of samples of written and spoken language from a wide range of sources). They type in the words 'get a grip,' and they are taken to a page with 50 examples of this expression (a concordance), each used in a sentence.

---

[3] Comments from people not in the class are possible only if the blog is set up that way at the beginning. This is a choice teachers have to make—public or private blogs.

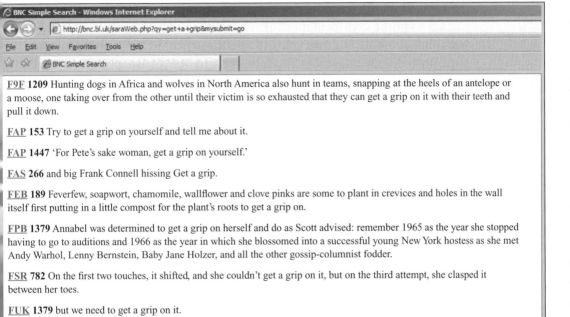

Screenshot 14.1   A partial concordance: the expression 'get a grip' from the BNC.

The teacher asks then what they notice about the phrase 'get a grip.' The students quickly realize that it is always, or almost always, followed by the preposition 'on.' In checking further examples, they see that it can sometimes be followed by the preposition 'of.' They note that it was also used as a command 'Get a grip!' They discuss whether or not this form has a different meaning from the phrase with 'on' in it. With the teacher's guidance, they see that 'get a grip' could be used literally to mean a physical hold or more metaphorically to mean in control. They then go to an online dictionary and type 'get a grip on' and find out that it means 'to obtain mastery or control over something or someone' and that it can also occur with the verb 'have.' The teacher asks them to make up a few sentences with the phrase, which they then read out loud as she checks.

They also do a corpus search and create a concordance for Tuk's word 'segue.' They discover that it is only used infrequently—there were only two instances in the entire 100-million word BNC. Moreover, one of them was in the name of a company, and both instances were found in written texts. They concluded that the Indonesian student was probably right. It probably is not likely to be used often in conversation. Tuk says that she will let him know.

The teacher tells the students again to turn back to their computers in pairs. The teacher directs the pairs to a YouTube site, where they watch a rock band performing its latest hit song. The students watch the video and listen to the song. Then the teacher tells them, 'Please now work together with your partner to post a comment on your reactions to the performance. What did you think about it? Did you enjoy the performance? Why?' They follow the same procedure with another YouTube site, this one focusing on diet-related health concerns. Most of the pairs focus on the postings on their page and work together on writing and co-editing clever and relevant comments in response. One of the pairs asks the teacher which is correct: 'There's a lot of reasons to like this performance' or 'There are a lot of reasons to like this performance.' The teacher replies that the second sentence is correct according to the grammar rule, but sentences like the first sentence are often used by native speakers of English these days.

The final step in the lesson is for the students to do a quick review of their wiki project. For this step, they work in small groups, with each working at one computer. Each group has decided upon a particular Thai dance to research and write about. There is not time in the class on that day to add any new material; the teacher tells them they will do this in the next class. For now, the members of each group are helping each other decide what they need to add or how to improve what is on the wiki. Later in the semester, they will be making group presentations in class on their dances, using PowerPoint slides.

The assignment for the next class is threefold. Students should:

1 Update their blogs.
2 Visit and update their Facebook pages and respond to classmates' pages.
3 Think about and do some research on the wiki topic. They should each write a rough draft of the new material that they want to add, and e-mail it to the teacher before the next class. The teacher will comment on their drafts, return the drafts to them electronically, and archive, or save the students' drafts in an electronic portfolio that she has created for each student.

Thinking about the Experience

Let us review some observations on the lesson and see what principles underlie them.

Observations	Principles
1 As the class begins, there is lively chatter about the assignments that the students have been working on.	Students find online tasks to be motivating.

2	The teacher asks the students to form a circle where they can see each other face to face.	Language learning takes place through social interaction.
3	Students choose comments from their blogs to share.	Students are autonomous in what they share about themselves.
4	The language that they work on comes from comments that language learners in other parts of the world have made on their blogs.	Students work on authentic language, which comes from interactions with others through online or virtual communities.
5	The teacher works with the students, and the students work together to understand a confusing message and to determine how to respond to it.	Learning to negotiate meaning is important.
6	Students use their native language to discuss a response.	Use of students' native language can aid comprehension.
7	The teacher is not focused on specific language items, but rather responds to what language emerges as a result of the students' online work.	There is less interest in linguistic structure and more interest in helping students deal with specific communicative situations using the language resources that are available to them.
8	Students have created a Facebook page with their profile.	Students construct their online identities in a way that is comfortable for them.
9	Students read their Facebook pages in pairs.	Language is learned by using it.
10	Sunni says 'Let's drink coffee.' While this is grammatically accurate, it is not the way that an English speaker would convey this message. However, the teacher does not correct him.	Native speaker usage is not necessarily what the aim is.
11	They consult a concordance and an online dictionary to work on a phrase.	Students are taught to use the tools that technology provides. Reflecting on language and developing language awareness are important.

12 Students observe what precedes and what follows a particular word or phrase.	Language consists of patterns, including collocations, or words that go together.
13 They observe that 'segue' is not used very frequently.	Knowing the frequency with which a word is used is part of learning to use a language.
14 Students watch YouTube videos and write a response.	Students need to become literate in the new technology.
15 Students co-edit their responses.	Students can learn from each other.
16 In response to a student question about which sentence is correct, the teacher answers that one of the sentences is correct according to the grammar rule, but the other is used by native speakers of the language.	Language is changed through use. It is a dynamic and evolving entity.
17 Students choose what to write and which topics to research.	Students have a good deal of freedom in choosing what they will engage with in and out of class.
18 Students are to write a rough draft of their wiki update and e-mail it to the teacher. She adds it to each student's electronic portfolios. The teacher reads the updated version and gives them feedback.	Teachers use archives of online student work to evaluate and to guide them.

Reviewing the Principles

1 What are the goals of the teacher?

The teacher seeks to provide students with access to authentic language. The language should be used in interaction with others and in relation to knowledge creation. Learning to use technology to support one's language learning is also important because it makes students more autonomous learners.

2 What is the role of the teacher? What is the role of the students?

The teacher's role is to plan activities that students accomplish via technological means. Then the teacher monitors their work and guides the students as they learn the language. The students' role is to be actively involved in using the language, in taking risks with the language by connecting with others, and in exploring information via the target language. Students help each other to learn.

3 What are some characteristics of the teaching–learning process?

Learning languages through the use of technology brings learners into contact with authentic language use. Student-generated language is what is focused upon. Since it is understood that language learning is a non-linear process, there is no particular pre-set order to the language items that are learned. Language is emergent, dynamic, and continuously evolving. It is influenced both by the topical focus and by the personal relationships that are developing. Cultivating students' language awareness is important. Much online work involves reading and writing; therefore, a good portion of class time involves speaking and listening in the target language. A language is learned by using it (**emergentism**—Ellis and Larsen-Freeman 2006).

4 What is the nature of student–teacher interaction? What is the nature of student–student interaction?

The teacher guides the process while students enjoy a great deal of autonomy over what is focused on and on how the tasks are achieved. Student-to-student interaction can take a number of forms, including students working together on websites or blogs, editing one another's writing, and participating in online discussions, called 'online chats.'

5 How are the feelings of the students dealt with?

Students are motivated by online tasks. They are able to choose how they wish to represent themselves in their profiles on social networks and in online communities. They enjoy autonomy in what they want to focus on and learn about.

6 How is language viewed? How is culture viewed?

Language is seen as a tool for social interaction, relationship building, and for knowledge creation. It is used for communication. Native speaker usage is not necessarily the model or indeed the goal. Language consists of patterns. Some language patterns are stable, and others are reshaped through use. Students learn about the everyday life or culture of speakers of the target language through their online interactions, such as those from e-pen pals. They can also 'visit' and learn virtually about different parts of the world.

7 What areas of language are emphasized? What language skills are emphasized?

Personal statements, sharing of opinion or facts, reporting and reflecting are emphasized. Computer use naturally requires the skills of reading and writing, although speaking and listening may also be worked on depending on the type(s) of technology used. Because of the emphasis on the written medium, class time can be profitably spent in face-to-face interaction.

8 What is the role of the students' native language?

A student's native language can be used for communication and support for learning the target language, as needed.

9 How is evaluation accomplished?

Evaluation is handled via an electronic or virtual portfolio of student work that a teacher archives.

10 How does the teacher respond to student errors?

Given the dynamic environment that technology affords, editing one's own work is an ongoing process. Therefore, errors are not a preoccupation of the teacher. Language use is creative and forgiving. New forms and uses of language are constantly emerging. Students have a record of their interaction and can always return to it to improve it, if they want to or if the teacher directs them to.

Reviewing the Techniques

Technology Used for Providing Language Learning Experiences

Here is a brief review of some of the options that teachers use. This review includes options not featured in the Experience above but ones that you should be aware of. It would not be possible to include all of the options within a single lesson, and, of course, the options are always increasing—given the rate of development in the field.

- **Blogs**

  One rich source of language texts are blogs, which can be thought of as online diaries or journals. The word comes from a combination of 'web' + 'log.' Blogs can be private and controlled with passwords, or public, depending on the desire of the author. Most blogs allow for visitors to post comments. Since blogs are written by people remarking on their travels, daily life, current events, etc., they are a rich source of authentic material for reading, discussion, and study. Blogs are available in many languages and are often created as an open source, which makes them searchable via any browser and search engine. Some blogs are specifically devoted to the author's language learning process or his or her experience in teaching a language. Searching on the web for 'language learning blogs' will yield some interesting sites. Students can also be encouraged to create and write their own blogs as a regular assignment or ongoing reflective activity. In this way, they are not always writing only for the teacher. Since blog entries are chronologically ordered, students and teacher can create a progressive archive of student work.

- **Computer-assisted Language Learning Software**
There is a wide variety of Computer-assisted Language Learning (CALL) software (computer programs) and/or websites available for use by language learners. Some of the CALL programs are open source, which means that they are free and can easily be downloaded onto individual computers; others can be purchased. Some CALL programs focus on specific elements of language such as vocabulary or grammar practice. Others have a reading comprehension focus or provide guidance and practice for improving pronunciation. As with any materials for teachers or learners, there is a range of quality and usefulness among CALL programs.

- **Digital Portfolios**
We saw in the lesson that we observed that the teacher was compiling a digital archive or portfolio of student work. In this way, the teacher has a file of student work that she can add to throughout the term. The European Language Portfolio is a standardized portfolio assessment tool that students can use to document their language learning experience and proficiency.

- **Distance Education**
One of the applications of technology to language teaching is in the direct delivery of language instruction via the web. An advantage of web-based instruction is that it provides access to languages that might not be available otherwise. For instance, recently the University of California, Los Angeles (UCLA) went live with its web-based instructional programs in Azeri and the Iraqi dialect of Arabic. This development allows UCLA to send language instruction to other campuses of the University of California system, and in turn to receive instructional programs in Danish, Filipino, Khmer, and Zulu from the University of California, Berkeley. Such exchanges present a partial solution to the problem of keeping

alive the less commonly taught, even endangered, languages. Although most research suggests that blended or hybrid instruction, which is some combination of face-to-face and distance education, is better than total distance education, obviously distance education is better than having no opportunity to study a language at all.

- **Electronic Chatting**
Electronic chatting is a synchronous activity: At least two people must be online simultaneously in order to chat. While the great majority of chats are in writing, there is also a fast-growing number that also offer voice or video communication. Skype is perhaps the best known example (for web address, see page 218). It allows for real spoken communication across countries and continents. It could also be used locally, of course. For example, the teacher might have students conduct an interview of a local celebrity, using the target language.

- **E-Pen Pals**
Once the use of e-mail became somewhat common, it was natural to use it for communicating with electronic or 'e-pen pals.' Sometimes, the pen pal connections originate out of relationships between 'sister schools,' extended family ties, or the personal networks of language teachers. Similar to the original pen pal idea, students are encouraged to share in writing about themselves, their lives, and their cultures in the target language. There are a number of models or designs for the e-pen pal approach. Sometimes, teachers provide guiding questions that students can use to communicate with their e-pen pal (such as 'How would you describe your town?' 'What is distinctive about your community?' 'What would a day in your school be like?' 'Tell your pal about your family.'). Another approach has students focusing on specific topics, such as current events.

- **Electronic Presentations**
Microsoft's PowerPoint is a tool that allows presenters to use templates with a variety of formats to create slides for presentations. They can be multimedia, using text, images, sound, animation, and video. The slides are presented by a computer hooked up to an LCD projector. PowerPoint is being used by increasing numbers of teachers and students for in-class presentations.

- **Electronic Text Corpora**
Electronic text corpora are collections of language texts, most often written, but sometimes spoken texts in transcript form. The texts have been digitized and are therefore computer-searchable. By entering a word

or a phrase into a website, a concordance, a list with the target item as it is used in limited contexts, is produced. Knowing the distribution and frequency of linguistic forms can be very helpful to language learners. Some of the corpora are free to use, and others you must pay for. Corpora for specific purposes or professions are also available.

Corpus analysis, a form of linguistic research, provides data on the real-world uses of words and collocations across various **genres**, **registers**, and language varieties. Pedagogically, it can be used to support data-driven learning, that is, language study where learners analyze language features based on corpus evidence. Certain corpus linguists have based language teaching materials mostly or entirely on their corpus findings (Sinclair 2004; McCarthy 1998; Biber et al. 1998). Other methodologists advise that teaching materials should not be corpus-driven, but rather corpus-informed.

- ### Cell Phone-based Applications: Text Messaging and Twitter

With the rapid expansion of the use of cell or mobile phones throughout the world, language learners have found new ways of learning. Users of text messaging and Twitter have developed their own form of language. Twitter is an instant messaging system that lets people send brief (no more than 140 characters) text messages to a set of interested people on any activity or event in which they are participating or opinion they wish to offer. The language used is typically informal, where the written language 'sounds' more like spoken language. For example, 'R U OK?' (Are you OK?) is a commonly used expression.

- ### Podcasts

Podcasts are digital audio and visual recordings that can be created and downloaded (moved from the Internet to an individual computer). You can watch and share such recordings on YouTube. Most YouTube recordings are available to anyone who has a high-speed connection to the Internet. The range of topics is vast, including actual videos from language classrooms, lectures, and small vignettes from everyday life.

- ### Social Networking

Social networking sites include Facebook, My Space, LinkedIn, to name a few of the dozens that are in existence. The purpose of such sites is for participants to share thoughts, activities, photos, videos, and links to websites with others whom they are connected to through their social network site. Through the network provided at the site, one can share a key event or idea with many other participants simultaneously. The whole class can have fun with these. Students do not have to be highly proficient in a language in order to participate. You should be aware, though, of privacy concerns. Once you or your students post a message online, it can be available to anyone who is a friend or a friend of friends. You need therefore to educate yourself and others on Internet safety.

Screenshot 14.2   Example of a Facebook site

• Wikis

The prefix 'wiki' comes from the Hawaiian expression 'wiki wiki', which means 'quick', and it refers to a quick way to create and edit web-documents. Wikis can be very useful in collaborative writing tasks. Multiple authors— a group of students—can write one text together. A good wiki-tool will keep track of authorship of the different versions/parts of the document that the students are creating. In this way the teacher can have a record of the students' writing as a process. The other concept associated with wikis is *wabi-sabi*. It refers to things always being changeable—never finished, never perfect.

Wikipedia is a shared online encyclopedia (for web address, see page 218). What makes it unique is that anyone can contribute information on a topic, so the information is always being updated.

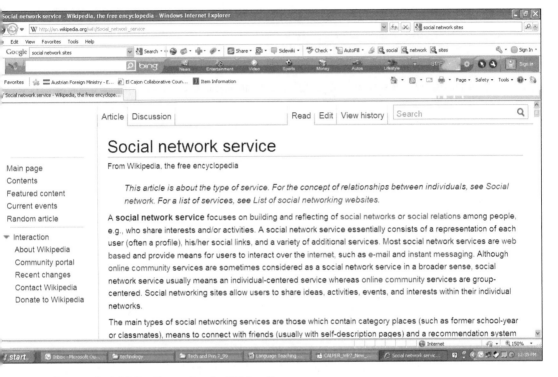

Screenshot 14.3   Example of a Wikipedia page

Not everything that is published on Wikipedia is accurate; however, information and knowledge about a topic change, and the good thing is that wikis are able to reflect these changes.

For example, for the concept of global warming, a user-participant begins by describing what he knows about the topic. Within days, several other participants add to what was shared by the first. Over weeks and months, the information about global warming becomes richer and deeper. Then, participants add links to other, related Wikipedia topics, such as fossil fuels, changing weather patterns, the Kyoto agreement, etc. More references are added each week, and gradually the Wikipedia explanation of global warming has become enriched through the shared efforts of all those who choose to participate.

Conclusion

Technology is always evolving, and new forms of connection are constantly being developed. We realize, therefore, that any technology we refer to in this chapter will likely change in the coming months. Still, we felt that it was important to discuss the use of technology in providing enhanced language learning experiences.

Although this is the last methodological innovation we introduce in this book, it does not mean that we have saved the best for last or that technology should be used by everyone. For one thing, not everyone has access to the technology described here, although having even one computer in class can be helpful. For another, the use of technology is not any more neutral than any other method or medium. For example, Reeder, Macfadyen, Roche, and Chase (2004) claim that certain e-tools for communication and education are based on Western-style notions of efficiency, and they question whether they are necessarily appropriate for international groups of learners. Nonetheless, there is no doubt that technology will have an increasing presence in education. What is important from our perspective is that teachers be knowledgeable about technology, and if they choose to use it, that they do so in pedagogically sound ways. We agree with van Lier who wrote:

> … if [technology] is to be a positive force in education, [it] should not be cast as an alternative to classroom teaching, or as replacing the teacher, but as a tool that facilitates meaningful and challenging classroom work. (van Lier 2003: 2)

With this in mind, can you see yourself integrating the use of technology with your teaching approach? Which of the techniques presented in this chapter are you likely to make use of? How will you build into your teaching what students do outside of the classroom?

Activities

Ⓐ Check your understanding of how technology can be used in language teaching.

1　What is the difference between the use of technology to provide resources for teaching and the use of technology to provide enhanced language learning experiences? What are some examples of each?
2　How can technology be used to construct authentic social relationships, both virtual and face-to-face?

B **Apply what you understand about using technology for language teaching.**

1   If you cannot set up your classroom in the same manner as the one described in the Experience, how could you combine face-to-face discussions with time students spend on a computer elsewhere such as in an Internet café?

2   What is your position on the emergent nature of language in a technology-driven classroom? Should all usages be accepted?

References/Additional Resources

Biber, D., S. Conrad, and R. Reppen. 1998. *Corpus Linguistics: Investigating Language Structure and Use*. Cambridge: Cambridge University Press.

Chapelle, C. 2003. *English Language Learning and Technology*. Amsterdam: John Benjamins.

Egbert, J. 2008. *Supporting Learning with Technology: Essentials of Classroom Practice*. Upper Saddle River, NJ: Merrill/Prentice-Hall.

Ellis, N. and D. Larsen-Freeman. 2006. 'Language emergence: implications for applied linguistics.' *Applied Linguistics* 27/4: 558–89.

Heift, T. and M. Schulze. 2003. 'Student modeling and ab initio language learning.' *System* 31: 519–35.

Kern, R. 2006. 'Perspectives on technology in learning and teaching languages.' *TESOL Quarterly* 40/1: 183–210.

Kramsch, C. and S. Thorne. 2002. 'Foreign language learning as global communicative practice' in D. Block and D. Cameron (eds.). *Globalization and Language Teaching*, 83–100. London: Routledge.

Larsen-Freeman, D. 2003. *Teaching Language: From Grammar to Grammaring*. Boston: Heinle/Cengage.

—— and L. Cameron. 2008. *Complex Systems and Applied Linguistics*. Oxford: Oxford University Press.

Lewis, G. 2009. *Bringing Technology into the Classroom*. Oxford: Oxford University Press.

McCarthy, M. 1998. *Spoken Language and Applied Linguistics*. Cambridge: Cambridge University Press.

Morrison, G. and D. Lowther. 2005. *Integrating Computer Technology into the Classroom*. Upper Salle River, NJ: Pearson Education.

Oxford, R. and J. Oxford (eds.). 2009. *Second Language Teaching and Learning in the Net Generation*. Honolulu HI: National Foreign Language Resource Center.

Pritchard. A. 2007. *Effective Teaching with Internet Technologies*. London: Paul Chapman Publishing.

Reeder, K., L. Macfadyen, J. Roche, and **M. Chase.** 2004. 'Negotiating cultures in cyberspace: Participation patterns and problematics.' *Language Learning and Technology* 8/2: 88–105.

Sinclair, J. (ed.). 2004. *How to Use Corpora in Language Teaching*. Philadelphia: John Benjamins.

Thorne, S. 2006. New Technologies and Additional Language Learning. *CALPER Working Papers Series*, No. 7. Pennsylvania State University: Center for Advanced Language Proficiency, Education and Research.

van Lier, L. 2003. 'A tale of two computer classrooms: The ecology of project-based language learning' in J. Leather and J. van Dam (eds.). *The Ecology of Language Acquisition*, 49–64. Dordrecht: Kluwer Academic.

——. 1998. 'All hooked up: An ecological look at computers in the classroom' in J. Fisiak (ed.). *Studia Anglica Posnaniensia* XXXIII, 281–301. Berlin: Mouton De Gruyter.

Vygotsky, L. 1978. *Mind and Society: The Development of Higher Mental Processes*. Cambridge, MA: Harvard University Press.

Warshauer, M. 2003. *Technology and Social Inclusion: Rethinking the Digital Divide*. Cambridge, MA: MIT Press.

Warschauer, M., H. Shetzer, and **C. Meloni.** 2000. *Internet for English Teaching*. Alexandria, VA: TESOL Publications.

Additional Resources

There are also two online journals: *Calico Journal* (see below) and *Language Learning and Technology* (see below).They can be helpful in keeping up-to-date with language learning and technology.

Websites

http://www.eslcafe.com/

http://www.facebook.com

http://www.youtube.com

http://www.natcorp.ox.ac.uk

http://www.wikipedia.com

http://www.skype.com

http://www.calico.org

http://llt.msu.edu

15

Conclusion

Introduction

Now that we have considered the methods individually, it will be useful to view them collectively. The table on pages 222–3 has been compiled to summarize each method/approach/methodological innovation with regard to which aspects of language/culture are focused upon, how the method seeks to promote language learning, and the associated language teaching practices. What is in the table is selective, highlighting only major features of each method or approach.

While this table provides a useful summary of the methods/approaches concerning the global categories of language/culture, learning, and teaching, there are three limitations to presenting information in this form. One is that this table fails to capture the dynamics of methodological change. Second, it obscures the similarities that exist among the methods. Third, there are certain areas of difference that are not revealed by treating the categories globally. Each of these three areas will be discussed in turn.

The Dynamics of Methodological Change

While it is true, as was mentioned at the beginning of this book, that all of these methods are being practiced today, it is also true that they are not equally distributed in classrooms around the world. In some parts of the world, certain older language teaching methods, such as the Grammar-Translation Method, have endured for years. Similarly, the Direct Method has been preserved in particular commercial language teaching enterprises, such as the Berlitz Schools.

In other parts of the world, some of these methods have had more influence during certain times than at others. For instance, in the USA in the 1950s and 1960s, although other language teaching methods were practiced, the Audio-Lingual Method was clearly dominant. When Noam Chomsky challenged the view that language was a set of patterns acquired through habit formation, its influence began to wane. Following its decline, the field entered into a period of great methodological diversity in the 1970s and early 1980s (Larsen-Freeman 1987), a period in which a number of 'innovative methods' emerged, such as the Silent Way (1972), Community Language Learning (1976), Total Physical Response (1977), Suggestopedia (1978), and the Natural Approach (1983).

Interest in developing students' communicative competence reunified the field in the 1980s. Although certainly the Communicative Approach has not been universally adopted (Ellis 1996; Li 1998), many teachers around the world report that they use CLT, even if their interpretation of its principles varies greatly. It seems then that it is primarily evolving conceptions of language that spurred change.

By way of contrast, innovation in the language teaching field in the late 1980s and 1990s has been stimulated by a special concern for the language learning process. New methods propose that language learning is best served when students are interacting—completing a task or learning content or resolving real-life issues—where linguistic structures are not taught one by one, but where attention to linguistic form is given as necessary. These views of language learning have been informed by research in second language acquisition. Also giving learning a special focus are methodological innovations of the late 1980s and 1990s. These include teaching learning strategies, using cooperative learning, and planning lessons in such a way that different intelligences are addressed.

In the 2000s so far, it seems that changes in the language teaching field have been made in response to two influences from outside the field. One is the continuing development of technology. Much of the language learning in the world takes place in classrooms, though this may be changing with the possibility for more autonomous learning, aided by technological advances. For example, in a new study conducted in Austria, it was reported that 15 percent of Austrians over the age of 15 have learned one or more foreign languages outside of high school or university in the last 10 years. Much of the autonomous learning is taking place through social networking sites, listening to popular music, and watching undubbed movies and television shows. With increasing access to popular media available in different languages through the world wide web, it is clear that the potential of technology has hardly been realized. Then, too, it is likely in the foreseeable future that there will be more corpus-informed teaching materials and more courses delivered entirely online or in blended format, combining online with face-to-face instruction.

The other external influence comes from **globalization**. While globalization also may not be a new phenomenon, there is no doubt that with growing transnational population flows, there has been increased demand for workers having proficiency in different languages. Further, seeing language proficiency as a means for economic advancement has also led to the perception that knowledge of languages is an indispensable tool. This has resulted in calls for starting language instruction at younger and younger ages and for enhanced efficiency in instruction, such as the 'two-for-one' promise of content-based teaching. Moreover, this utilitarian view of language has meant that language is taught apart from culture,[1] with cultural values often being deemed irrelevant.

Responding to the potential for exploitation that can accompany globalization is a critical approach to pedagogy. In critical pedagogy, language is not seen as something politically neutral, and it is not the exclusive property of native speakers. There is also an appreciation for how much of one's identity comes from speaking a particular language or languages (Norton 2011). Therefore, some believe that holding learners to native-speaker standards is inappropriate and unnecessary. As Ortega (2010) notes, in much SLA research, monolingualism is taken as the norm, with the goal of second language acquisition being an unnecessary, and often unattainable, monolingual-like performance in another language. Instead, it should not be monolinguals with whom emergent bilinguals (Garcia and Kleifgen 2010) are compared, but rather other proficient users of the target language.

In the category of external influences in the language teaching field could also be governmental national and international language policies. For example, in the USA there has been growing support for the teaching of languages deemed 'critical' for political or security purposes (Larsen-Freeman and Freeman 2008), and in countries comprising the former Soviet Union, Russian language programs have been terminated.

While teachers' roles may be redefined by technology, their responsibilities have multiplied in other ways. For instance, with proponents of the Participatory Approach reminding us of the political nature of language teaching, some teachers are assuming the role of advocates—not only advocates on behalf of their disempowered students, but also advocates on such topics as the treatment of immigrants, environmental issues, ethical issues concerning globalization, social issues such as AIDS education, and international education issues such as calls for world peace education (Gomes de Matos 2006). Such teachers feel that they can no longer be content to teach language in classrooms ignoring issues in their own and their students' lives outside the classroom walls (Clarke 2003).

[1] Although some (Kramsch 2011) see this as an impossibility.

Method/Approach/Innovation	Language/Culture
Grammar-Translation	Literary language Culture: Literature and the fine arts
Direct Method	Everyday spoken language Culture: History, geography, everyday life of target language (TL) speakers
Audio-Lingual Method	Sentence and sound patterns
Cognitive Code Approach	Grammar rules
Silent Way	Unique spirit/melody
Desuggestopedia	Whole, meaningful texts; vocabulary emphasized
Community Language Learning	Created by a community
Comprehension Approach: Natural Approach, *The Learnables*, and Total Physical Response	Vehicle for communicating meaning; vocabulary emphasized
Communicative Language Teaching	Communicative competence Notions/functions
Content-based Instruction	Language is a medium
Task-based Language Teaching	Language is meaningful—useful for accomplishing certain tasks in the world
Participatory Approach	Political Not the property of native speakers of the language
Learning Strategy Training, Cooperative Learning, and Multiple Intelligences	
Technology in Language Teaching and Learning	Dynamic, ever changing

Language Learning	Language Teaching
Exercise mental muscle.	Have students translate from target language (TL) texts to native language.
Associate meaning with the TL directly.	Use spoken language in situations with no L1 translation.
Overcome native language habits; form new TL habits.	Conduct oral/aural drills and pattern practice.
Form and test hypotheses to discover and acquire TL rules.	Do inductive/deductive grammar exercises.
Develop inner criteria for correctness by becoming aware of how the TL works.	Remain silent in order to subordinate teaching to learning. Focus student attention; provide meaningful practice.
Overcome psychological barriers to learning.	Desuggest limitations: teach lengthy dialogues through musical accompaniment, playful practice, and the arts.
Learn nondefensively as whole persons, following developmental stages.	Include the elements of security, attention, aggression, reflection, retention, discrimination.
Listen; associate meaning with TL directly.	Delay speaking until students are ready; make meaning clear through actions and visuals.
Interact with others in the TL; negotiate meaning.	Use communicative activities: information gaps, role-plays, games.
Learn language through engaging with meaningful content.	Teach language and content at the same time—have objectives and activities for both.
Learn by doing.	Engage in tasks with clear outcomes.
Learn from working on real-life issues of power.	Dialogue with students, pose problems, and problem solve.
Learn how to learn.	Teach learning strategies, cooperation; use a variety of activities that appeal to different intelligences/minds.
Language emerges through use. It is reshaped by experience.	Provide enhanced learning experiences in which students are more autonomous.

Table 15.1 Comparison of different methods and approaches

Despite the recognition within the field that decision-making authority for educational matters should rest with local educators, there seems to be a resistance to this notion from outside the field. As Clarke (2007) argues, teachers should have the say in educational matters, but this is not always the case, given today's political reality. Decisions affecting education beyond the control of teachers can be seen in the increasing reliance on language examinations and in the demand for more effective preparation and in-service professional development for teachers. There are also widespread calls for establishing standards. As Richards (2008) expresses it:

> The standards movement has taken hold in many parts of the world and promotes the adoption of clear statements of instructional outcomes in educational programs as a way of improving learning outcomes in programs and to provide guidelines for program development, curriculum development, and assessment.
> Richards (2008:172)

Of course, examinations, teacher education, and standards are not in and of themselves worrisome. Everyone wants education to be conducted to the highest possible standards, but how that is to be accomplished is what is disputed. We will return to this point later in the chapter, but for now we will discuss the similarities and differences of the methods presented in this book, and summarized on pages 222–3.

Similarities among Language Teaching Methods

In displaying the essential features of the language teaching methods in table form, it is the salient differences that get highlighted. Not apparent from this display is the fact that these methods overlap in significant ways as well. Despite there being continued debate on what communication entails, and on the means to bring it about, it is nevertheless true that one of the most important similarities in many of these methods is that their goal has been to teach students to communicate in the target language.

Those who advocate content-based, task-based, and participatory approaches have another thing in common. They rely on analytic syllabi, believing that the best way to achieve communicative proficiency in a language is to use it, not learn it bit by bit. In other words, students should learn to communicate by communicating.

Another similarity, which has only recently become obvious, is that all of the language teaching methods described in this book are practiced in classrooms in schools. With the increasing influence of technology, this may not be the case in the future. Classroom instruction is already often supplemented with visits to the computer lab. In certain situations, distance education may make classes, fixed schedules, and learning in face-to-face groups obsolete.

Finally, it is interesting to note that most of these methods seem to treat culture implicitly, having no clearly articulated view of it or its teaching. Certain methods, such as Desuggestopedia, make use of the fine arts, but the arts themselves are not the object of study; rather they are drawn upon to facilitate the acquisition of the target language. Where culture is included, it may be seen as a 'fifth' skill, another skill to teach in addition to reading, writing, speaking, and listening. Alternatively, as noted earlier in this chapter, there may be a deliberate attempt, in the case of those who teach international languages, to omit explicit teaching of culture, even though it is known that culture values are transmitted through language (Kramsch 1993) and language teaching methods.

Complementary and Contradictory Differences among Language Teaching Methods

There are also differences among the methods, which get lost on a selective table such as ours. There are two particular kinds of differences. The first is one we might call complementary differences. While each method may emphasize a different perspective on a learner, a teacher, or learning, taken together, they do not necessarily contradict each other, but rather help us to construct a more complete view. For instance, the language learner is not only a mimic, but is also a cognitive, affective, social, and political being. The same applies to the role of the language teacher—not only is the teacher a model, a drill conductor and a linguist, but possibly also a counselor, facilitator, technician, collaborator, learner trainer, and most recently, an advocate (Larsen-Freeman 1998a).

The other type of difference is one that is contradictory. For instance, notice that the use of the students' native language in the Direct Method and Comprehension Approach (Chapter 8) is proscribed, whereas in the Grammar-Translation Method and Community Language Learning, it is prescribed. Most recently, the restriction to avoid use of the students' language has been challenged, with the students' L1 not being seen as an impediment to, but rather as a resource for language learning (Widdowson 2003; Cook 2010).

Witness also the divergent views regarding the level of control of the input that learners receive, from highly controlled input in the Audio-Lingual Method, to less controlled in the Natural Approach, to virtually uncontrolled in task-based, content-based, and participatory approaches. Contrast the views regarding what to do with learners' errors, which range from doing everything to prevent them in the first place (Audio-Lingual Method), to ignoring them when they are made under the assumption that they will work themselves out at some future point (for example, TPR).

There are no doubt other differences as well. However, it is the existence of contradictory differences that leads us to the question we will be discussing next: How is a teacher to choose?

Choosing among Language Teaching Methods

At the end of this book a reasonable question to ask is, 'Which method is best?' After all, while we have seen that many of the methods presented in this book have characteristics in common, there are also some fundamental differences among them. And so in the end, one does need to choose. However, there is a two-part answer to the question of which method is best. The first is to remember what we said at the beginning of this book: There is no single best method. The second part of the answer to this question is that for individual teachers and their students, there may be a particular method that they are drawn to—which it is not likely to be a decision a teacher reaches once and for all. It is also the case that a teacher will have to make many other decisions besides that of choosing a method. In any case, the matter of deciding needs some careful thought because:

> … if we intend to make choices that are informed and not just intuitive or ideological, then we need to expend no little effort first in identifying our own values, next in tying those values to an appropriate set of larger aims, and only then devising or rejecting, adopting or adapting techniques.
> (Stevick 1993: 434; see also Edge 1996)

The first step in the Stevick quote, identifying values, is what this book has been all about. Our goal has been that you will use the principles and techniques in the methods we have written about as a way to make explicit your own beliefs about the teaching/learning process, beliefs based upon your experience and your professional training, including the research you know about. Of course, a study of methods is not the only way to make your beliefs explicit, but unless you become clear about your beliefs, you will continue to make decisions that are conditioned, rather than conscious. In a way, this set of explicit beliefs could be said to be your theory, which will inform your methodological choices. It will also be your theory that will interact with those of others. As we wrote in Chapter 1, ' Engaging with the professional beliefs of others [their theories] in an ongoing manner is also important for keeping your teaching practice alive.' Furthermore:

... if the teacher engages in classroom activity with a sense of intellectual excitement, there is at least a fair probability that learners will begin to participate in the excitement and to perceive classroom lessons mainly as learning events—as experiences of growth for themselves.
(Prabhu 1992: 239)

This has been true for Tim McNamara. He describes what transpired after he interacted with the theories of others in a Master's degree program:

I became an observer in my own classroom, of myself and, in particular, of my students, and kept thinking about what I was doing and what alternatives there might be. Once I had developed an appetite for that understanding, it never left me. To learn that a site of practice was also a site for thinking gave a dimension to my experience of teaching which has remained with me.
(McNamara 2008: 302)

Larsen-Freeman frames it this way:

A theory helps us learn to look (Larsen-Freeman 2000). It allows us to see and name things that might otherwise have escaped our attention. Our intuitions may be quite sound, but conscious awareness of why we do what we do allows us to make a choice—to continue to do things the same way or to change the way we do them. A theory also stimulates new questions in teachers, as well as in researchers ... Additionally, our theories help us make sense of our experience.
(Larsen-Freeman 2008: 291)

For some teachers, the choice among methods is easy. These teachers find that a particular method resonates with their own values, experience, and fundamental views about teaching and learning. It fits with what they are trying to achieve, and it is appropriate for their students and their context. We might call the position such teachers adopt, when confronted with the issue of methodological diversity, one of absolutism: One method is best for them. What makes it so is because it is the one the teacher knows, having been trained in it, and/or because it is consonant with the teacher's thinking (values, beliefs, assumptions), and/or because there is research evidence supporting it. Such teachers may choose to become specialists in a particular method; they may even pursue advanced level training in it.

Before being persuaded that one method is absolutely best, however, we should remember methods themselves are decontextualized. They describe a certain ideal, based on certain beliefs. They deal with what, how, and why. They say little or nothing about who/whom, when, and where. Each method put into practice will be shaped at least by the teacher, the students, the conditions of instruction, and the broader sociocultural context. A particular method cannot, therefore, be a prescription for success for everyone. As Parker Palmer has said, 'When person A speaks, I realize that the method that works for him would not work for me, for it is not grounded in who I am' (Palmer 1998: 147). What makes a method successful for some teachers is their investment in it. This is one reason why the research based on methodological comparisons has often been so inconclusive. It sought to reduce teaching to the faithful following of pedagogic prescriptions—but teaching is much more than this.

> A good system of education … is not one in which all or most teachers carry out the same recommended procedures, but rather a system where all, or most, teachers operate with a sense of plausibility about whatever procedures they choose to adopt and each teacher's sense of plausibility is alive or active and hence as open to further development or change as it can be.
> (Prabhu 1987: 106)

As Allwright and Hanks (2009) note:

> Arguing against standardisation, then, is very different from being against standards. We want teachers to work to the highest standards they are capable of, but that is a very personal professional matter and one that is much more difficult if institutions insist on standardisation, making everyone work in precisely the same way.
> (Allwright and Hanks 2009: 9)

Some use this concern of coercion to argue that there can be no right method for everyone. They point out that some methods are more suitable for older learners; others for younger—or that some might be more appropriate for beginning-level language study, but not for intermediate or advanced. They say that some methods clearly call for a level of language proficiency that not all language teachers possess. They warn that methods should not be exported from one situation to another (Holliday 1994). We might call this position **relativism**. Each method has its strengths and weaknesses, relativists believe, but they are not equally suited for all situations. Different methods are suitable for different teachers and learners in different contexts. Such a position rings true for many teachers. They may have found themselves, when reading of a particular method in this book saying, 'This would never work where I teach.' While there is no doubt some truth to this position, and certainly teachers are in a good position to judge the feasibility of a method, it would be a mistake to reason that every situation is so unique that no similarities exist among them. Indeed, 'it is a very large claim that the process of language acquisition—a basic human attribute—itself varies according to contextual factors' (Prabhu 1990: 166). Indeed, learners are very versatile and can learn well sometimes despite a given method rather than because of it. What is true, though, is that there are sociopolitical reasons or demands on teachers which may make one method more acceptable than another in a given context.

There is another version of the relativist position, one that we might call **pluralism**, which many other teachers find reasonable. Rather than deciding to adopt or reject methods in their entirety as being suitable or unsuitable for a particular context, they believe that there is some value to each method. Instead of believing that different methods should be practiced in different contexts, they believe that different methods, or parts of methods, should be practiced in the same context (Prabhu 1990). For example, by playing the believing game, they see that the multiple perspectives on language represented by methods in this book—that language is literary, deals with everyday situations, is made up of patterns, rules, sounds, vocabulary, notions, and functions, is meaningful, comprises texts, is used for interactions, and is a medium through which to learn certain content, accomplish certain tasks, or become empowered—are all true. Moreover, if language is complex, then it makes sense that learning it is also complex, and therefore that **associationism**, habit formation, rule formation, interactionism, emergentism, etc. can all be true or at least partially true, although no single truth necessarily accounts for the whole of language acquisition. Then, too, although teachers know that there are many similarities among students, they also know that 'each group has its own special characteristics, and that successful teaching requires the recognition and acknowledgement of this uniqueness' (Bolster 1983: 298, cited in Larsen-Freeman 1990; Allwright and Hanks 2009).

When teachers who subscribe to the pluralistic view of methods pick and choose from among methods to create their own blend, their practice is said to be eclectic. Remember, though, that methods are coherent combinations of techniques *and* principles. Thus, teachers who have made their beliefs explicit—have constructed their own theories—and fashion a teaching approach in accordance with their theories (which may very well make allowances for differences among students), could be said to be practicing **principled eclecticism**. They are in effect creating their own method by blending aspects of others in a principled manner.

We should hasten to add that from an external perspective, it may be difficult to distinguish eclecticism from principled eclecticism. Remember that a method involves both thoughts and actions. We would not want to label teachers' methods simply by what is visible—their actions. It would only be in listening to teachers talk about their practice that we might be able to tell. Teachers who practice principled eclecticism should be able to give a reason for why they do what they do. When asked whether or not they would use a role-play, for instance, they will likely invoke the common teacher response, 'It depends ….' 'It depends,' they will say, 'on what we are practicing,' or 'on whether or not we have done a role-play recently,' revealing that their teaching philosophy might include such principles as the need to match a particular target language point with a particular technique or on the need for variety among teaching activities. They might even say that it depends on what time of day it is or what day of the week it is, recognizing that they frequently have to make decisions resulting from the complexity of classroom reality, including what is happening socially among the participants at the time (Allwright 1984; Allwright and Hanks 2009; Nunan 1992; Prabhu 1992; Clarke 1994).

Now the answer 'it depends' might be seen by some to be a sign of teachers' avoiding taking a position. But 'it depends' answers might be taken by others as signs of the wisdom of practice. For, after all, teaching is a contingent activity that requires a response in the moment. It is also true that with us human beings, there is often a gap between our intentions and our actions (Clarke 2007), despite the fact that 'we are all seeking coherence in the world—ways of aligning our behavior with our convictions …' (ibid. 2007: 200). Of course, even if we were to achieve total congruence between our beliefs and our actions, we cannot control everything in our interaction with our students. In complex systems, sometimes unintended consequences occur (Larsen-Freeman and Cameron 2008).

And finally, it is true that many methodological decisions are outside the control of teachers. They must teach for a test, for instance. Or they may have a class where students come with negative attitudes toward the study of language. Fanselow (1987) observes that perhaps as little as two percent of the variance that contributes to learning may be controlled by the teacher. And yet as he says:

> But so what? If learning equals one hundred percent, and lack of learning means anything less than one hundred percent, the two percent we are responsible for makes the difference between learning and not learning. (Fanselow 1987: 11)

Teaching as the Management of Learning

Teachers who teach as if their practice causes learning, while recognizing that they are not in control of all of the relevant factors, and that at the very least they are in partnership with their students in this enterprise, can be true managers of learning.[2] We are not speaking narrowly of classroom management, but rather more broadly of someone who can live with the paradox of

---

[2] Allwright (1984) was perhaps the first to use this term.

knowing that teaching does not cause learning, all the while knowing that to be successful, one must act as if it does. A manager of learning 'is concerned with the quality of the educational environment and the learning opportunities it affords—and explicitly with the values and ideals we wish to promote in our educational work' (van Lier 2003: 51).

It is this commitment to creating learning opportunities that motivates a teacher to make informed methodological choices. Teachers who are managers of learning recognize in general that a number of methodological options exist, but they are guided in any particular moment by a compass consisting of a set of values, professional knowledge and experience, and a commitment to (particular) learning outcomes. Such teachers do not despair in methodological profusion; they welcome it. They know that the more tools they have at their disposal, the better off they are in having a large repertoire to choose from when a teachable moment presents itself. They recognize that they must focus students' attention on the learning challenge, and then step back and respond in service to their learning.

When asked if they would use a particular technique—say, assign a particular reading passage, ask a particular question, they answer, 'It depends.' There may be times when a pattern drill is appropriate, or giving a grammar rule, or an interactive task, or an activity which involves negotiation of meaning, depending on the learning challenge or what the students are struggling with at the moment. 'It depends' statements provide us with evidence of the highly complex, interpretive, contingent knowledge which teachers/managers must possess in order to do the work of teaching.

Learning to Teach: A Developmental Process

But there is another important dimension to the question of teaching methods that must be considered. And that is that learning to teach is a developmental process (Freeman 1991); indeed, while there may not be any strict sequence of developmental stages in teaching, learning it is said to be a lifelong process. Thus, before concluding, Larsen-Freeman offers a brief autobiographical sketch of her own development as a teacher, as an illustration, one not meant to be a model (Larsen-Freeman 1998b).

> When I was first learning to teach, I was trained in a particular method. Fortunately for me, I was oblivious to alternatives. I practiced one method exclusively, using the books that I had been given. I was learning to teach and all of my attention was on trying to the best of my ability to adhere to the method, while learning the classroom routines and maintaining some sense of decorum in the meantime. I was the teacher (while learning to be one) and was teaching (while learning to do so at the same time).

After a while, I grew dissatisfied with my teaching. I found that it had reached a level where I could give less attention to what I was doing and more to what my students were learning. The consequence was that I did not like what I saw. I felt that there had to be a better method than the one I was practicing. I sought further education. What I discovered from this education was that although there were other methods, there was very little agreement on the best way to teach. What was important though was for me to be able to rationalize what I was doing. I felt during this phase of my development that I was no longer learning to teach. My view of teaching had changed. I knew a lot, but I realized that there was a lot more to learn. I found that I was learning teaching. I no longer was preparing to do something. I was experiencing it, and I was learning a great deal from the experience.

Learning teaching has sustained me for many years—and still does, even though my area of concern is now less language teaching than language teacher education. One of the problems with relating my experience in this fashion, is that it appears that my development as a teacher is a linear process, with each stage being discrete. This is not the case. I am still learning to teach in some respects (such as every time I meet a new group of students for the first time), and I am still learning teaching. In fact, I am still learning about the subject matter that I have been teaching for over forty years! However, I believe I can identify an additional chapter in my own story because I realize in retrospect that during my learning teaching phase I was still operating under the assumption that at some point I could master teaching. Sure, there would always be some new developments in the field, but for the most part, I thought I could make room for them without upsetting my practice very much. I was mistaken. I finally came to realize that I could never master teaching. Practically everything I needed to know, including my students, was always changing.

Language, learning, teaching are dynamic, fluid, mutable processes. There is nothing fixed about them (Larsen-Freeman 1997; Ellis and Larsen-Freeman 2006). I would characterize my third stage then as just learning. This is not the willful learning of teaching, but the egoless following of learning. Further, this learning is not a gerund; this learning is a participle. It is not something that results in a static product; it is a dynamic process. Learning in this sense means being open to what comes, relating to it, and becoming different in its presence (Caleb Gattegno, personal communication). And by so doing, when I am able to do it, I am learning all the time.

Let us restate that we are not being prescriptive. Larsen-Freeman was simply describing her own experience. Different teachers no doubt have their own stories to tell. And surely one can mature professionally in this field by deepening one's practice in a particular method, rather than by switching methods. But what may be more common than is usually acknowledged is that each of our stories unfolds over our lifespans as teachers (Freeman and Richards 1993). And what seems to lead to the unfolding of the story is an eagerness to want to teach better—to reach more students more effectively and more compassionately.

For this reason, teaching is perhaps best served by teachers' cultivating an **attitude of inquiry** (Larsen-Freeman 2000). Much is unknown about the teaching–learning process, and those teachers who approach it as a mystery to be solved (recognizing that some aspects of teaching and learning may be forever beyond explanation) will see their teaching as a source of continuing professional renewal and refreshment.

Conclusion

By confronting the diversity of methods in this book, and by viewing their thought-in-action links, we hope that you will be helped to arrive at your own conceptualization of how thought leads to actions in your teaching, and how, in turn, your teaching leads to the desired learning in your students. What we hope your reading of this book has also done is challenged you to identify your values, and to question them, perhaps leading to reaffirmation, perhaps not. But teaching is not only thinking and holding certain values; it is also action. We hope, therefore, that this book has encouraged you to experiment with new techniques—to try them, observe the consequences, make adjustments, and then to try them again.

In order to move from ideology to inquiry, teachers need to inquire into their practice. They need to reflect on what they do and why they do it, and they need to be open to learning about the practices and research of others. They need to interact with others, and need to try new practices in order to search continually for or devise the best method they can for who they are, who their students are, and the conditions and context of their teaching. It is to this quest that we hope this book has in a small way contributed.

References/Additional Resources

Allwright, D. 1984. 'The importance of interaction in classroom language learning.' *Applied Linguistics* 5/2: 156–71.

—— and J. Hanks. 2009. *The Developing Language Learner*. Basingstoke: Palgrave Macmillan.

Bolster, A. 1983. 'Toward a more effective model of research on teaching.' *Harvard Educational Review* 53/3: 294–308.

Clarke, M. 1994. 'The dysfunctions of the theory/practice discourse.' *TESOL Quarterly* 28/1: 9–26.

——. 2003. *A Place to Stand: Essays for Educators in Troubled Times*. Ann Arbor, MI: University of Michigan Press.

——. 2007. *Common Ground, Contested Territory. Examining the Roles of English Language Teachers in Troubled Times*. Ann Arbor, MI: University of Michigan Press.

Cook, G. 2010. *Translation in Language Teaching – An Argument for Reassessment*. Oxford: Oxford University Press.

Edge, J. 1996. 'Cross-cultural paradoxes in a profession of values.' *TESOL Quarterly* 30/1: 9–30.

Ellis, G. 1996. 'How culturally appropriate is the communicative approach?' *English Language Teaching Journal* 50/3: 213–18.

Fanselow, J. 1987. *Breaking Rules: Generating and Exploring Alternatives in Language Teaching*. New York: Longman.

Freeman, D. 1991. 'Mistaken constructs: Re-examining the nature and assumptions of language teacher education' in J. Alatis (ed.). *Georgetown University Round Table on Languages and Linguistics 1991: Linguistics and Language Pedagogy*. Washington, DC: Georgetown University Press.

—— and J. Richards. 1993. 'Conceptions of teaching and the education of second language teachers.' *TESOL Quarterly* 27/2: 193–216.

Garcia, O. and J. Kleifgen. 2010. *Educating Emergent Bilinguals*. New York: Teachers College Press.

Holliday, A. 1994. *Appropriate Methodology and Social Context*. New York: Cambridge University Press.

Gomes de Matos, F. 2006. 'Language, peace and conflict resolution' in M. Deutsch, P. Coleman, and E. Marcus (eds.). *The Handbook of Conflict Resolution* (2nd edn.), 158–75. San Francisco: Jossey-Bass.

Kramsch, C. 1993. *Context and Culture in Language Teaching*. Oxford: Oxford University Press.

——. 2011. 'Culture' in J. Simpson (ed.). *Routledge Handbook of Applied Linguistics*. Oxford: Routledge.

Larsen-Freeman, D. 1987. 'From unity to diversity: Twenty-five years of language-teaching methodology.' *Forum* XXV 4: 2–10 (Special Anniversary Issue).

——. 1990. 'On the need for a theory of language teaching' in J. Alatis (ed.). *Georgetown University Round Table on Languages and Linguistics: The Interdependence of Theory, Practice and Research*. Washington, DC: Georgetown University Press.

——. 1997. 'Chaos/complexity science and second language acquisition.' *Applied Linguistics* 18/2: 141–65.

——. 1998a. 'Expanded roles of learners and teachers in learner-centered instruction' in W. Renandya, and G. Jacobs (eds.). *Learners and Language Learning*. Singapore: SEAMEO Regional Language Centre.

——. 1998b. 'Learning teaching is a lifelong process.' *Perspectives* XXIV 2: 5–11.

——. 2000. 'An attitude of inquiry.' *Journal of Imagination in Language Learning* V: 10–15.

——. 2008. 'Does TESOL share theories with other disciplines?' *TESOL Quarterly* 42/2: 291–94.

——. 2011. 'Key concepts in language learning and education.' in J. Simpson, (ed.). *Routledge Handbook of Applied Linguistics*. Oxford: Routledge.

—— and **L. Cameron.** 2008. *Complex Systems and Applied Linguistics*. Oxford: Oxford University Press.

—— and **D. Freeman.** 2008. 'Language moves: The place of "foreign" languages in classroom teaching and learning.' *Review of Research in Education* 32: 147–86.

Li, Defeng. 1998. 'It's always more difficult than you plan and imagine: Teachers' perceived difficulties in introducing the communicative approach in South Korea.' *TESOL Quarterly* 32/4: 677–703.

McNamara, T. 2008. 'Mapping the Scope of Theory in TESOL.' *TESOL Quarterly* 42/2: 302–5.

Norton, B. 2011. 'Identity' in J. Simpson, (ed.). *Routledge Handbook of Applied Linguistics*. Oxford: Routledge.

Nunan, D. 1992. *Collaborative Language Learning and Teaching*. Cambridge: Cambridge University Press.

Ortega, L. 2010. The Bilingual Turn in SLA. Plenary delivered at the Annual Conference of the American Association for Applied Linguistics. Atlanta, GA, March 6–9.

Palmer, P. 1998. *The Courage to Teach*. San Francisco: Jossey-Bass.

Prabhu, N. S. 1987. *Second Language Pedagogy*. Oxford: Oxford University Press.

———. 1990. 'There is no best method—Why?' *TESOL Quarterly* 24/2: 161–76.

———. 1992. 'The dynamics of the language lesson.' *TESOL Quarterly* 26/2: 225–41.

Richards, J. 2008. 'Second language teacher education today.' *RELC Journal* 39/2: 158–77.

Stevick, E. 1993. 'Social meanings for how we teach' in J. Alatis (ed.). *Georgetown University Round Table on Languages and Linguistics 1992: Language, Communication, and Social Meaning.* Washington, DC: Georgetown University Press.

van Lier, L. 2003. 'A tale of two computer classrooms: The ecology of project-based language learning' in J. Leather and J. van Dam (eds.). *Ecology of Language Acquisition*, 49–64. Dordrecht: Kluwer Academic Publishers.

Widdowson, H. G. 2003. *Defining Issues in English Language Teaching.* Oxford: Oxford University Press.

Glossary

Active phase: the second phase of a Desuggestopedia lesson, in which students actively work with the language they have been introduced to in the receptive phase.

Adjunct model: students enrolled in a regular academic course also take a language course linked to the academic course.

Advance organization: a learning strategy focused on improving reading skills by learning to preview and to skim to get the gist of a reading passage.

Affective filter: a metaphorical filter that is caused by a student's negative emotions, which reduce the student's ability to understand the language spoken to them.

Analytic syllabus: '[O]rganized in terms of the purposes for which people are learning language and the kinds of language performance that are necessary to meet those purposes' (Wilkins 1976: 13).

Antonym: a word with the opposite meaning to another word, e.g. 'cold' is the antonym of 'hot.'

Apprenticeship of observation: a term to describe the fact that teachers come to teacher training with ideas about the teaching/learning process formed from the years they have spent as students themselves (Lortie 1975).

Associationism: a learning theory that assumes that language learning takes place when learners associate forms with their meanings.

Attitude of inquiry: a teacher's commitment to inquire and reflect on his or her teaching practice, learning from every experience (Larsen-Freeman 2000).

Authentic language: language used in a real context.

Banking method of education: a more 'traditional' form of education where the teacher 'deposits' information in the students, making the assumption that the teacher knows what the students need to learn.

Bottom-up approach to reading instruction: a learning to read approach that begins with students learning the basic elements of language, e.g. sound–symbol correspondences.

Cognate: a word with a similar appearance (and usually a similar meaning) across languages.

Cognitive code approach: an approach in which learners are seen to be actively responsible for their own learning, engaged in formulating hypotheses in order to discover the rules of the target language.

Cognitive strategies: learning strategies which involve learners interacting and manipulating what is to be learned.

Coherence: a property of discourse where sentences are connected in a meaningful way.

Cohesion: a property of discourse where sentences are connected with explicit linguistic forms, such as conjunctions.

Communicative approach: an approach to language teaching that makes learning to communicate central.

Communicative competence: knowing when and how to say what to whom. Being communicatively competent in the target language means being able to communicate appropriately with others.

Community of practice: a group of people who share a common interest and/or a profession. As they share information, they learn from each other (Lave and Wenger 1991).

Competency-based instruction: adults study certain vital life-coping or survival skills, such as how to fill out a job application or use the telephone.

Comprehensible input: language that is understood by students. The teacher ensures that she or he is understood by using pictures, gestures, and occasional words in the students' native language.

Comprehension approach: a general approach that includes methods that give importance to input, especially in the form of listening comprehension.

Computer-assisted language learning (CALL): instruction that uses computer or web-based technology to teach language.

Concordance: a computer-generated list of words or phrases, used in limited contexts.

Conditioning: associated with behaviorism, conditioning is a process whereby students learn to respond correctly to stimuli through shaping and reinforcement.

Conscious and subconscious planes: communication takes place on two planes. On the conscious plane, the learner attends to the language. On the subconscious plane, the learner receives messages about the ease of the learning process. Learning is enhanced when there is unity between the conscious and subconscious planes.

Constructivism: students are actively involved in constructing their own knowledge through experience and problem solving (Dewey 1913).

Control and initiative: a teacher exercises lesser or greater control in the classroom, which influences how much initiative students are encouraged and able to take (Stevick 1980).

Cooperative learning: students learn from and with each other in groups.

Counsel: in Counseling-Learning/Community Language Learning, the teacher does not offer advice, but rather 'counsels' the students by showing that he is really listening to them and understanding what they are saying. This is typically demonstrated by an 'understanding response.'

Critical discourse analysis: the study of how identity and power relations are constructed in language.

Critical pedagogy: instruction that is premised on the belief that 'what happens in the classroom should end up making a difference outside of the classroom' (Baynham 2006: 28).

Deductive grammar teaching: the teacher explains grammar rules to students, who then apply them to different examples.

Discourse or suprasentential level of language: the organization of language as texts, e.g. how sentences go together to make up a paragraph.

Discrete-point test: an analytical approach to language testing in which each test question assesses one distinct feature of the language.

Display question: a question to which both teacher and student know the answer, but that is used by the teacher to find out what a student knows or is able to do.

Doubting game and believing game: the doubting game requires someone to evaluate an idea using logic and evidence. The believing game requires taking on the perspective of the originator of the idea, to see it through his or her eyes. It is important to play both games. The goal is to understand an idea fully before judging it (Elbow 1973).

Emergentism: a language learning theory that sees language as emerging from meaningful language use. Speakers' language is shaped and reshaped by experience.

Endangered languages: languages that are in danger of disappearing due to the declining numbers of people who speak them.

English as a lingua franca: the language used by millions of non-native English speakers, primarily for use in multilingual language contact situations.

Fidel charts: color-coded Silent Way charts that show sounds of the language and the various ways the same sound can be spelled.

Five minds: a theory focused on cognitive abilities or 'minds' that individuals need to develop in order to be successful in a changing world (Gardner 2007).

Focus on form: the teacher directs learners' attention briefly to linguistic structure while the learners are engaged in a meaningful activity.

Functions: speech acts, such as inviting, promising, introducing one person to another, that are performed within a social context.

Generative words: from Freire's work in literacy education, words that are important to the people in their community, which are used to teach basic decoding and coding skills.

Genres: different types of language texts, e.g. poetry or scientific writing.

Globalization: the expansion of businesses internationally.

Grammaring: an approach to teaching grammar that treats grammar as an ability to use grammar structures accurately, meaningfully, and appropriately, rather than as a set of static rules to be applied (Larsen-Freeman 2003).

Graphic organizer: a diagram used by teachers to help students organize and remember new information.

Human computer™: in Counseling-Learning/Community Language Learning, the student chooses which aspect of language to practice and controls how much to practice it. The teacher repeats correctly what the student says as often as the student desires.

i + 1: language that is just in advance of students' current level of language proficiency ('i').

Inductive grammar teaching: the teacher gives students examples with a particular grammar structure. The students figure out the rule.

Infantilization: Desuggestopedia teachers consciously create an environment in which students can release their fears and become 'childlike' in their classroom interactions.

Information gap: an activity where not all the information is known by all the participants. They have to share the information they have in order to complete the activity.

Inner criteria: students develop their own inner criteria for correctness— to trust and to be responsible for their own production in the target language (Gattegno 1972).

Input enhancement: promoting students' noticing of a particular language feature, such as putting in boldface type a particular structure in a reading passage.

Input flooding: promoting students' noticing by using particular language items with great frequency.

Language for academic purposes: language studied so as to be able to participate successfully in academic contexts.

Language for specific purposes: language studied in order to participate in a specific activity or profession, e.g. German for business purposes.

Learning strategies: 'the techniques or devices which a learner may use to acquire knowledge' (Rubin 1975: 43).

Linguistic competence: mastery of the linguistic structures of the target language.

Literacies: literacy in the unique forms, vocabulary, and norms of different discourses, e.g. those of politics or business.

Metacognitive strategies: learning strategies that are used to plan, monitor, and evaluate a learning task, e.g. arranging conditions for learning, setting long and short-term goals and checking one's comprehension during listening and reading (Chamot and O'Malley 1994).

Minimal pair: pairs of words which differ in only one sound, e.g. 'ship' and 'sheep.'

Multicompetence: being able to use more than one language in a way that one's needs are met without necessarily imitating monolingual native speaker use.

Peripheral learning: students learn from what is present in the environment, even if their attention is not directed to it.

Pluralism: the belief that there is some value in each method.

Plurilingualism: an individual's language proficiency in several languages.

Principled eclecticism: teachers build their own method by blending aspects of other methods in a principled manner.

Recast: a form of corrective feedback in which a teacher reformulates correctly what a student has said incorrectly.

Receptive phase: the first phase in a Desuggestopedia lesson where a dialogue is read with musical accompaniment and read a second time at normal speed.

Register: the level of formality of a text.

Relativism: the belief that each method has its strengths and weaknesses and that therefore different methods are suitable for different contexts.

SAARRD: in Counseling-Learning/Community Language Learning, this acronym represents the six elements necessary for nondefensive learning: S = Security; A = Aggression (students are given the opportunity to assert themselves); A = Attention (students' attention is focused); R = Reflection; R = Retention (integration of the new material takes place within the whole self); D = Discrimination (sorting out the differences among target language forms).

Scaffolding: language support provided by a teacher, which enables learners to communicate something they could not do otherwise, e.g. building a complete utterance together with the students.

Sheltered Instruction Observation Protocol (SIOP): effective practices for sheltered instruction (Short and Echevarria 1999).

Sheltered-language instruction: an instructional approach that allows for the integration of language and content by supporting students' understanding of the content in the target language.

Social/affective learning strategies: learning strategies where learners interact with other persons or pay attention to the affective domain to improve learning (Chamot and O'Malley 1994).

Strong and weak version of the communicative approach: in the weak version of the communicative approach students are learning to use English; in the strong version, students use English to learn it (Howatt 1984).

Synonym: a word with a similar meaning to another word, e.g. 'sick' is a synonym of 'ill.'

Synthetic syllabus: a syllabus comprising linguistic units: grammar structures, vocabulary items, functions, etc. It is the learner's responsibility to synthesize the linguistic units for the purpose of communication (Wilkins 1976).

Task: an activity, with a clear outcome, in which learners communicate meaningfully.

Task-supported teaching: teaching with meaningful communicative tasks, without excluding the possibility of using tasks with a grammatical focus.

Top-down approach to reading instruction: a learning to read approach that begins with students engaging with the general ideas of the text as a way in to understanding the text.

Understanding response: a response from a listener that paraphrases what the speaker has just said, without questions, opinions, or judgments.

Whole-person learning: teachers consider not only their students' intellect, but they also have some understanding about the relationship among students' feelings, physical reactions, instinctual protective reactions, and desire to learn.

Workplace literacy: the skill adult learners need at their workplace to read and write about relevant content.

World 'Englishes': different varieties of English, each spoken in a country that was a former British colony, e.g. Indian English.

World wide web (www or 'the web'): a way of accessing information over the Internet.

Zone of proximal development (ZPD): an area of learning potential lying between the learner's ability to operate independently and the learner's ability to operate with the help of a teacher or a more competent peer (Vygotsky 1978).

Index

Direct Method 26–7
Grammar-Translation method 14

Rajagopalan, K. xii, 4
Rardin, J. 95
reading aloud 25–6, 32
reading comprehension questions 21
realia, pictures and objects, use of, *see also*
  pictures
  Audio-Lingual method 42
  Communicative Language Teaching 126
  Content-based Instruction 139
  Desuggestopedia 74, 77
  Direct Method 25–8
reasoning-gap tasks 159
recasts 97, 151, 155
receptive phase 79
Reeder, K. 216
reflection:
  reflective listening 99
  student 92, 95, 99
  teacher xi
  relativism 228
repetition:
  input flooding 150
  lack of in Silent Way 61, 62, 77
  necessity of in Audio-Lingual method 42
repetition drill technique 37, 47
Richards, J. x, 224, 233
Riggenbach, H. 150
right brain hemisphere, addressing 107
Rinpoche, S. 7
rods, as tool in Silent Way 54–7, 66
role-playing:
  Communicative Language Teaching
    118–19, 121, 127–8
  Desuggestopedia 82
Rubin, J. 181
rule formation, language learning as 51

Samuda, V. 150, 151
Savignon, S. xi, 115
scaffolding 138, 139
Schleppegrell, M. 139
Schulze, M. 200n
'second language', non-use of term 13
Seidlhofer, B. 166
self-correction 27, 29, 32, 65, 66, 99, 177
self-evaluation 97, 175, 177
self-expression, language for 61–2
self-reliance 62
Sheen, R. 150
Sheltered Instruction Observation Protocol
  (SIOP) 141

sheltered-language instruction 141
Sherris, A. 134
Short, D. 141
Shulman, L. xi
silence, as a tool 59, 60, 63, 66
Silent Way 6, 51–69, 220
Sinclair, J. 213
single-slot substitution drills 37, 47
Skehan, P. 132, 157
skim reading 183–4
Skinner, B. 35
Skype 212
sleep, learning during 63, 77, 79
Snow, M.A. 131, 132
social/affective learning strategies 186
social context of language:
  Audio-Lingual method 42
  Communicative Language Teaching
    115–30
  Community Language Learning 85–102
  via technology 200
  Vygotskian principles 142
social networking sites 201–2, 203, 213–14
social skills, teaching 186–90
songs, use of 74, 78
sound-color charts 52–8, 62, 65
speaking:
  coming after listening 103
  in Grammar-Translation method 18
  primacy of speech in Audio-Lingual
    Method 44
  primacy of speech in Direct Method 28,
    29, 31
speaking when ready 110, 112
specific purposes, language for 132, *see also*
  Content-based Instruction
standards, calls for more 224, 228
Stevick, E. 2, 3, 226
Stoller, F. 185
student–student interaction:
  Audio-Lingual method 45
  Collaborative Learning 186–90, 220
  Communicative Language Teaching 123
  Cooperative Learning 186–90, 220
  Direct Method 31
  lack of in Grammar-Translation approaches
    19
small group tasks 99–100, 120, 123
students helping each other 59, 60, 63, 93
  Task-based Language Teaching 155, 156
  via online means 209
subconscious plane, accessing 77
substitution drills 37–9, 43, 45, 47
suggestion in teaching, *see* Desuggestopedia